CONNEXA

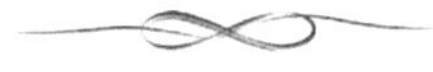

By Samantha White

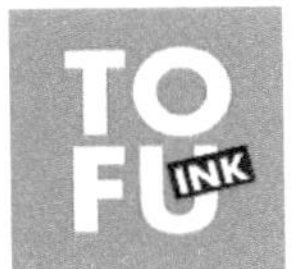

Contents

1

Samantha White writes stories that mix science fiction, fantasy, and horror, because why choose just one? Life hasn't always been easy, but years of facing chronic health challenges have taught her how to adapt, persevere, and keep moving forward. She believes that strength comes from within and lives by a simple motto: do what you can, when you can, how you can and make tomorrow better. With a supportive family behind her, she turns life's challenges into inspiration for the stories she tells.

Connexa is the tale of overcoming abuse, power, and the expectations of our elders crushing us beneath a cloud of lust and hate. It focuses on the struggles of a child named Emma who was born at the dawn of the eighteenth century. A child born to a woman who sells her off for medical experimentation before she was even born. They must learn to navigate life without the help of her elders, despite this and the neglect they are watching and learning. Others move through the Shadows trying to help her while they are trapped themselves because of the choices they made in their pasts.

Thanks to the help of these few good souls they discover love, hope, and happiness which allows them to discover who they were at heart. No matter the torture, experimentation, and neglect that they threw into their face did they falter in their journey. Simply allowing the challenges to polish them into a hero who could survive in the hell into which they had been born. Through the fires of pain, loss, and rejection they learn how to be the hero that can be a beacon of hope to those caught in the Shadows.
We all crave control. Over our environment, over our possessions, and even control over the people around us. This drives some to commit horrors and others to create beauty in the world. Emma is a product of this eternal fight between the light and the dark within us. This is her origin story and it is not a pretty one, at all. Will these experiences

taint her soul? Or will she find a way to make peace with who she must become? Read on, if you dare to look upon the truth of the 1800s.

I want to thank my greatest supporter Matt for always standing behind me. I would also like to thank Nancy for giving me the confidence to write stories.

Introduction

Darkness is an ever expanding, ravenous creature that hungers endlessly for the light. Every single living creature must choose whether they wish to live for the light or wallow in the darkness. In a universe of infinite possibilities, comes endless opportunities, and endless chances to be swallowed up by the darkness. If you let the darkness in it will consume you whole, twist you up, and drive you to become filled with hatred and anger. The darkness wants to drain the light out of you, it wants you to fail, because in failure you are vulnerable. Standing in the light is far more difficult but also far more rewarding. It is harder to fight for what is good in the world, to tell the darkness that you will not be its pawn, that you will not give into your pain, into your misery.

How do I know? I have been fighting the darkness for nearly eight hundred years. I have seen the darkness win, seen it beat down and fracture the light again and again and again. I have watched the light break. But, I have also seen the light come back. I have seen the light triumph over the darkness again and again and again. It happens when good people do good things, when they stand up against the darkness, and refuse to be broken. I have rambled enough for one setting. Please, let me introduce myself. I am Mother. I have been given the wondrous opportunity to not only serve the light but to foster it in the hearts of others. To always protect it from the ravages of the darkness and through this pursuit of service, I have given life to countless worlds and destroyed countless others. I have used the power of the light to build an empire dedicated to fighting the darkness and defending the light. Now it is time for new heroes to take up the mantle, to defend the light, for my time grows ever shorter. It is time for my daughters to serve the light and keep the darkness at bay. It is time for the many worlds to learn the truth.

Do not mourn for me when I am gone, for I have lived a full life and served the light with honor and integrity. The Stahl are coming and when they arrive the light will take another beating. It may not win this time. We certainly didn't win the first time or the second, but that was because I stood alone.

This time my daughters will stand with me and I will give the last of myself to ensure they return to the darkness from whence they came. Ensuring that the light continues to shine, but I am getting ahead of myself. Let me tell you my story and the stories of my daughters. Let me show you how everything has come to be and why we must prepare to fight the darkness once more.

PART ONE

A First Time for Everything

Shadow Log: Grace, Barrington, Rhode Island, January 4, 1800

Grace ported into an idyllic, little, snow covered park, using a tree to hide her sudden appearance and instantly pulled her cloak tighter. She hated the cold with a passion only met by her hatred of the Useptis. It made her joints ache, her skin crawl, and made her unusually sleepy, but people kept settling in frozen hellholes. Grumbling to herself, she stomped around the tree sending up little puffs of fresh snow with each step, and found a good vantage point of the wrought iron gate that denoted the entrance to the park. She leaned against the frozen trunk of an old maple and became so still that if you had walked by her she would have gone unnoticed unless she moved.

A short, fat, pregnant woman waddled into view with excruciating slowness that made Grace grind her teeth in annoyance. The woman was bundled up so tightly that it was almost impossible to see that she had long mouse-like hair or that her eyes were green with specks of brown. Grace's nose crinkled as the woman waddled closer making it clear she didn't make frequent use of any of the bathhouses. Already impatient and cold, Grace let out a calming breath, and took a single step towards the woman making her scream in shock. "Dear God! Where did you come from?" She demanded to know in a nasally whine.

"I have been waiting for your arrival." Grace replied calmly. Grace had learned early in life that if she was ten minutes early for any meeting that it was much less likely for her to be ambushed. Even humans were dumb enough to try at times. It also afforded her the time she needed to mentally prepare for the burden of boring conversation. Everyone seemed to think the entire world was about them, their problems, and their desires. It often made Grace wish murder was an acceptable option. However, she had made herself the head of The Shadows which meant such interactions were necessary.

Rule number one was to never let them know when they were getting under your skin. Never let them see your emotions lest they take advantage of you or use them against you. Thus Grace kept an iron fist closed around her emotions during every meeting which while frustrating kept her safe and allowed her to continue growing The Shadows.

"Well! I… I didn't see you there!" The woman protested loudly.

Grace watched her squirm, letting herself enjoy the woman's misery for a long moment before she realized her own foolishness. She was only expanding the amount of time she would be stuck out in the cold with snow crusting her hair. Pulling out an envelope she got down to business.

"This is your contract, it states that you will be given a monthly stipend to care for the child, a small home on the edge of town, and proper medical care during your pregnancy and delivery. In exchange you will allow us to monitor the child with weekly unsupervised visits that will last about an hour."

The woman accepted the brown envelope without any hesitation. Watching the woman tuck the paperwork into her cloak, Grace felt a spark of hope flare to life at the thought of the meeting ending soon, at being able to port back home, and sitting before a roaring fire; sipping bourbon. She even allowed herself a brief, tiny smile, before suppressing it. But with one sentence the woman smashed that hope into a thousand pieces.

"I was thinking we could possibly renegotiate my fee."

In a flash of movement, Grace had the woman by her collar, and pressed against the nearest tree. She leaned in close, trying to not breath in the noxious fumes of the woman's rotted teeth, and let her see the anger bubbling just beneath the surface of her control. The woman whimpered pleadingly, her hand going to her belly almost protectively as a stream of hot steamy urine began to leak out of her stockings.

"Let me be clear, I want your child. I have no qualms about simply cutting it out of your womb while you scream in agony and terror." She growled into her ear.

The woman began to shake in her grasp, fear clearly making it difficult for the woman to get air in with the tiny little gasps she could manage. Grace smiled coldly, let the woman drop back onto her feet, and stepped clear instinctually.

"I'm sorry, I just miss my husband and…" The woman started to wail.

"I don't care." Grace cut her off coldly.

There was no way she was going to stand in the falling snow, inhaling the disgusting vapors of this woman while listening to her moan and complain about how her husband was dead and everything sucked. Grace had her own problems to deal with and she already had a headache. Giving the woman an icy glare, she made it clear that she was not going to be manipulated or forced into doing anything she didn't want to do.

"I'm sorry." The woman whimpered quietly.

Begrudgingly, Grace gave her a cold smile, reached into her cloak, and pulled out a second much smaller envelope. It took all of her remaining will to force herself to not plunge a dagger into the woman's scrawny little neck and watch her turn the snow crimson.

"Here is your first stipend and the address to your new home. I have also included a necklace that when held tightly will alert us to any emergency you may be having. If you use it in a non-emergency situation, I will kill you."

Grace savored the woman's terror as she meekly nodded her head in agreement, snatched the second envelope from Grace's hand, and fled; waddling away with surprising speed. Letting out a contented sigh, Grace walked back to her hiding spot, and ported back to base. Nothing, not even an emergency was going to keep her from her evening curled up in front of the fire, after all, she had earned it.

Shadow Log: Theodore, Barrington, Rhode Island, December 25, 1800

It was odd to be working on Christmas, odd to have no one waiting for him to come home, odd to feel so alone and uncared for. But that had become his life just over ten years ago when his wife had been murdered and a patient of his had died due to his negligence. He was a Shadow now, reduced to following orders, and experimenting on children. Reduced to being a pawn for a woman who didn't understand that the big picture was made up of thousands of little ones.

Looking down at the angry screaming bundle that was his most recent patient, he couldn't help but feel a pang of regret mixed with loss at what could have been.

How had he let himself fall into The Shadows trap? How had he let Grace become his master? How many children would die because of his inability to save them? These questions haunted him almost as much as the conditions in which most of these little ones lived. Uninsulated shacks that were freezing in the winter and scorching in the summer with parents that were better suited to being cared for rather than caring.

Shaking himself out of his thoughts, he lifted his arm up, unstrapped his Shadow-band, and set it on the table. Switching on the voice recorder, he slowly turned back to the child, wishing he could just grab her, and port away to somewhere safe where he could protect her from The Shadows, but The Shadows had already made that impossible.

He rubbed the tiny scar on the back of his head remembering the awful headache that had come from the chip being inserted in his brain. That chip could be activated remotely and could cause his death instantaneously or worse, knock him out so that he could be captured. Removing it would also bring immediate death. It also meant that one day all of his secrets would become known to The Shadows, but that day hopefully wouldn't come anytime soon.

Realizing he was only stalling the inevitable, he bent down, and with great care collected the child from her crib. Pulling her close, he rocked her gently until her cries faded away, and were replaced by happy coos. Letting out his pent up breath, he unswaddled her with great care, and set her on the table next to his recorder. Tickling her belly to make her laugh with one hand, he laid out his tools with the other, and prepared for the task at hand.

"Subject five shows no abnormal outward signs of distress, no sign of skin deterioration is present at this time, and the subject seems to have a healthy appetite."

Hesitation froze him in place for a long moment before he was able to carefully strip the girl of her tiny dirty nightgown. Not wanting to make her cry, he carefully took his measurements making sure to not let the cold metal of the instruments touch her naked skin. Tickling her belly again, he gently held her down, she wouldn't like what he was about to do.

"The subject weighs 16 pounds, ten ounces. Subject's blood pressure, blood sugar, and white blood count all are within normal range for a seven month-old infant. It should be noted that the infant's pupils have begun to take on a more oval appearance as well as turn gray."

He stuck the three point needle into the bottom of her foot, listening to her ear piercing screams, and injected the black serum into her. With that done, he quickly redressed her, and swaddled her back into her blanket. Pulling her close to his chest, he did his best to bring her comfort, and began to sing quietly to her.

"Over in Killarney, many years ago
Me Mother sang a song to me in tones so sweet and low,
Just a simple little ditty, in her good ould Irish way,
And I'd give the world if she could sing that song to me this day.
Too-ra-loo-ra-loo-ral,
Too-ra-loo-ra-li,

Too-ra-loo-ra-loo-ral,
Hush now don't you cry!
Too-ra-loo-ra-loo-ral,
Too-ra-loo-ra-li,
Too-ra-loo-ra-loo-ral,
That's an Irish lullaby.
Oft, in dreams I wander to that cot again,
I feel her arms a huggin' me as when she held me then.
And I hear her voice a hummin' To me as in days of yore,
When she used to rock me fast asleep Outside the cabin
door."

Staring down into her calm eyes, he realized just how much
he missed his home and his family, but he was a Shadow and
those things were gone. Wiping away his tears, he stood up
softly, and tucked her back into her crib.

"Shot administered at 0800 with no exploding veins or black
lines appearing." He whispered as he turned off the recorder.
"I'm sorry, Precious One." He whispered sadly.

Maybe it was because it was Christmas or maybe it was
because it was the day his wife died; but he felt forlorn, lost,
adrift. It felt wrong to just leave the child to her fate, yet he
understood that it was the only way to keep her alive, at least
until the experiments killed her. Seeing that his hour was
almost up, he quickly packed up his tools, gave the girl one
last loving look, and ported to his next appointment.

Shadow log: Ruth, Barrington, Rhode Island, April 12, 1801

Panic is a funny thing, it seems to seep into your bones
making your skin clammy, and then your heart nearly
explodes in your chest from beating so hard. It makes you do
stupid things that you would normally never do and makes
you into a rabid beast when you are backed into a corner
with no way out. For Ruth it made her want to disappear
from the world, to fade into the background, and completely

be ignored. Unfortunately, there was no real way for her to do that so she settled for the next best thing.

Today that panic had driven her to shove her body into the tiny cupboard in which her mother kept the silverware. It was uncomfortable and slightly painful to hold herself in the position required to remain hidden but the fear was enough to keep her there. Peeking out from her hiding spot, she could just barely make out the swollen ankles of her heavily pregnant mother, and the dirt encrusted boots of an unknown male.

"I'm sorry, Mrs. Weston but your husband was caught under a boulder that was being hoisted. The crank broke and it fell directly on his right hip. He'll survive but won't be able to work anymore. If you want to visit him I can take you to the office, he shouldn't be moved until the bones start to fuse back together."

The wail her mother let loose could have woken the dead in the family plot behind the house. Ruth flinched, banging her head against the top of the cupboard just hard enough to see stars, but thankfully another scream from her mother drowned out her own cry of pain. Trying to sob quietly, Ruth carefully closed the door to try and keep the noise she was making from reaching her mother's ears, and felt the emotion begin to overwhelm her.

Ruth didn't understand everything the man was saying but did manage to comprehend that her father was badly hurt. It broke her heart to think about him lying in his office screaming in pain with no one there who loved him.

She heard her wailing mother get dragged out of the room, each thud and thump increasing the stress she was trying to suppress. Finally, it became too much to bear, she exploded out of the cabinet in a blur of motion only to be caught by the maid. Letting the busty woman cradle her in her arms, Ruth allowed everything she was feeling to come out in one big, snotty, tear filled breakdown. Once she had cried herself dry, the maid sat her down gently in a chair, and began the task of cleaning up.

"You really shouldn't hide in cabinets, it is very naughty." Priscilla chastised lovingly in a very heavy African accent.

"I heard Mama coming and panicked since she has been in such a bad mood lately." Ruth muttered uncomfortably.

"Pregnancy like hers is likely to do that to a woman." Priscilla said dismissively.

Ruth chewed her cheek, listening to her mother wail from upstairs as a hole opened up in her chest. Looking up at the ceiling, she felt sure she was going to not be a big sister, it just didn't feel right. She wanted to be a big sister, wanted her mother to be happy, but she only got the hole in her chest when the babies came out unmoving. Feeling fresh tears, Ruth scrubbed angrily at her face wanting to be strong for her mother. Father wouldn't be home for this one, wouldn't be there to hold her hand, and provide comfort. Those duties were hers now and she could only feel panic at the thought. Suddenly, Priscilla rested her calloused hand lightly on Ruth's hand, jarring her out of her thoughts.

"You are strong enough to handle this." Priscilla promised. Ruth nodded, still feeling unsure but wanting to be a big girl. It was time to put her emotions aside and help her family not break under the stress. Time to put all the lessons her mother taught her to the test. She didn't feel ready but that didn't matter because nothing really mattered anymore.

Shadow Log: Theodore, Shadow Base, South Dakota, February 15, 1802

Sitting in his slightly too cold lab Theodore struggled with his demons. He was now responsible for the entire Emergence Program, five hundred and sixty two children and counting. Most of which, the data suggested, would not live beyond the age of five, and those that did would be dead by fifteen. The guilt weighed heavily on his soul, no manner of drugs or alcohol could make him forget the pain he was now responsible for. So, he remained sober and focused instead on trying to change the odds. If he could save just one of his girls then he would have made a difference but that was currently an impossible task.

His thoughts kept bringing him back to Subject five, her DNA was already mutating in an almost predictable manner which meant he had a chance to save her. But the problem came from the how; how to keep her DNA from turning into mush. Blinking up at the clock, he instantly became aware of the time he had spent staring endlessly at her test results. Six hours and nothing had changed, he was no closer to any answers, it was time to ask for help. He calmly reached over and smacked the call button for his nurse.

She was an average woman who struggled with food addiction which made her not only over weight but unpleasant in her smell. Yet, she was surprisingly intelligent and often had decent insights into people. Knowing she was busy bandaging up a wounded soldier, he popped open his salad, and tried to force himself to eat. He was no good to anyone if he starved himself out of guilt anymore than if he shrank from his duties. Sometime later, the door to his lab slid open and the telling odor of his nurse flooded the room. Bracing himself, he spun away from his lunch, and gave her a large smile.

"Mildred," He said, trying to sound happy.

Mildred gave him the stink eye as she lowered herself slowly onto a stool, her fat folds making it completely disappear under her weight. Theodore gagged as a fresh wave of hell washed over his nostrils.

"I'm very busy today, so drop the pleasantries and tell me what you want." Mildred barked.

Theodore nodded in agreement as he rolled out of her way so that she could take a look at the test results. She gave them a cursory look before reaching out and stealing a handful of salad with her grubby hand.

"Looks like the Subject is mutating properly to match Grace's DNA…Wait look at the strands. She's related to Grace! How is that possible? I thought Grace was the only survivor when the Useptis crashed into her village." Mildred exclaimed excitedly.

Theodore pushed her out of his way, leaned in close to the screen, and put Grace's DNA next to Subject five's. To his surprise, he found that Subject five was indeed related to Grace. From the looks of it she was probably the great, great grandchild of a sibling. But that made no sense… unless… one of her brothers must have somehow survived the crash but hadn't been hit by shrapnel. He'd been left without powers and able to have children. Grace had only survived because her DNA melded with the Useptis DNA embedded in the shrapnel giving her a massive boost in cell regeneration but leaving her barren.

"I can't believe it." He whispered in shock.

"Should we, I don't know, tell Grace?" Mildred asked, sounding equally shaken.

"NO! She'll do something insane, you know how she hated her family. We have to be smart about this if we don't want to end up in The Room." Theodore said with a loud shudder. Mildred returned the shudder as that thought set in.

"You're right, the older she gets the more crazy she is acting. We have to protect Subject five because she'll probably end up as our next boss."

Theodore nodded, not really listening anymore, this meant that Subject five had a real chance of surviving the experiments if he could find a way to control her mutation. The only way he could think of doing that was by facing his greatest fear.

"Do you think the rumors are true? That Grace managed to finally capture one of those Useptis?" He asked quietly.

"Aye, she's keeping it at the Clover School until she can create a secure ward here. The soldier I was working on had the displeasure of being there when it happened." Mildred said, her excitement clearly growing.

"Everything we know about DNA and science in general we learned from them. I have to find a way to get it to help us." Theodore sighed.

The Useptis were terrifying on paper and he was sure that they would be even more so in person. His lip quivered at the mere thought of being trapped in a room with one of them but he had a duty to further the Emergence Program. But more than that he knew deep down he felt a deep fatherly love for the girl and wanted to do everything he could to keep her alive. He had to help get her out of the terrible conditions in which she was living. Had to give her mind a fighting chance amidst all of the horror in which she lived.

"Do you think someone living in an abusive home stands a chance of being good when they grow up?" He asked quietly. The moment the words left his mouth he regretted them, he had just shared too much, and put himself in a vulnerable position. And while he didn't think Mildred was likely to betray him, he felt anxiety spring to life inside of him. Tapping his foot nervously, he waited for Mildred to finish chewing her stolen salad, and answer him.

"Have you considered that Grace became so twisted because she pushed everyone who ever cared about her away? That she refused to be loved or taken care of by anyone?" Mildred asked gently.

Theodore blinked both in surprise and in anger, not at Mildred but at himself. He wasn't sure why he hadn't thought about that or why he hadn't thought about the environmental impact of the experiments. Looking back at the screen, he traced the mutations with his fingertips, and allowed his thoughts to drift.

He couldn't force Grace to do anything she didn't want to but maybe he could convince her to let him do more extensive cognitive testing. Then he might be able to help Subject five overcome the horrors of her upbringing.

Turning back to Mildred he said, "Thank you, your insights, as always, have been super helpful."

She nodded, stole a handful of food from his untouched lunch, and waddled out of the room. Staring at the remainder of his lunch, he calmly pushed it into the trash, and let out a small groan. There was a lot to do before he would be allowed to get close to the captured Useptis and a lot more data to collate. Looking at Subject five's DNA he was sure she would be fine for a few more years as long as someone showed her a little bit of love. Cracking his knuckles, he switched back to the reports, and got back to work.

Shadow Log: Grace, Shadow Base, South Dakota, October 17, 1803

Sitting alone in her office, listening to the crackling of the fire, staring at the unprocessed pile of paperwork, Grace wondered why she had been chosen. Why she had not only survived but mutated all those years ago. Tracing the huge scar that covered the left side of her abdomen, she closed her eyes allowing herself to remember the pain of that ship smashing into her home. To remember the terrified mutilated faces of the survivors after the Useptis had started feeding. If she hadn't mutated so quickly she would have been food like the rest of them.

She had fled that day with her baby brother but chose to give him away and lie to everyone about being the only survivor. It had been to protect him from the life she was building, to keep him safe from the sting of those memories. No child needed to know he came into the world as his mother was being eaten alive, and so she had done what had to be done and cut him from her life.

In two hundred years she hadn't tried to get in touch with anyone who might know what happened to him. Hadn't allowed herself to think about him or to regret giving him a better life. But as she grew older and her body began to slow, she found it difficult to not wonder if she had done the right thing. It remained the biggest regret in her long life.

"The past is the past, leave it there." She ordered herself sternly.

Pouring herself a shot of bourbon, she turned her attention to the more immediate problems that The Shadows were facing. The frequency of crashes seemed to be increasing at an alarming rate as if the Useptis could sense their window of opportunity closing. This made Grace really want to smash something or to just repeatedly stab someone to death. Yet, she was stuck in her own self created prison as an administrator. The paperwork alone that The Shadows required to keep running smoothly was enough to drive her insane but then there was the staffing issues, research oversight, and crash monitoring that all required her attention. A normal human wouldn't be able to keep up which was why she was separating those things into their own individual departments with their own oversight management.

She knew that the human body could only take the strain she put hers under for so long before it broke and she was beginning to worry about what would happen if she died. The thought of dying didn't really bother her, it was the thought of failing to complete her mission that left her laying awake at night. The thought of Earth falling to the Useptis and the humans becoming nothing more than cattle. That was why she labored against exhaustion and pain to prepare for the possibility that she would one day not be there to protect her planet.

A knock resounded through her office, startling her out of her thoughts, and causing her to accidentally send her stack of papers erupting across her entire office. Sighing at herself, she quickly blurred through the office collecting every stray piece of paper, and returned to her desk. Finding herself surprisingly short of breath, she dropped into the comfort of her chair, and took several sips of water. Smoothing the wrinkles from her uniform, she straightened her back, and tried to look stern yet regal.

"Enter." She ordered loudly.

A tall, lanky, badly burned man shuffled calmly into the room looking entirely unimpressed with the show Grace was putting on. With an air of exhaustion, he bent down, collected one of the papers Grace had missed, and walked over to her. Setting the paper on her desk, he dropped effortlessly into the metal chair across from her, and gave her the most disapproving glare imaginable. Squirming slightly under his gaze, Grace forced a cold smile, and pretended like she didn't care what he thought.

"Thank you for coming so quickly, these are for you." She announced a bit more loudly than she had intended.

The man chuckled as he watched Grace fidget almost imperceptibly. After a few heartbeats, he accepted the proffered folders, and turned his unwavering focus to the pages within them.

Feeling strangely tingly with relief to be free from his scrutiny, she poured him a glass of water, and downed the rest of the pitcher.

"You want me to be your successor?" The man muttered in shock.

Smiling happily at no longer being the uncomfortable one, Grace leaned back in her chair, and put her feet up on her desk.

"You have been in more battles than anyone else here besides me and you have shown that you are willing to do whatever it takes to win. Benjamin, I honestly can't think of anyone better suited to the role."

Benjamin gave her an almost dirty look, dropped the folders on her desk, and leaned back with his arms crossed tightly against his chest.

"I burned half my face off protecting a nunnery. I don't think that qualifies me to lead an organization that spans twelve countries." Benjamin grumbled.

Grace let the smile drop from her face as she slowly lowered her feet and set back up. Giving him her most disapproving look, she bit her lip, and let out a quiet growl.

"I was a child who only understood how to work the fields when I was thrust into the role of leadership. I have thrived because there is no other choice. As will you." She said sternly.

Benjamin flinched, his body going from tense to ready for battle in an instant. Standing up abruptly, he sent his chair crashing into the floor, and placed his hand on the hilt of his dagger.

"I have given my life willingly to The Shadows because you pulled me out of the gutters, but I will not be bullied into doing what you want. If you're asking nicely then I would be honored to continue my service but otherwise I'm done." He spat.

Grace let out a relieved little laugh, pushed the glass of water over to him, and gave him a huge smile.

"I knew I had picked the right man for the job." She reassured him.

Ignoring the drink, Benjamin grabbed the folders from her desk, and stormed out. Grace finished the water herself, let loose a happy little sigh, and decided to celebrate. Grabbing a cinder weed cigar from her desk drawer, she carefully trimmed it, and lit up.

It didn't take long for the walls to turn all shiny and all of the colors to start to blend together. Shortly after that her skin began to shimmer and a warm tingle ran down her spine as her muscles relaxed. Breathing in, she found that she could taste the air, and it tasted wonderful. Laughing, she could see the sounds dancing through the air and feel them vibrate against her skin. The world certainly was wonderful.

Shadow Log: Theodore, The Clover School for Girls, March 16, 1804

Standing in the shadow of the captured Useptis, Theodore finally understood everything that the Shadow agents had been talking about. Understood why it took twelve well trained humans to even stand a chance at taking one down and why out of those twelve only four were likely to return alive.

The Useptis stood at just over seven feet tall with the head of a mouthless spider, the torso of an ape, the lower body of a horse, a bladed tail, and six huge muscular arms all covered in a dark blue coarse fur. He could smell something akin to lemon mixed with sulfur which made the hair on his arms stand at attention and made it hard to think. He had been told that the Useptis had genetically engineered their bodies for combat, but to see it in action was as terrifying as it was inspiring.

Shaking off his fear he stepped to the edge of the so-called safety zone and said, "I don't know where to start but I think you can help me."

The creature leaned down, taking a few clopping steps forward, and sniffed curiously at the air.

"Fear is not necessary. If Anton wanted That One dead, That One would be dead. Tell Anton what it is That One needs." A small object hanging from the creature's neck said.

"The Shadows are trying to recreate Grace before her body burns out and the responsibility for this falls on my shoulders. But I don't want someone who can't think for themselves, The Shadows have enough pawns what we need is…"

"Anton understands. That One has a person in mind?" Anton cut him off.

"Theodore, my name is Theodore. This is the girl's folder." Theodore watched him flip through the folder excruciatingly slowly all while making strange grunting noises. He felt like he was back in school trying to impress his professors.

Instead he was waiting for an alien with infinitely more knowledge to grade his work which was infinitely more terrifying.

"Good work for a human… but the subject will die in a few years without correction." Anton finally said.

"Thank you, I think, will you help?" Theodore replied uncomfortably.

"That is why At'It'Ut'Tuuuti'Eta'Vor was brought here."

"That's your real name?" Theodore questioned with genuine curiosity.

"That is This One's real name but humans can never understand our language so This One took the name of the man it crushed with its ship. This One will show Theodore how to add to the blood it is using." Anton sighed.

Theodore nodded in relief as he tried to work out how to memorize the overly complicated name. Giving up, he decided to just focus on helping Subject five before Grace ended up getting her killed.

"This One won't hurt Theodore so come close and learn." Anton ordered sternly.

Steeling himself, Theodore crossed the safety line, and walked over to the monitor that Anton was using. Seeing several lines of advanced genetic code he immediately knew he was in for a long night.

Shadow log: Ruth, Barrington, Rhode Island, June 1, 1805

Ruth could feel panic starting to close in again but this time there was no hiding, no running, no escape. She was expected downstairs to help entertain her father's guests and her own feelings on the matter didn't matter. Just like they never mattered, not since the accident, not since her mother had gone catatonic leaving her to deal with her father's spiral into a deep depression. Even from where she was standing, she could hear the rowdiness of the poker game, and knew that soon more of the family's silver would be missing in the morning, and that would be if they were lucky. Shuddering as much as the tightly laced corset would allow, she corrected her posture, and gracefully descended the stairs.

The 'gambling room' was formerly the dining room, but now instead of nice china on display there was a makeshift bar complete with a smoking section. Instead of a nice table there was a scratched up table with broken down chairs, all supporting mysterious stains. Instead of polished floors there were barely maintained boards that creaked under your feet. At first Ruth had managed to be the woman of the house and with Priscilla's help had kept everything pristine, but when her father had gambled Priscella off to one of his buddies everything fell apart. The beatings had begun since she could no longer handle all of the cooking, cleaning, and yard work by herself. No manner of logic could convince her father to keep his belt in his pants when he was drunk. Ruth had lost count of the times her mother had sat there in her bed unmoving as she howled and begged for the pain to stop. This was her new life, her new reality as a caregiver to a man who could barely walk a few feet before having to rest. It was miserable and there was no escape.

Walking into the room, she was surprised to see a tall, and well distinguished woman seated as the honored guest. Women weren't allowed to gamble, to drink and smoke, to have fun. So, why was this one so different? Blinking away her shock, she obediently walked over to the bar, and began prepping six drinks, six smokes, and gathering the biscuits she had made earlier. Working slowly with her back to the room she took the opportunity to listen in.

"Bit early in the evening for big bets don't you think?" Charles, her father's oldest friend, asked.

"Evening is a perspective, it's been evening all day for me!" Her father shouted.

The entire room flinched at the volume of his voice which made Ruth spill a little of the whiskey on the bar. Moving quickly, she wiped it up hoping that her father hadn't noticed the mistake. Steeling herself for the booty grabs and disrespect, she carefully gathered up her skirts with one hand, and grabbed the tray with the other.

"Come now, Arthur, there's a lady at the table." Mark, a fairly new face to the group, protested.

"Grace is no lady." Her father chuckled.

"Aye, she can kill us all with her pinky." Benjamin laughed dryly.

Ruth blocked out the continuing conversation as her full concentration fell on not spilling a single thing. She walked over and sat the first set of refreshments on the table. Her father grabbed her ass right on the freshest bruise which she knew he had done on purpose but she didn't react beyond navigating around his hand, not another drop was spilled. Grace was suddenly standing over her father and a fresh bruise was blossoming on his cheek from where she had slapped him. Ruth, stunned, now eyed the burned man wondering if he was telling the truth or exaggerating, but could only see serious fear in his eyes. She cautiously tuned back into the conversation.

"Being a pig is never acceptable. Now apologize to your daughter." Grace growled angrily.

Her father muttered a half assed apology while rubbing his cheek in what was clearly shock. Grace gave him the most disappointed look imaginable before she calmly reached out, grabbed his ear, and twisted it so that he had to twist his head to avoid losing it. His cry of pain made Ruth smile internally but she made sure to remain serene on the outside, fearing what would come once the guests had gone.

"This really isn't necessary." She said shakily.

Grace gave her father's ear a good yank making him scream in pain and said, "Nonsense, a gentleman should understand how to behave in polite society." Grace replied coldly.

"I'm sorry, I'm so sorry!" Her father shouted loudly.

Grace raised an eyebrow expectantly at Ruth, who quickly nodded in agreement, and Grace released his ear. Ruth hurriedly set out the rest of the refreshments undisturbed as Grace nonchalantly returned to her seat.

"Ruth, dear, would you please head upstairs and get out of those ridiculous clothes before you pass out?" Grace asked sweetly.

Ruth froze not knowing how to respond or how to get out of the beating that was surely coming her way. Watching her father rub at his ear, she felt that pesky panic flare back to life, and had to struggle to keep the tears in check. Grace gave her a long look before she clicked her tongue and turned back to Arthur.

"Don't you think Ruth should be tending to her mother rather than putting on a show for us? I can handle pouring a few drinks and for that matter so can you." Grace said in a tone that made arguing impossible.

Her father nodded meekly, not wishing for things to escalate further, Ruth curtsied quickly, and fled the room. She raced up the stairs, fighting for every breath as the corset compressed her ribs, and darted into her room. Shaking uncontrollably, she sagged into her makeup chair, and tried to not pass out from the lack of air. Suddenly stern fingers were unlacing her dress and loosening her corset so that she could suck in huge deep breaths of fresh much needed air.

"Just breathe," Grace cooed softly as she pulled her into a hug.

Ruth's shock gave way to relief and she felt so safe snuggled up in Grace's arms almost like it was her mother comforting her. But she knew the moment had to pass which just made her sob even harder. She let out all of her pent up emotions into those strong arms which just held her tight while gently stroking her hair. Until her tears dried up on their own, she stopped shaking, and was able to breathe normally. Grace gently squeezed her one last time, before she took a firm step back, and gave her a huge smile.

"There that's better, now we can talk." She announced.

Ruth watched her drop onto the edge of her bed wondering who this woman really was and why she had taken such an interest in her? The entire evening hadn't made any sense and that left her feeling very uncomfortable.

"I know how confused you must be feeling right now and I commend you for your poker face. I run an organization that specializes in protecting people and I was thinking that you would be a good fit for recruitment." Grace explained.

Ruth stared at her trying to decide if she was being pranked or not. It felt wrong to have a complete stranger see her worth when her own father couldn't. But it also felt like the hope she had been hunting for and she was afraid of missing her only chance to escape.

"Why me? It can't just be because of my poker face." Ruth demanded to know.

"You tuned everything out to focus on a single thing with a concentration that is beyond remarkable. With effort, support, and the right resources you could be a very good agent capable of saving a lot of lives." Grace gushed.

Ruth blushed, her eyes darting to the floor uncomfortably at the compliment, and nervously began to fidget with the collar to her dress. It had been a long time since anyone had taken the time to notice her efforts, much less compliment her. It felt surprisingly nice, but she had no idea how to handle it. Realizing Grace was waiting for her to say something, she returned her gaze to Grace's eyes, and gave her a small smile.

"I am not used to kind words, thank you. But, I do sense that there is a cost to admission to your organization." She said cautiously.

"There is a cost to everything; it is a fact of life. The cost is high, some see it as too high, but I can promise you that it is essential to ensuring the commitment needed to serve." Grace said cautiously.

Whatever the cost, it had to be pretty extreme for Grace to be so worried about telling her. But listening to the ruckus down stairs only made Ruth remember how she had gotten the bruises covering her butt and legs. Remember the way her father now looked at her, like she was a piece of meat for him to consume. She remembered her mother's vacant eyes, ragged breathing, and the smell of her sores. She remembered how badly she wanted her freedom from her family's burdens, to escape being married off to some rich jerk who wouldn't love her.

"I'll pay it, whatever it is." She whispered.

There was an unknown fierceness to her voice that surprised her and made her see that the panic she felt bubbling inside her wasn't hers. She was simply carrying it for her family and she was tired of lifting their burdens without support. She wanted a family that would be there for her when she needed them like Grace had already shown she was willing to do.

"I want you to end your mother's suffering and give your father a chance to heal. Not only will I make sure you are accepted into my organization, but will also clear your father's debt, and I will try to get him the help he needs." Grace said, sounding almost regretful.

Ruth looked out the window, feeling a heaviness settle in her chest at the thought of ending her mother's life, but she already knew she would say yes. Her mother's soul had died when she gave birth to her third dead brother. What lay in her bedroom was just a shell waiting to die anyway and it would probably even be a mercy.

"How?" She asked simply.

"I'll get you a fast acting poison you can put in her morning gruel that will kill her painlessly." Grace replied without a hint of surprise.

Ruth nodded in agreement, not really having any words to describe the mix of anxiety, anticipation, and hope surging through her body. Turning back to the room, she found she was alone again with only her thoughts to keep her company, but hope had already started to creep back in. Hope that soon she would be able to escape the belt, the humiliation, and the pain. That, maybe, Grace really was going to give her the life she always dreamed of.

Shadow log: Grace, Shadow Base, South Dakota, May 10, 1806

Grace stared at the pile of reports Benjamin had dumped on her desk. Every single one showed her the same thing and each cut her to her core.

For years she had labored to build a safe space for the abandoned, lost, forgotten, and orphans. A place where they could not only feel safe but could also fight for a better world. Now they hated her, despised really, and she only had herself to blame. In trying to keep them safe she had inadvertently suffocated them which had made them feel unsafe.

It hurt a lot to know they felt this way, but this wasn't about her. It was about her family, the family she had built, and bled for. It was about them having a chance to feel safe in their own home so that they wouldn't end up dead in an alley somewhere. It was time for her to begin the process of stepping down and taking a more active field role in lieu of leadership. Time for her to stop putting her needs ahead of theirs and be the mother they needed.

She sagged into her chair, poured herself a drink, and tried to get her head in the right space. It would still be a few years before she could officially step down but she could take the first steps to repairing the damage she had done. Downing her drink, she poured herself another one, and flipped on her monitor. Once it had started, she opened up her report application, and started to type.

Shadows,
I have been fighting the Useptis for so long that I have lost track of what really matters. I forgot how important each of you is and how much you do to ensure our planet is safe. I can't apologize for the pain I have caused without first

showing you that the apology is sincere. In an attempt to repair some of the damage I have done as of today May 10, 1806 I will be effectively stepping down as your leader. It will take a few years for the transition to be complete but moving forward Benjamin Reyes will be leading us into the future. He is a good man, who has shown loyalty and honor in his service and I know he will lead you with that same integrity. I am sorry for any pain and suffering my actions have caused and hope that one day you will be able to forgive me for my transgressions. For better or worse I tried to do what I felt was necessary to protect you and in doing so I became your new nightmare.

Please, forgive me,

Grace

Her hands shook slightly as she hit send, her heart aching at the mere thought of what she had just done, and downed another glass of bourbon. She wished she knew what it was like to be able to get drunk, to feel hungover, and to be normal for once. But that wasn't the life she was meant to lead and the one she had was filled with excitement and purpose. It was one she was proud of even if she had made mistakes, now she only needed to clean up those mistakes, and ensure The Shadows continued under a capable leader.

Shadow Log: Theodore, Subject Five's home, July 23, 1807

It had been far too long since he had been able to visit Subject Five, his duties as head of the Emergence Program left him with little time to do house visits. Those duties he had left to his nurses so that he could focus on keeping Grace away from the truth. But now Five was starting to become her own person, to learn how to be a human, and he wanted to be there to show her love. To sing to her again, to teach her how to be kind, and how to think for herself. Without air-conditioning the tiny shack not only was oppressively hot but also incredibly rank. He was sure he would never get used to the smell of urine and feces baking in the summer heat anymore than he could get used to the new bruises constantly appearing all over Subject Five's body. At least he was trying to make a difference in her life, to show her what love was, to hide her from Grace and her agenda. Yet, somehow, it didn't feel like he was doing enough or could ever do enough to end her suffering.

Her mother finally tossed him the key to the closet where she kept her daughter and sluggishly dragged her lazy ass out of the shack. Using a handkerchief he carefully collected the key, walked over to the closet, and unlocked it. Bracing himself for what he might find, he slowly pulled the door open. The girl crouched huddled against the farthest wall away from the door, her long hair matted to her head. The nightgown she wore barely hid the deep purple, pale green, and dark blue splotches covering her skin much less the various sores sprouting from her body. Swallowing his disgust along with his paternal instincts he crouched down, held his hand out to her, and waited.

After what felt like an eternity, she finally crawled forward, and cautiously took his hand. Giving her an encouraging smile, he carefully helped her out of the closet, doing his best to cause her as little discomfort as possible, and tenderly wiped a smear of blood from her face. Feeling his heart break, he turned his face away from her in an effort to keep her from seeing his tears. But she took his face gingerly between her fingers and softly kissed his forehead.

Giving him the smallest kindest smile, she let go of him as she took a step fearfully backwards.

"I'm Theodore, but you can call me Theo if you want. I'm here to get to know you a bit better. I don't want to just stick another needle in your arm." Theodore whispered softly. The girl cocked her head thoughtfully, looked down at his shoes, and shook her head with what seemed to be disapproval.

Seeing how broken down she was broke his heart and made him want to forget about his oath of service. The only thing that kept him from sweeping her up into his arms and porting away was the knowledge of what she was becoming. Knowing that with his help she could potently find a way to change the entire world. But none of that would be likely to happen if he tried to run away with her.

"Hurt?" She asked as she pointed to the tiny track marks already dotting her arm.

Theodore flinched. He couldn't imagine being so sure that everyone wanted to hurt him, to break his spirit. It made him feel even sicker than the smell of the shack which made him thankful he was doing his best to help.

"No! I will never hurt you without cause!" He protested just as loudly.

"Why?" She asked, her eyes seeming to pierce his very soul.

"Because you are smart, resourceful, and in need of a friend." He mumbled uncomfortably.

Number Five thoughtfully chewed on his words looking like she wasn't sure if she trusted him or not.

He tried to think of a way to reassure her of his intentions, and decided that taking things slowly would be his only option to win her trust.

"How about we take it one day at a time? Hmmm? Have you ever had a bath?" He asked gently.

"Bath?" She asked back suspiciously.

Giving her a big smile, he held out his hand, and said, "Let me show you."

After a long pause she finally took his hand, her tiny frail fingers wrapping loosely around two of his. He understood that it would be a long road before he would be able to earn her trust enough to teach her what she would need to know to fulfill the role he had in mind for her. But he was willing to put in the work and to protect her from Grace no matter the cost. There was no way he was going to let that woman win.

"You didn't give me your name." Theodore said so suddenly that the girl flinched.

"I have none." The girl replied with emotionless simplicity.

Feeling a pang of sadness, Theodore closed his eyes briefly, and let out a heavy sigh.

"Alright, let's see Mary, Amelia, Cora, Emma…"

"Emma." The girl crowded excitedly.

"Emma it is." Theodore chuckled.

"Mama's name is Rose." Emma said matter of factly.

"Emma's a better name anyway." Thedore replied.

He gave her hand a tender little squeeze as they reached the bathhouse feeling a small spark of joy flicker to life inside his chest. The girl would certainly be a challenge, but the fact that she had managed to learn so much without any true interaction meant he had a good chance of helping her; especially with Anton as his advisor.

Shadow Log: Grace, Shadow Base, South Dakota, June 15, 1808

Waking up in the infirmary Grace found herself drowning in fiery pain. Every muscle spasmed, causing red-hot agony to race through her veins. Opening her mouth to scream, the only noise that managed to escape was a quiet little whine as drool flooded down her chin. Her lungs scorned the fresh air making the pain spiral into agony and as they seized her head began to pound. Drowning inside her own body, she willed herself to move, but found herself trapped within the cycle of horrific torment.

Someone injected something into her veins as a tube was shoved rudely down her throat and straps were applied to keep her seizing body in place. The pain receded slowly only to be replaced by a thick fog that weighed her down in heaviness. Groaning uncomfortably, she let the medication wash away the horror from her veins, and drifted peacefully into darkness.

Time vanished beneath the waves of distant agony as Grace found herself standing in the center of an infinite darkness that cradled her with surprising gentleness. She turned in a slow deliberate circle, making sure to take in the vastness of the darkness cradling her, and began to wonder if she was dying. Screwing her eyes tightly closed, she struggled to control her breathing, and tried to remember how she had been hurt. But all she could find within her memories were blurry images mixed with distorted sounds all covered in streaks of black goop.

"It is known as the Black Death, my people are immune and can carry it for years before giving it to a victim. It is both a parasite and a plague that is certain to destroy you." Anton said.

Yelping in surprise, Grace spun around, and gave Anton a nasty glare. She wasn't surprised that he had suddenly invaded her thoughts because she knew of his telepathic abilities. But she was surprised to hear him speak so casually about the thing trying to destroy her body. She took a long moment to clear her thoughts and cleanse as much of the anger from herself as possible.

"What exactly is the Black Death?" She asked calmly. Anton's eyes smiled menacingly as he gave her an icy reply, "The Black Death Anton gave That One is a parasite that infests the stomach first then spreads slowly out into the bloodstream eventually reaching the brain. Once that happens it slowly digests That One from the inside out." Grace swallowed hard as she tried to keep her panic and terror in check. She wanted to smash Anton into a thousand pieces for daring to tell her the truth, but knew she had to put the mission first. Shaking with fear, anxiety, and apprehension she felt her knees buckle in slow motion.

"Did you do this to me?" She finally managed to ask.

"That One tried to make Anton betray Anton's values. Anton refused so That One tried to hurt Anton. Anton had no choice but to remove That One's arm and give That One the parasite." Anton said, like it all made sense.

Choking on her rage, Grace tried to lunge at him, but found her body trapped by an invisible force. Seething, she let loose a howl of pure hatred as her left hand slowly dissolved until it was just a stump ending at the elbow.

"How am I supposed to finish my mission now!" She raged as she tried to break free.

"Anton suggests That One prepares for death; it only has a few years left with treatment." Anton sneered coldly.

Grace ground her teeth, tears creeping down her cheeks as she struggled to come to terms with her failure. Staring down at the stump that had once been her arm she felt a mixture of anger and remorse begin to pump through her veins. She could feel fire racing through her blood, her stomach churning with a cold rage, and the chill of impending doom settling on her skin. Letting her emotions out in a single howl, she wept for what had been lost, and allowed herself to grieve.

When she looked up again Anton was gone, leaving her alone with her grief, trapped in her own personal hell. Wiping away her tears, she cumbersomely dragged herself to her feet, feeling determination flood her.

She may have failed but she had known for a while that her body was slowing down. Had known she needed to prepare for the day she would return to the earth. Anton had just accelerated the process and made the Emergence Project that much more important. When she woke, she would find Theodore, review his progress, and give him some much needed motivation.

Shadow Log: Theodore, Subject Five's Home, November 7, 1809

If there was a God he had to be a very cruel one or a practical joker with a dark sense of humor. Either way, he didn't enjoy being the center of his attention. He wasn't ready to do his duty, to serve Grace's agenda, but ever since the attack she had been an unending pain in his butt. Glancing at his watch, he felt his heart skip a beat, and knew the cruel hand of fate was about to strike.

Turning his attention to Emma, who was working on an advanced math text, he reached out, and took her hand. Holding it with firm gentleness, he tried to find the words he needed, but found himself struggling to even breathe. He bowed his head, closed his eyes, beating himself up for being a coward.

"Emma, no matter what happens I want you to remember that no matter how dark it gets or how painful, you are strong enough to beat it." He whispered fervently.

Emma looked up at him with big scared eyes, her lower lip quivering slightly as she met his gaze. He felt his chest tighten, his heart pounding against his ribs rapidly, and a sharp stabbing pain raced down his right arm. Letting go of Emma, he clutched at his chest, trying to catch his breath but found it impossible.

Knowing that time was running out he grabbed the table desperately, "I love you." He managed to choke out before he passed out…

He woke up some hours later, feeling like he had been thrown across a room by a Useptis, and found himself staring up into the impatient eyes of Grace. Yelping in surprise, he rolled away from her, and set up causing the world to spin uncontrollably. Groaning unhappily, he dusted himself off, and tried to get a sense of his surroundings. He was in a small grove of willow trees by a raging river. It smelled like peat, moss, and horse dung which told him this had to be part of Grace's private garden.

Licking his upper teeth, he muttered, "That was needlessly cruel."

Grace laughed, looking smugly at him with a cruelty that was frightening, and replied coldly, "Cruel is you getting attached to a test subject. Cruel is you trying to hide her from The

Shadows to keep her from her treatments. You have seriously compromised Operation Emergence and that is unforgivable. But The Shadows don't have a replacement for your expertise, so I have decided to be merciful and simply send you to The Room for… let's say five treatments."

Theodore felt everything go cold as bile slowly crept up his throat and air became scarce. The Room was every Shadows' worst nightmare and he had walked right into it. Into being tortured but somehow he knew Emma would be worth it, worth the pain, so long as Anton kept his word and took care of her. Looking back up at Grace's smiling face, he smiled back, letting her see that he wasn't regretful, and gave her a little chuckle.

"Emma doesn't deserve the school. She will not only outlive you, but will out shine you. You will be nothing but a footnote in history but she will be praised for saving Earth." He spat triumphantly.

Grace slapped him hard enough to send him stumbling until he tripped over a root and fell on his ass. Spitting blood onto Grace's shoes, he laughed, letting her know that he was done with being afraid. Letting her know that he would no longer be afraid of her or whoever succeeded her. Smiling defiantly, he picked himself up, and spat the rest of the blood onto Grace's uniform.

"Thousands have died for your crusade, for you, and you don't even care about them." He growled angrily.

"I have never forgotten the dead but I have to focus on the living." She shouted back.

"Arrest me," he said drily.

Shaking her head in disappointment, she stepped behind him, and slapped a pair of cuffs on him.

"The Shadows shall rule the Earth but you are worm food." He laughed.

She angrily hit him over the head just hard enough to render him unconscious.

Shadow Log: Emma, Barrington, Rhode Island, November 12, 1810

Emma had moved beyond hating Rose for the terrible condition in which she lived. She could never forgive the woman for the abuse she had dished out over the years, but she could set it aside for her own sanity. It was hard enough to spend days forgotten, locked in the closet, starving, and covered in pressure sores. But what bothered her the most were the men who walked by her prison at all hours of the day, completely unwilling to even acknowledge her existence, much less offer aid.

Winter was the worst, the cold air washed in from outside turning her prison into a frozen hell from which her tattered, dirty, threadbare nightgown offered little protection. So, she would crouch huddled in the corner, wishing her matted hair offered more warmth, and dreaming of the day she would be free. At least the door had a couple of good peep holes that allowed her to study the men coming to pleasure themselves with Rose. It also allowed her to hear everything going on in the tiny apartment which was both a blessing and a curse with how loud the men were when they were locked in the bedroom.

She had learned early on in her life to be quiet no matter how painful, terrifying, or uncomfortable things were. Had learned that the sock filled with rocks was worse than anything the closet had to offer. Even with the horrors of having to clean out the overflowing chamber pots, that silence was the only way to not make her mother angry. It made losing Theodore even harder. He, at least, had listened when she spoke and encouraged her to think for herself instead of blindly following orders.

Footsteps echoing against the snow laden wooden walkway outside drew her attention to the door. A man, not too heavy or too light, was slowly making his way to the door. His steps were hesitant, probably because he could smell the horrific odor of the un-emptied chamber pots, and Rose's unwashed body from the street. His steps also seemed to carry a heavy burden that was definitely not physical. This was not a man who had been here before, Emma crept closer to the closet door letting her curiosity get the better of her as she pressed her eye to her favorite peephole.

The front door crept open with excruciating slowness allowing a gust of frozen air to rush into the apartment making Emma almost move herself away from the door, but she feared missing what was about to happen. It was a Monday, which was the day Rose always got high and bathed on making his appearance very peculiar. The man stepped into view, just a black silhouette framed in the brightness of the early morning sun. He hesitantly stepped inside, pressing a handkerchief firmly over his mouth and nose as he gagged on the smell.

He was tall, almost tall enough for his top hat to brush against the ceiling. His limbs seemed to be strangely gangly and muscular all at once and looking closer Emma could tell that his face was very angular. Two large brown eyes set just above his crooked nose, and even though she couldn't see them she knew that he had very thin lips. His three piece suit was clearly tailored to him and very well made which meant he was rich. His whole demeanor made it clear he didn't want to be here, making Emma squirm with anticipation.

Thump, thud, crash, sounds exploded from Rose's bedroom as she attempted to stumble drunkenly out of her bed. Listening closely, Emma traced Rose's stumbling steps to the door, and listened to it swing open only to hear it crash into the already dented wall. Right on cue she spit a wad of blood and mucus into her favorite corner and sauntered into the living area.

Emma couldn't hide her smile as she watched the stranger recoil in horror, his eyes going wide as Rose appeared without a stitch of clothing on. Seeing how offended the man was at her nakedness, she calmly turned her back on him, and pulled a dirty robe off of the wall. Slipping into it, she nonchalantly tied it shut, and leaned against the doorframe. Rose opened her mouth to speak but before a single word could escape her mouth she was wracked with a bone shaking cough. Sounding as if death was trying to strangle her, she bent forward coughing so fiercely it was surprising a lung didn't slip from between her lips. Suddenly, she hurled a glob of black, goopy, blood filled mucus mixed with spit at the man's feet making him recoil in horrified shock. Making a miraculous recovery, Rose took a few steps towards the man, and gave him a toothless smile.

"You from the school?" She drooled.

The man looked positively shaken as he stared down at the globs of spittle now splattered across his boots, clearly at a loss for words as he tried to suppress the urge to flee. Emma felt hope beginning to blossom in her chest at the mention of a school but she suppressed it. Emma was never that lucky. Seeing the man regain his composure she refocused her attention on what was about to happen.

"Indeed, I am. I was expecting…Uh, nevermind, you must be Lady Crimson, I am Mr. Moore." He introduced himself, sounding very formal.

A string of drool dripped down Rose's chin and came to rest in her cleavage, going completely unnoticed by the woman but having the effect of horrifying Mr. Moore even further. It was clear to Emma that the man was extremely close to losing his nerve.

"That be me. Best lay in town." Her mother drawled, her words slurring slightly.

"Let's get this over with. Where is the girl?" Mr. Moore said in a tone that was filled with authority.

"Hold onto your cock, I'll get her." Her mother huffed. Emma quickly scrambled back into the corner farthest from the door as her mother came stomping over and began to fumble with the lock. Trying to not let her panic get the best of her, Emma knelt down on her bruised knees, bowed her head, and carefully placed her hands palm down on the floor. The door was thrown loudly open, making Emma flinch involuntarily as she sucked in a scared little gasp of air. Her mother reached in, grabbed a handful of hair, and unceremoniously dragged Emma out of the closet. She roughly slammed her into the closet frame without a care in the world and dropped her at Mr. Moore's feet. She gave Emma a quick kick to the ribs for crying at the sudden pain and dragged her to her feet.

Without a word, Mr. Moore mercilessly grabbed her chin with his right hand, squeezing it painfully as he turned her head back and forth. Whimpering despite herself, Emma tried to ignore the pain and humiliation as the man's steely gaze picked out every one of her flaws. Sighing unhappily, he let her go, and without even looking at her forced her back to her knees. Giving her mother a disapproving look, Mr. Moore took several steps backward, and gulped in a couple lung's worth of fresh air. Looking a bit more centered, he came back inside, and pulled out a coin purse.

"Per your contract, you are entitled to one final payment before I relieve you of the girl." Mr. Moore said.

He dropped two gold coins at her mother's feet, making her hiss like an angry goose, and stomp her feet unhappily. Bending over, her robe fell completely open as she picked up the money, and tossed it forcibly at Mr. Moore's face. She stomped over to him, slapped Emma in the face knocking her out of the way, and jammed her finger angrily into his chest.

"What do you take me for? Hmmm? A fool?!" She demanded to know.

Globs of spit showered down on him, making him recoil blindly, his heel catching on the doorsill, he crashed into the outer wall causing a fairly large hole to appear. Clearly shaken, he desperately tried to wipe the saliva off of his skin, but he only succeeded in smearing it everywhere. Giving up, he straightened his suit, and gave her mother a dirty look filled with loathing.

"Now you damage my home! You'll have to pay for that!" Her mother screeched.

Emma did her best to remain invisible, knowing far too well how much damage the woman could cause when she was angry. At this point, she wasn't sure if the closet or the school would be better. But she did know that she would have no say in the matter and it was better to just stay out of it until her fate was decided. Mr. Moore dropped a bag of gold in her mother's hand, giving her a murderous look.

"You are lucky I don't simply end your miserable life." He hissed.

The man reached down to wrap his hand tightly around Emma's arm but immediately let go. A horrified look flooded his face as his hand came away encrusted with a mysterious, foul, slimy, clear substance that smelled even fouler. Shaking his head in disbelief, he tried to wipe his hand off on the nearest wall only to have it come away covered in black sludge. Looking sick, he reached down, grabbed Emma roughly by the waist, and threw her over his shoulder. Without another word, he stomped away, angrily muttering to himself as he hurried towards the main street.

Emma felt a mixture of fear, worry, and joy begin to overwhelm her. It was one thing to live as her mother's slave, to be familiar with her tormentors, and to know what to expect. But quite another to be taken into the unknown by a man who had just bought her. A man who clearly knew who she was and had come specifically for her for some unknown purpose. She wanted to flee, to escape to somewhere warm where no one could hurt her anymore but the fear left her unable to move. Only the mention of the school was holding back outright panic.

Before she knew what was happening Emma was dropped unceremoniously into the snow causing her to yelp in surprise and pain. Shivering, she pulled her knees up against her chest, and tried to look small hoping he would just forget about her. Freezing water suddenly came crashing down over her making her howl in shock as every nerve in her body screamed from the cold. Someone roughly grabbed her nightgown, ripping it rudely from her body, leaving her shivering naked in the snow. The rest of her dignity disappeared as the largest man she had ever seen brutally scrubbed the grime from her body with a piece of burlap. Her skin burned from the harshness of his actions as her toes went numb from the frozen ground. Just before Emma was sure she would freeze to death the man slipped a new nightgown over her head, plucked her up, and dumped her onto the floor of a black two horse carriage.

Hearing Mr. Moore laughing with his companion, Emma curled in on herself trying to not let him see her cry, and began to shiver violently. Suddenly, Mr. Moore draped several thick woolen blankets over her as he climbed into the carriage and took his seat. Despite the scratchiness of the blankets, Emma wrapped them tightly around her body, and tried to get warm. The carriage began to move swaying gently as the horses gained speed, every once in a while she could feel the carriage shake as it crossed a rough patch of road, or was jarred by an unexpected bump.

"I had my fun and took my anger out on you. That wasn't fair and I am sorry for the pain I caused. I know you're hungry and thirsty, so, please let me rectify that." He whispered gently.

Staring up at Mr. Moore, angry, but confused, she carefully sat up, and let him see how much pain she was in. She didn't expect him to care or to even respond. He had made it clear he wasn't interested in her feelings or her thoughts, but she needed to know how far he would go to make her disappear. She needed to understand her place in this new world. To her surprise he simply gave her a small smile, took a sip of water from a canteen, and offered it to her.

Emma didn't trust him, but he was right about her being thirsty and she was starving. Her hand trembled as she carefully accepted the canteen and brought it to her lips. She closed her eyes, letting the cool water flood her mouth, before she swallowed it. It tasted like winter and spring all mixed up with fall and it was absolutely wonderful. Before she could stop it, a single tear slipped out of her left eye, and raced down her cheek. She fearfully wiped it away hoping that Mr. Moore hadn't seen it lest she be punished.

"Tears aren't shameful, they're our emotions escaping our bodies so that we can heal." He said gently.

He handed her a small tin, gently stroked her cheek, and turned his attention to the window giving her space to process. Before she knew what was happening she was sobbing quietly as she tried to understand why he was being so nice to her. It felt unnatural, like at any moment he would turn back to her and slap her for being foolish. But, he let her cry herself dry, leaving her to the quiet swooshing of the carriage, allowing her to compose herself.

After what felt like an eternity her tears dried up, allowing her to carefully peak into the tin. Inside she found five circular disks that smelled a lot like her mother's chocolates. Bracing herself for a terrible taste, she pulled out one of the disks, and gave it a nibble. Fresh tears leaked down her face as the most wonderful chocolatey taste filled her mouth.

"They taste good." She whispered in shock.

Mr. Moore replied with a smile.

Unable to contain her enthusiasm Emma ate the entire tin of cookies while taking long drinks from the canteen. It was so very wonderful to be able to eat something that wasn't watered down, unseasoned grits or oatmeal. Smiling for the first time since Theodore's death, she leaned back against the seat, and pulled the blankets tightly around herself.

"Thank you," she whispered sleepily.

She drifted off to sleep, feeling Mr. Moore's eyes bore relentlessly into her, finding it impossible to keep her eyes open. The tin rolled out of her hand as the carriage hit a large bump in the road and Emma lost consciousness.

Shadow Log: Jacob, Rhode Island, November 12, 1810

The sights outside his carriage were almost as bleak as the darkness creeping into his heart. For years his job had been to help children find a new life with a true purpose. Now, he collected pets for Grace like some kind of lap dog who jumped when told to jump and was obedient over intelligent. Staring out at the wasteland that had been vibrant fields only months before made him feel an anger begin to bubble inside of him. All he wanted to do was to disobey, to stop hurting the girls he was now forced to collect, but he was afraid. The tiny scar on the back of his head began to itch in tune with that anger, a reminder of his oath of service.

The carriage shifted ever so slightly indicating someone else had ported in and even without looking he knew who it was. The smell of lilacs mixed with vanilla and lemon was a dead give away that his master was checking up on him. His shoulders tensed and his spine straightened as he prepared for the confrontation he knew she was about to start. She hated it when people ignored her calls, almost as much as she hated it when her toys stopped acting like toys.

"Hello Grace." He said calmly.

He refused to look at her knowing that even if it was the smallest act of rebellion it would anger her greatly.

Sometimes, you just had to take a stand in any way you could that wouldn't lead to your death. You just had to draw a line in the sand and say no more or risk being washed unceremoniously away with the tide. This Emma was his line; even an idiot could tell she was special to the woman which meant he might have a way out.

"Mr. Jacob Moore, you've been ignoring me." Grace purred angrily.

"Have I? Perhaps running a torture camp for you has been a bit of a strain." He replied.

He smiled for a split second, proud of himself for speaking his mind, and then he wiped it away for a more serious expression. Turning to face Grace; he was pleased to find her clutching a handkerchief over her mouth with a sour look written across her face. There was nothing in this world quite like the lingering smell of human excrement and he had known walking into Emma's apartment that he'd have to burn his favorite traveling suit. The whole carriage was rank with it already and it looked like Grace's enhanced senses were struggling.

"She was locked in a closet covered in bedsores, whoever you replaced Theodore with wasn't doing his job," Jacob said disapprovingly.

Grace reached down to stroke the girl's face with surprising tenderness just before she calmly stuck a concealed three point needle into the girl's arm. Turning her attention back to Jacob, she gave him a terse smile, and dropped her hands on her lap. They sat for a long while just admiring the passing scenery before Grace stirred and gave him a haunted look.

"I'll be dead before long, returned to the earth once more like everyone must one day. That doesn't scare me, I used to think nothing did, especially after the Useptis ate my village. But recently, I have come to realize that I am afraid of leaving the family I built without protection. Twelve men leave, two return able to fight again, two return maimed, and eight return in body bags. This experiment started before you were born and today remains the same with only paltry results. My methods have grown extreme, I know that, but I will not fail. Not in this!" She explained.

He could see real pain in her eyes, real distraught at losing her edge, and he felt bad for her. But that didn't excuse her inability to see how much damage she had already caused to so many children.

"Six hundred and forty one girls have arrived at the Clover School for Girls since your tenure there. Of those girls forty one remain and one of them is lying at your feet. The rest have had their bodies burned in the basement by my hand." He replied coldly.

Grace flinched, her face growing angry as she unhappily tapped her leg with her robotic hand. It was clear to Jacob that the woman had already started to lose her mind to the parasite living inside of her but as of yet he hadn't found a way to get her to listen. Nor had he found a way to contact her superiors to have her removed from his school.

"Their deaths are regrettable but I have buried over fifty thousand souls in my tenure with The Shadows and when I stop being able to hunt that number will represent the losses in six months. I can't allow that to happen, I won't be responsible for that, I cannot take that guilt with me to my grave." Grace said with firm conviction.

Jacob wasn't sure why he was trying to argue with a lunatic fanatic, it was pointless since he could never change her mind. Glancing down at Emma's sleeping form, he felt his heart break at the horrors she had already faced in life. Break at his responsibility in what was about to happen to her, and at what he was already responsible for.

"That One has options." Anton said into his mind.

Jacob's head reverberated against the carriage wall as he jumped in shock at the suddenness of the contact. It had been years since the alien had spoken to him and then it had only been to threaten to rip out his guts and feast upon them. It made no sense for him to speak now unless he knew something that Jacob didn't and was for whatever reason attempting to help.

"Okay, I'm listening." Jacob thought loudly.

"No need to shout, humans are loud enough already with all of their constant thinking." Anton chastised angrily.

Smiling involuntarily Jacob turned to Grace and asked, "Is that all or do you want me to report for disciplinary action as well?"

Grace sneered at him, looking like she would like to drive her fake hand into his chest, and rip out his heart. But instead she disappeared in a flash of light, leaving him alone with his thoughts and the alien listening in. Unless, you counted the drugged Emma who wouldn't wake until they were close to the school.

"That One was tasty, Anton had issues not eating more of it." Anton purred.

Jacob wrinkled his nose in disgust at the thought of Grace being tasty to eat and tried to not vomit from the visual image as it combined with the smell of his clothes. Shuddering, he got his stomach under control, and turned his attention back to Anton.

"What is your plan?" He asked sternly.

"Anton knows that Emma is Grace's hive member. Anton has been working with Theodore to help refine the genetics of Emma; but the Useptis in her needs trauma and pain to bind to her human parts. Let Grace think she is winning, focus on the mind, protect it, guide it." Anton said.

An uncomfortable slithering inside his head told Jacob that Anton had stopped paying attention and that he was becoming more sensitive to the invasion of his thoughts. He worried for a moment about how many times Anton had listened in without him knowing and realized that Grace had made a huge mistake.

The Useptis might only be able to speak to certain humans with the right DNA but they could hear everyone's thoughts. It meant Anton probably already knew everything about The Shadows and was remaining their prisoner for another reason, but that wasn't his problem, the girls were. If Anton was willing to help him solve his Grace issue then he didn't care if Anton won or not. The Shadows had taken him in and protected him, but that had been over twenty years ago. They had shown their true colors by making Grace his issue and he felt no loyalty to them or their agenda. It was time to start a revolution.

Shadow Log: Emma, The Clover School for Girls, Rhode Island, November 13, 1810

Emma woke to find herself strapped securely to a freezing, cold, metal chair that cut uncontrollably into her lower back and the bottom of her legs. Testing the restraints on her wrists with a couple of sharp upwards yanks she found they were a lot stronger than she was. The one holding her head to the headrest was squeezing just tight enough to be very uncomfortable and cause her head to pound angrily. And she wasn't even sure that she could feel much below the straps holding her feet to the legs of the chair.

It hurt badly, but pain was something that she understood how to handle. Closing her eyes, she took a deep breath, and did exactly as Theodore had taught her. She imagined taking the pain and putting it in a box where it wouldn't bother her. It took her a few moments before she was able to get it under control and focus on her surroundings.

Opening her eyes, she took a second deep breath, and began to look around. From what she could see she was sitting in the middle of an old barn that looked like it would be better suited to be torn down than anything else. The dirt floor in her field of view was surprisingly well packed and clean, almost like someone was keeping it that way. What scared her was the strange tools laid out on a metal tray to her left. While she couldn't see most of them she could make out enough to know they weren't for anything good. Hearing a door open behind her, she took a deep breath, and held it anxiously.

The man who stepped into her eyeline was short, pudgy, and balding. He moved with a deliberateness that only came from age and experience, but his face held a cruelty that made her very uncomfortable. Looking into his steely blue eyes she couldn't detect a hint of emotion as he started looking over his tools. Unable to hold her breath anymore she let it out in one explosive burst that seemed to delight the man.

"I'm going to ask you a series of questions, I will know if you lie to me, and will cause you pain. Do you understand?" He asked in a very matter of fact way.

"Yes Sir." Emma replied calmly.

"Good, do you have excessive bleeding when cut? Does it come out so quickly that it can barely be stopped?"

Emma glared up at him, wishing she had the courage to tell him where to stuff his tools, but she didn't. So, instead she just made her discomfort known through her eyes. Making sure that she didn't flinch away from his coldness despite a healthy fear building in her chest.

"No." Emma spat.

The man pulled out a binder filled with sheets of paper that were already covered in handwriting and started adding data to it.

"Have you sustained any injuries that have left extensive scarring on your body?" He finally asked, still focused on his papers.

"No. I need to pee." Emma said firmly.

The man eyed her for a long moment before he calmly turned his attention back to his papers.

"Then pee." He muttered, sounding like she was wasting his time.

Emma shifted uncomfortably not wanting to just pee all over herself. She had done enough of that in her life to know that she didn't want to give this man the satisfaction. She could tell he enjoyed the suffering of others just from the way he moved, he was just like her mother. Time to put the discomfort from her mind and focus on not letting him know how unhappy she was.

"How well do you see? Any blurriness?" The man chuckled, clearly knowing how unhappy she was.

"I see everything perfectly." She growled.

"Good, we are ready to begin." He said happily.

Emma wanted to fight the restraints, to struggle to get free, to pee all over his feet, but she didn't do any of that. Instead, she did the one thing she knew would piss him off and held completely still. Controlling her breathing, she closed her eyes, and began singing silently to herself.

"Over in Killarney, many years ago me Mither sang a song to me in tones so sweet and low."

The pain coming from her right upper arm was difficult to ignore as the man dug a needle repeatedly into her arm leaving behind a very visible black design. But focusing on remembering the words to the lullaby made it easier to remain unreactive. Unfortunately, it also reminded her of Theodore and how much she missed him. It still hurt, like his dying in front of her was only yesterday. Grief seemed to be nothing but an evil parasite trying to worm into her mind.

An half hour later the man sat his tools down and bandaged her wound without a word. A satisfied smile crossed his face as he started to hum a sad little diddy. Emma looked up into his eyes, gave him a huge smile, and peed all over his shoes.

"Told you I had to pee." She growled defiantly.

The man stared forlornly down at his feet, a look of disbelief plastered across his face, and then backhanded her so hard that her teeth rattled together. Emma laughed, enraging him further, but he simply stomped away. His feet made a sloshing, squishy, little squeak with each step that turned her defiant laugh into a genuine one. So much for him being able to enjoy his work but he had no one to blame but himself.

Shadow Log: Jacob, The Clover School for Girls, Rhode Island, November 13, 1810

Jacob stared down at his hands, seeing nothing but blood, and tried to still his racing heart. It was impossible to not feel guilt and regret for his past actions, but it was his most recent ones that had him so disturbed. He had just come from burn duty, seeing those innocent little faces going up in flames always left him feeling hollow, and made him so angry. Angry that he could no longer protect his charges, no longer protect his friends, and no longer protect his daughter. He had let his anger win once all those years ago, it had led him to being trapped in this no win situation, and he was determined to not let it happen again.

"You alright, Jacob?" A male startled him out of his thoughts.

Jacob blinked repeatedly, trying to desperately remember where he was, and why he was there. His surroundings told him exactly where he was and why he had come there. He was standing just inside the old chapel which had been converted to a makeshift infirmary when Grace had converted the school for her purposes. The ten cots to his left were for girls who most likely would not survive the day, for girls he would be burning soon, and for girls who had been marked for death. The ten to his right were for the girls that had been experimented on and just needed some treatment before being released back into the general population. Shuddering unhappily, Jacob turned to face the nurse who was patiently waiting for an answer, and realized he might be about to ruin the poor man's life.

The man was only fourteen, an intern in the nursing program, training to be a doctor. He was tall, muscular, and had dreamy blue eyes which contrasted handsomely with his short blonde hair. Typical of the Winchester family as was his overall kindness, gentleness, and intelligence.

"I have a request that could turn out rather dangerous, and Johnathan I won't be offended if you don't want to hear me out." Jacob finally managed to blurt out.

Johnathan simply nodded, grabbed Jacob by the arm, and pulled him into a supply closet. He quickly locked the door before sliding a short shelf over to block the doorknob. Turning back to Jacob, Johnathan gave him a little nod, and then smiled brightly.

"You hired me when no else wanted to because of my last name. Neither of us signed up to bury children who have suffered more than most adults ever will. What do you need?" Johnathan asked fiercely.

Jacob licked his lips nervously, took a deep cleansing breath, and took a moment to think out his next words.

"There's a new girl that just arrived, Subject Five, she is different from the rest, and we have to protect her without Grace knowing." He said firmly.

"How do we do that? This Five will be in a cell by the end of today, and then Philips will get to handle her care…" Johnathan asked in bewilderment.

"She is going to hate me for betraying her trust when I bought her, plus I'm an authority figure, and she has already been abused. You will have direct access, the ladies swoon over you, and you can give her the friend she needs to stay sane. I'm also going to have Mary befriend her and give her a sense of purpose." Jacob explained.

"I can try, but Philips is a suspicious fellow and he was ranting this morning about someone new peeing on his favorite boots." Johnathan sighed.

Jacob chuckled happily, it was awesome that she had enough presence of mind to know how to resist, and that meant Theodore had done a great job preparing her. Theodore might be the key to ending this if he could be found, it might be a good idea to visit the basement, and have a long talk with Anton.

"Sounds like Five is already fighting back, that's good even if it complicates things. I suggest that you don't give Philips a chance to figure out what you are doing or he'll hurt you." Jacob warned.

"He punishes his nurses for failing with a strap that has little metal balls on one side. Once it's strapped to an arm or leg it becomes painful quickly, but leaves only a few bruises, and is something I know how to handle." Johnathan promised.

"If that's the case, let it happen, sneak out, and show your father. The Winchester family has a ton of pull in these parts." Jacob suggested.

Johnathan got the biggest shit eating grin on his face, gave Jacob a nod of agreement, and glanced anxiously at the door.

"I have to go or it'll be worse than the belt for sneaking out." Johnathan warned.

Jacob nodded, waved at the door, and said, "Go, but please be careful Grace will kill you before she lets anyone disrupt her work."

Johnathan hurriedly unlocked the door, slipped out, and hurried away. Jacob felt a bit of the weight weighing him down lift a little as he watched Johnathan walk away. It felt right to be working to undo Grace and that made him happy, but his next task was going to be much worse. Straightening his suit vest, he took a moment to prepare, and snuck out of the closet.

Shadow Log: Grace, The Clover School for Girls, Rhode Island, November 13, 1810

Grace stepped into the processing barn, her senses immediately getting assaulted by the smell of urine, ink, and blood. Her stomach growled, making her cringe, she would never get used to the sudden hunger that the smell or sight of blood brought on. Rubbing the stump of her arm, she took a deep breath to steady herself, and walked up to the girl.

"Subject Five, I think you're the first girl to ever get under Philips's skin." She said calmly.

The girl stared up at her, unflinching, and completely calm. It reminded her a lot of her in the early days, even her pupils were narrowing like hers did, and she felt a spark of hope under all of the heaviness weighing on her heart.

"The name is Emma." The girl growled angrily.

Grace smiled, reached down, and stroked the bruise blossoming on the girl's face. She was a fighter, strong and fierce, and she would be a fine replacement…if she survived.

Grace took a step back, taking a breath, she couldn't get attached to the girl, and let go of her emotions. She took a single step backwards, gave her a cruel look, and let her see the coldness within her.

"Moving forward you will only be referred to as Subject Five. At least until you prove you are worthy of a name." Grace growled.

The girl went cold, a look of rage flashing momentarily across her face, and then it was gone, replaced by a frozen glare. The girl showed potential, too much potential to let her know the truth, and Grace knew in that moment she had to take a step back. Grinding her teeth, she turned her back on the girl, and walked over to the door.

"I will send in a nurse to finish your processing." She hissed before slamming the door angrily.

She wasn't angry at Emma or even at herself, she was angry that this damn parasite was taking everything away. She was angry that she was slowly losing herself to something that was eating her soul a little at a time. What stung the most was that she was the only one truly to blame for her current predicament, and instead of fixing it she was just letting it happen.

"Protect your family." She whispered to herself as she walked away.

Shadow Log: Emma, The Clover School for Girls, Rhode Island, November 13, 1810

Emma was furious at the audacity of these people for stripping her name from her, for treating her as property, and for having let herself feel hope. She should have known that they weren't to be trusted, should have tried to escape, tried to fight back. But she was too small, too broken down, too untrained to take on men who wanted to keep her prisoner, at least for now. Theodore had promised her that one day no one would be able to tell her how to live her life which meant that all she had to do was be patient and learn all she could about those who meant her harm.

She heard the door open once more and braced herself for whoever was coming. To her surprise a young, handsome man with kind eyes came over and began working on unstrapping her from the chair. She sensed a reluctance to cause her any further harm which worried her greatly. It didn't make any sense, didn't fit into her experiences with the school, and was like nothing she expected. This made her fear a trap of some kind or a test that she would somehow fail, since she didn't yet understand all of the rules. It was for these reasons that she remained on guard yet obedient once the straps were removed and she was marched unceremoniously outside.

The snow made her feet ache as it smushed wetly between her toes and made her want to shriek. She tried to ignore the discomfort but the debris littering the forest floor hidden beneath the snow made it impossible to keep her footing much less keep from cutting her bare feet. An almost inaudible whimper slipped out as her ankle twisted, making the man stop short, and turn to face her. Seeing the pain on her face, a guilty look filled his eyes, and he took a single step towards her before he froze uncertainly, looking like he was afraid of scaring her.

"May I carry you the rest of the way?" He asked with surprising gentleness.

Emma took a step away from him before she could catch herself, chewing unhappily at her lip, she gave him a nod of approval fully expecting him to treat her with extreme roughness. But he approached slowly, giving her a chance to prepare herself, before he carefully scooped her up, and cradled her softly to his chest. Wrapping her arms around his neck, she snuggled into his warmth, and started to wonder if he wasn't going to hurt her after all.

He carried her to a medium sized building with a low roof, and a single wooden door recessed into its front. It sat just inside of the treeline like some sort of predator waiting to ambush its prey. The pockmarked stone walls were covered with dead vines and its roof seemed to sag slightly under the weight of the snow resting upon it. Despite its appearance Emma felt nothing but peacefulness coming from the building as the man gently deposited her at its door. He fished out an old rusty key, quickly pushed the door open, and ushered her into the steam that came billowing out. The inside was just as worn as the outside, the stone floors worn smooth by the feet of its many visitors, and the stairs descending into the hot spring looked near to worn out. Looking around she could see a row of benches sitting along the far wall with a row of towels hanging above them, but besides that the room was barren. She turned to face the man, raised a questioning eyebrow, and waited.

"Sorry if I scared you at the barn, the guards were watching, and I can't afford to get caught being kind to the girls or I get punished. My name's Johnathan, I work as a nurse in the infirmary…obviously. What's your name?" He asked quietly.

"Emma." She replied suspiciously.

"Nice to meet you, please fetch a towel, and get yourself cleaned up. I'm going to stare at this door like my life depends on it to give you some privacy." Johnathan said. True to his word Johnathan turned his back on her and stared intently at the door. Smiling to herself, Emma began to worm her way out of the urine soaked nightgown, and tried to think. Johnathan seemed to be one of the good ones, but this place had more layers than an onion. She wanted to trust him but that felt foolish, especially after she'd let her guard down earlier, and ended up drugged. Grabbing a towel, she laid it out by the edge of the pool, and jumped into the water.

The heat was a shock to her frozen body, but that faded away quickly, leaving her to moan with pure bliss. She sank into the water, letting it wash away the horrors still clinging to her skin, and let herself settle on the bottom. She had incredible lung capacity according to Theodore but to her water was a second home. It cleansed her, leaving her feeling relaxed, but she knew staying under too long would be a bad idea. She surfaced in a spray of water to see Johnathan shifting worriedly on the edge of the pool.

"So much for enjoying the pleasures of the door." Emma laughed.

Johnathan blushed, quickly turning his back on her, and hung his head shamefully.

"You are one of the good ones." Emma sighed happily.

"I try to walk in the light of the lord." Johnathan replied quietly.

"Can you tell me what to expect once I'm finished here?" Emma asked hopefully.

"The new arrivals are taken to registration, scanned in, and put in their cell until the next release period. I'd try to get some rest while you can, after the release you'll see Philips again, and I guarantee that you angered him greatly." Johnathan explained softly.

Rinsing the rest of the debris from her hair, Emma took a deep breath, and wondered if running was an option. Yet running didn't feel right, there were other girls here, and those girls didn't know how to withstand the pain like she did. They were defenseless, trapped in this hell, and she didn't feel right running away.

"Thank you for being kind." She whispered.

She climbed out of the pool, wrapped the towel around her body, and walked over to where Johnathan waited. He gave her a big smile, being careful to keep his eyes on her face, and led her over to one of the towel pegs. He gave it a quick pull causing a hidden door to appear next to it.

"Follow the hallway and you'll find registration, be careful there are some sharp rocks, and the lights completely suck. And Emma, please be careful, I don't want to have to burn your body." Johnathan warned.

Emma nodded nervously, chewed on her cheek for a moment, and stepped into the unknown. She wasn't a hero, wasn't a savior, but she was a girl who hated people like her mother. Theodore had taught her that running away was never an option with those people because when they inevitably caught you it would be extremely unpleasant. The only way out was through, was to fight them from within, and that was something she was good at.

Shadow Log: Ruth, The Clover School for Girls, Rhode Island, November 14, 1810

When Ruth had graduated from basic training, she had thought she was on to a life of glorious adventure, but instead here she was bullying children. Grace had made it clear that with her training, young appearance, and sweet demeanor that no one would suspect her of being a spy. The problem was that she hadn't signed up to be a glorified babysitter, trapped in a prison, reporting to Grace like some sort of pet. But if this was her first assignment then she would do it like no one else could and prove her worth. Today was a simple task, wake the new girl with a bucket of cold piss, and make sure she felt like the garbage she was. The doors to the girl's rooms were kept unlocked to encourage disobedience and to allow for more punishment to be administered. Taking in a steadying breath, she pushed open the door slowly, making sure to not spill the bucket of piss she held in her left hand, and stepped into the room. The room was a six foot by six foot stone gray room with a cot, a nightstand, and a chamber pot. It felt cold, uncaring, and bleak, almost like it didn't want an occupant, but that was just silly because rooms couldn't have feelings. Looking down at the black haired little girl sleeping peacefully, she felt sad that she had to wake her the way she was about to, but it was her job. Clenching her teeth, she hefted the bucket up, and threw its contents into the girl's face.

The girl came alive with an unholy shriek that turned Ruth's blood to ice. Before she could react, the girl launched herself off of her cot, and onto Ruth's chest. Ruth tried to push her off, to fight as the girl hissed evilly, and clamped her teeth down onto Ruth's ponytail. Ruth's training kicked in and she sent the girl flying off of her, but unfortunately the girl didn't let go of Ruth's hair, which meant that the ponytail went with the girl when she went flying through the air. Trying not to cry at the pain, Ruth clutched her head, and quickly scrambled out of the room. The girl's insane laughter as she spit the hair out of her mouth was haunting and Ruth knew it would haunt her dreams for a long while. Slamming the door, Ruth dropped to the floor, and looked down at her bloody fingertips. How had she let herself get jumped like that? How had she failed so miserably? Hearing the guards approach, she stumbled to her feet, and prepared herself for Grace's inevitable rage. So much for her being ready for the field, so much for being a good agent, she clearly had a ways to go.

Shadow log: Emma, Barrington, Rhode Island, November 14, 1810

Emma was furious that she was once again covered in pee, it was annoying that it kept happening, but now she understood what they were trying to do. Knowledge was power, it would allow her to control the narrative, and she was starting to gather her footing in this strange new place. Laughing hysterically, she picked the hair out of her teeth, and waited for the guards to come into her cell. There was no way she wasn't going to get beat up for ripping out that girl's hair and scalp. No way to avoid getting a personal visit from Philips, but that was a small price to pay for the fun she had just had.

Two guards threw open the door to her cell, looking around like they were sure they'd find a she-demon instead of Emma. Emma smiled at them, held up the ponytail, and swung it back and forth like it was a trophy she had just won. Throwing it at their feet, she dropped onto her knees, and placed her hands on her head. There was no way she would be able to resist and so she settled for being obedient unless provoked. They rushed in, cuffed her, and placed a bag over her head. Suddenly, a needle was stabbed into her neck and everything went black.

Emma woke to the worst headache she had ever experienced, immediately tried to look around, but she found that the bag was still over her head. She was still restrained and so she turned to her other senses to determine where she was. Closing her eyes to help her concentration she inhaled deeply through her nose. Old books, smoke, and a strange pungent smell that she couldn't identify all mixed with the smell of vanilla.

Hearing voices muffled by a wall or door, she turned her full focus to listening in, even stopping her breathing to help heighten the sounds.

"We subdued the subject, she's waiting in your office." A gruff male voice said.

"So, you're capable of doing part of your job…Give me the key to her restraints, I'll take it from here." Mr. Moore replied almost angrily.

A rustle, followed by a jingle, and then a growl; then a door opening. Footsteps coming closer, growing louder, and then the bag was lifted off of her head. Emma blinked uncomfortably as her eyes slowly adjusted to the light and Mr. Moore calmly freed her wrists. Rubbing her wrists in an attempt to restore circulation, she stared up at Jacob, and let him see her anger.

"I know you have no reason to trust me, no reason to care what I have to say, but I hope you're willing to listen." He said gently.

Emma hissed as she surged forward, to stand within a few feet of him, and spat on his chest.

"You have been a snake from the beginning, why would I do anything for you?" She demanded angrily.

Mr. Moore calmly took a few steps backward, wiped the spit off, and sat down at his desk. Looking mildly annoyed, he pulled a small wooden box from the desk, and then he gave her a small smile.

"For twenty years this place was a school that taught people how to stand up for what is right, and for themselves. The girl who attacked you this morning was part of the last class to come through before Grace took over and made it a prison. I didn't sign up to be a prison warden, anymore than you signed up to be here. Let me help you survive, please, I can't keep doing this; and please call me Jacob…Mr. Moore died with the school." He said unhappily.

Emma's anger fell away in a sudden burst as emptiness flooded her, shaking uncontrollably, she sagged back into the chair, and tried to focus on her breathing. She needed to sort out the truth of what she had just heard, to figure out how she could matter enough for a man like him to be truthful with her. She was definitely missing too many pieces of the puzzle, pieces she wouldn't get unless she played the long game, and was willing to let people help her. Sighing unhappily, she took a moment to prepare her thoughts, and gave Jacob a little nod.

"Fine, what happens next?" She asked quietly.

"I can't stop Philips from punishing you for hurting Ruth, but I can make it less awful or at least bearable. This box contains cinder weed, it will make the world easier to live in, but it will also alter your perspective." Jacob said.

Emma watched him open the box, pull out a cigar, and offer it to her. She had no idea why she would trust Jacob enough to take drugs from him, but she really didn't want to endure her punishment sober. So she accepted the cigar, let him light it, and took a deep puff of it. She held the smoke in her lungs for as long as she could before letting it out in an explosive cough.

"It won't take long before it will kick in, don't be alarmed if colors start to shift around you or you start to feel tingly." Jacob warned.

"Thank you," Emma whispered softly.

"GUARDS!" Jacob shouted loudly.

The bag went back over her head as a guard roughly cuffed her again, but the emptiness she felt made it easy to not resist as they dragged her away.

Shadow Log: Grace, The Clover School for Girls, Rhode Island, November 14, 1810

Watching Emma endure her punishment, Grace could tell even from her side of the one way mirror that Emma had smoked recently, and from the smell it was cinder. According to the logs it had to have been Jacob, the poor bastard had probably been trying to help the girl, but he didn't know cinder caused DNA to bond more easily to other species. He was unwittingly helping her which made her happy, and so she decided to just ignore his actions for now.

Watching Philp work was like watching a master painter at work, it was amazing how he could take a few grains of rice and a whip, and make a child beg for relief without ever having to use the whip except to keep the subject engaged. Genius really, he was used to breaking rulebreakers for her, and had transitioned to this work so easily.

Her wristband began to beep, loud, and urgently warning her of Useptis movement at the edge of the school. Sighing at the thought of missing the show, she ported away to the last spot where the alarm had been triggered, and took a look around. Moving with urgency, she stepped into the woods, smelling the tale tale smell of cloyingly sweet lemon that had started to go bad. It was the smell of alien blood which meant they were all in danger until she found it and killed it. Hearing the bushes shift behind her, she increased her speed, hoping she had time to reach her preferred battleground before it descended on her. She knew that in such a heavily forested area she would be at the disadvantage and in her current state that would mean death.

Just as she stumbled out of the trees the huge creature came crashing down on her, sending her careening face first into the frozen ground, and knocked the wind from her lungs. Choking for air past the bruises forming on her back, she dragged herself clear of its bladed tail, and rolled onto her knees. Letting out a quiet almost desperate curse, she rolled forward again, making the creature stumble blindly into her trap.

Dual blades came crashing down out of the tree limbs and impaled the creature with barbed hooks that sunk deep into the flesh of its torso. Letting out a warcry, she dodged its attempts at slashing her with its weapons, and rammed her sword into its first, second, third, and then fourth heart.

Panting from exertion, pain, and age, she lowered her weapon, and took a step back. Watching the thing's fifth heart slowly pump the blood out through its wounds she felt nothing but joy.

Switching over to the creature's mother tongue she asked, "How do you wish to die?"

"Death!" It shouted back.

Suddenly, the pain of every choice she had just made, came exploding out across her nerves making her fall forward, and collapse in a ball. Looking up at the thing's smug face she knew that this was where she died, this was the site where her ultimate failure happened. She stared it down refusing to allow it to see anything other than her refusal to quit.

Suddenly, with one exaggerated motion, the creature dropped its weapons on the ground, and ripped its own head off.

"This one is the only one allowed to kill that one," Anton said into her mind.

"Thanks, I think." She sighed.

Forcing her body to work again, she picked herself up, and quickly soaked the body in a salt mixture causing it to bubble and steam. Within minutes there was nothing left but a puddle of greenish black goop that could be washed away with a canteen of water.

The pain the parasite was starting to cause was becoming a real problem. She knew she was running out of time, her body was failing, and she had no more time to waste.

Thankfully, she had a promising subject that she could focus on. It was time to dial up the program and find her successor before she ran out of time.

Shadow Log: Ruth, The Clover School for Girls, Rhode Island, November 15, 1810

Ruth came up out of the slime bath, began vomiting up the sludge, and tried to clear the crap out of her eyes. The slime bath was the quickest easiest way to heal wounds but it sucked to have to endure the stuff slowly creeping its way into every orifice, every pore, every inch of you that it could. And once it had done its work you just had to throw it up, scrub it away, and try to get the slimy feeling off of you. Gulping fresh air into her lungs, Ruth rubbed her bald head, and felt an intense anger form as she thought of her failure. She was a trained agent, she was trained to handle fully grown adults, and she had let a snotty brat get the advantage. It stung to have failed so severely so quickly in her career.

"Failure hurts, especially the first one on duty." Grace said from the doorway.

Ruth grabbed a towel, wrapped it around her naked body, and tried to find her footing on the slippery floor. Finding it was impossible to not slide with the slime coating her body, she slid over to the nearest wall, and used it for support. Turning to Grace, she forced herself to smile despite the foul taste building in her mouth, and prepared for the lashing she deserved.

"I'm sorry, she caught me off guard…" She whispered.

"Indeed, but I know you won't let that happen again." Grace calmly cut her off.

Ruth blinked in shock, a confused look spreading across her face, and tried to understand why she wasn't in trouble. Her knees trembled under her weight, so she slowly lowered herself onto the floor, and gulped in more air in an attempt to calm herself.

"My first failure cost me my entire family…At least, your hair will grow back in time. Wear it with pride for without failure we are nothing. Failure comes from ambition and without it you don't grow." Grace said firmly.

Ruth nodded at a loss for words, bowed her head in shame, and smiled sadly. Grace slid a canteen of water over to her, closed the door, and walked away. Ruth rinsed out her mouth, feeling determined to make the most out of her second chance, and pushed herself up off of the floor. It was time to cleanse herself and return to work.

Shadow Log: Emma, The Clover School for Girls, Rhode Island, November 15, 1810

The klaxon sounded three times, reverberating Emma's cot with its loudness, startling her out of her meditation. It was time to meet the other girls, have breakfast, and try to learn more about her prison. Standing up quickly, she scratched at her dress, feeling sure they had picked the itchiest cloth available to make it out of, and walked to her door.

She froze with her hand on the knob, suddenly overwhelmed with worry, and struggled to breathe. It wasn't the thought of being disliked that worried her, it was the worry that somehow she would anger the guards, and end up in punishment again. She felt sick to her stomach at the thought of having to kneel on rice while reciting the code of conduct. At the thought of the whip meeting her calves again and again every time she mispronounced a word or stumbled over one of them. Jacob couldn't keep her high all the time and even if he tried she didn't want to live her life that way. "Fear is healthy, it keeps you sharp." She reminded herself. With a firm nod, she pulled the door open, and confidently stepped out into the hall. Stepping up to the railing to look down at the tables, she was shocked at the sheer number of girls collecting their trays. There had to be at least forty of them if not more and they all looked miserable. Grinding her teeth angrily, Emma let out a hiss, took a solid step back away from the railing, and pinched herself hard. Focusing on the pain, she forced the anger out of her system, and turned towards the stairs.

Suddenly someone grabbed her by the hair, dragged her backwards, and threw her stumbling into a supply closet. Regaining her footing, Emma turned around just in time for Ruth to punch her in the stomach. Emma collapsed onto her knees, all of the air escaping her in a sudden gush as pain followed up like an angry hornet. It made breathing impossible past her seizing stomach muscles and seizing lungs. Ruth took advantage of Emma's predicament, slamming her knee into Emma's face, and dislocating her nose. Choking on her own blood, Emma curled up on the floor, and tried to find a way to survive.

"You Stupid Little Snotty Brat!" Ruth howled angrily. Another blow landed on Emma's back, but this time instead of taking it, Emma let out a terrifying hiss, and came up into a crouch. Staring Ruth dead in the eye, she snapped her nose back into place without making a sound, and smiled evilly. Laughing like she was possessed, Emma charged forward on all fours, and tackled Ruth sending her spiraling onto the floor. Balancing on top of Ruth's chest, Emma leaned in close to the girl's face, and let her blood drip down into her mouth. Cocking her head to the right curiously, she ceased all noise, and gave her a huge manic grin. Licking some of her blood from Ruth's cheek, she drank in her terror, and let out one final hiss of warning.

"Nice hair cut." She cooed almost playfully.

"Get off of me!" Ruth screeched, sounding horrified.

Ruth struggled under her, fighting with all her strength to break free, but Emma simply leaned in close and squeezed her legs tighter. Just as Ruth was about to pass out from lack of air, the guards came crashing into the room, and ripped Emma away. Deciding that since punishment was inevitable she should at least earn it, she turned her rage on the guards, and went completely limp.

One guard tried to catch her as she began to fall but she twisted in his grasp and ripped a chunk of flesh from his arm with her teeth. Savoring the taste of his blood, she scratched at his face and neck, trying to draw as much blood as she could, and let out a demonic hiss that seemed to terrify him. His partner tried to help by pulling Emma away, and so she turned her anger on him. Screaming and hissing, she dug her teeth into any flesh she could, ripping out huge chunks every time he tried to pull away, and spitting them into his face. Suddenly a pipe collided with her head, stunning her just long enough for someone to be able to pin her down, and stick a needle in her neck. As everything faded away, she felt a great deal of satisfaction at the sheer amount of blood that now decorated the supply closet, and hoped no one would try something like this again.

Shadow Log: Jacob, The Clover School for Girls, Rhode Island, November 15, 1810

Jacob put his fear aside as he walked through the secret door that led to Anton's prison. Of course, there was no way to really contain a creature that had been bred into a pure killing machine over centuries, but it made most of the guards feel better that he was chained up and locked behind a stone wall. Jacob knew that he could die before he could even blink if Anton willed it, but so far the creature had shown no signs of aggression towards him recently. Looking around at Anton's lab, he had no idea what half the panels, tubes, and other equipment did. Yet he did know he never wanted to end up as one of the experiments trapped down here with him.

"Jacob finally had the courage to appear to Anton's face." Anton said dryly.

"Mock all you want, but we both know you would eat me if you got hungry." Jacob grumbled back.

Anton ignored him except for a single twitch of his bladed tail, Jacob grabbed the only wooden chair in the room, dragged it over closer to the door, and sat down. He knew he was being foolish but he felt safer with the wall to his back and the door to his immediate right.

"Emma has developed a taste for blood. Anton is happy." Anton said, jumping right to the point.

"Why is Emma nearly killing three people and making the guards think she is possessed by an evil spirit a good thing?" Jacob asked, feeling stupid.

"Useptis have the blood right for all Useptis youth as they come of age to allow them to Sprout into maturity; with all the hormones, body changes, and Ut It True they become very hungry for blood." Anton tried to explain.

"What is the last thing? I'm rusty on Useptis," Jacob replied dryly.

This earned him a stern look from Anton who understood his sarcasm and didn't appreciate it. Jacob smiled to himself, Anton was starting to remind him of his brother, may God rest his soul, and started to relax.

"Loose translation is the eruption of scales, but it is deeper than that. It is when their hearts become armored, their second stomach is grown, their tails grow sharp or blunt, their venom veins grow in, and their scales form beneath their skin. The ritual of blood allows them to have an outlet for the rage, itchiness, and other issues. It keeps them from killing mindlessly." Anton tried to explain.

If Jacob didn't know better, he would think he had offended the alien, but he knew Anton considered himself better than him which meant he found these types of conversations annoying in general. Anton's annoyed tone was directed at Jacob's ignorance and nothing more, but that didn't keep Jacob from eyeing the door nervously.

"Alright, how do I help Emma?" Jacob asked as calmly as he could.

"Find a cow or pig, cow be better. Make a big…pen in the forest for it, and then release Emma into the pen. Cut the cow, the blood will send her into a blood rage. Let Emma feast and when Emma is done, Emma will regain some control. She is also human, so this will trigger an eruption of her body and rapid puberty." Anton warned.

"That sounds horrible for the cow, but if it helps me get my school back from Grace, so be it." Jacob said firmly.

"It will be best if Emma ingests a large amount of cinder beforehand to aid with the bonding of DNA." Anton warned.

Jacob's brow crinkled, he wasn't a scientist, but he couldn't think of a reason that DNA would need bonding. Grace's blood had been being injected into the girl since she was a baby and should have already bonded with the girl. Staring at Anton's back, he worked up the courage, and asked, "Bonding of the DNA?"

"Grace gave Emma the markers needed for change but that alone would have killed Emma. Anton chose to use Anton DNA to provide stability, to use technology to keep her body from rejecting Anton, and to give Emma what Emma will need to thrive." Anton explained proudly.

Jacob felt sick, that poor child was already struggling with the insanity that was the world, and now would have to learn how to be both human and Useptis. She had gained two new parents without even knowing one of them existed and now he had to find a way to protect her. Looking over at Anton, Jacob felt a great weight settle on his shoulders as a horrible thought emerged.

"Have you done this with others?" He asked quietly.

Anton finally turned to face him, his many eyes effortlessly making Jacob's skin crawl, and took a few clomping steps toward him. Anton bowed his head almost shamefully and then a quiet whine escaped his butt.

"Anton agreed to serve Grace, Anton could not say no to Grace, and so Anton served. There is another, Anton protected her, hid her away in the hope she would become stronger, but Anton lost contact months ago. Anton does not know if she still lives." Anton said sadly.

Jacob was stunned, angry, and hopeful all at once, which made thinking into a near impossible task. He'd need to find a way to find that girl, to make sure she was safe, to know if she was still alive. Shuddering ever so slightly, Jacob shakily got to his feet, and bowed stiffly in Anton's general direction.

"Thank you for your honesty. I will heed your consul." He whispered respectfully.

Looking surprised, happy, and honored Anton returned the bow. Then clasped Jacob's hand and gave it a firm enthusiastic shake that nearly broke the bone.

"Did Anton do the handshake right?" Anton asked nervously.

"It's supposed to be a lot more gentle than that, it's like your bow. A greeting that says, "Let's start off or end with respect and less I'm trying to rip your arm off." Jacob groaned as he gingerly rubbed his now sore shoulder.

Anton nodded in acceptance of this criticism, turned his back on Jacob, and trotted back to his work station. Smiling despite the pain, Jacob left the secret room, and headed for the stairs.

"Father hurt?" A meek scared voice asked from the darkness. Jacob grinned, a big happy wide grin as his daughter came out from her room under the stairs. He pulled her into a big bear hug and held her until she squirmed away giggling heavily.

"I'm fine, which girl gave you that black eye this time?" Jacob sighed.

He gently took her chin between his fingers, examining the fresh bruise blossoming to life on her face, and clicked disapprovingly.

"Stair, slipped." Mary muttered unhappily.

"Oof, is there anything I can do to make it better?" Jacob asked.

He let go of her, took a step back, and gave her his best I support you look. It was hard to keep her safe, to make people understand that just because she was slow in the head that they had no right to hurt her. It was a task that grew harder by the day as Grace drove people insane. He worried for her safety, for her sanity, and for her life. But she refused to leave him, refused to be sent away, and that meant that all he could do was make sure she had everything he could possibly provide.

"Books?" Mary asked hopefully.

"I can do that and before I forget there's a girl here, Subject Five. She likes to be called Emma and she could really use a friend to cheer her up tonight?" He asked gently.

His actions put her at risk. He hated putting her between Grace and Emma, but he was fighting a war for their survival, and that meant she wanted to help.

"Happy Mary." Mary said proudly.

"I'm proud of you, Little Bean." Jacob whispered proudly. Mary's smile was the last thing he saw as she disappeared back under the stairs. He'd lost count of the times he had tried to get her to move into his apartment upstairs, tried to get her out of the dank basement, but she was happiest down here. And as her father he had to put her wishes ahead of his own as long as they didn't put her in danger.

Shadow Log: Emma, The Clover School for Girls, Rhode Island, November 19, 1810

Emma stared up at the ceiling of her tiny prison, studying the intricacies of the wooden roof, and planned for her release. Seven days in isolation, no food, no contact with anyone, just the tiny silent cellar. They wanted to break her, to make her theirs, but she was no stranger to isolation or hunger. They had been a regular part of her life prior to being bought and Theodore had taught her how to use them to her advantage. Time to think, to plan, and prepare were the greatest gifts you could be given. It didn't hurt that she could track time easily without tools, making it easy to tell how long she had left before the door opened, and she would be free to resume their plan for her.

It also made it clear they were drugging her twice everyday, once in the morning and once in the evening. She didn't lose time without someone or something rendering her unconscious and she kept losing an hour during those times. The fresh needle marks on her marked arm didn't magically appear either which could only mean that they were giving her something for some unknown purpose.

Of course, if she put together everything she had learned so far, she would conclude that the experiments Theodore spoke of were moving into a new phase. The woman, Grace, who had visited her in the barn had to be the one in charge which meant that if she died it would end. Not just for her but for everyone suffering under her reign. The question became could she kill? Could she end the life of another and still be able to live with herself? For four days and four nights she had meditated on these questions and she had finally arrived at an answer she could live with.

She would only kill as a last resort, to protect others from harm, and to ensure the safety of those too weak to fight back. She would only fight to ensure that those who couldn't fight would have a chance to survive. She would resort to violence only when diplomacy and subterfuge failed. This was a code she could live with, respect, and accept. This was how she wanted to live her life, as a protector of the innocent, and her first task was to kill Grace and burn this hellhole to the ground.

Three days until her release, three days before she could start figuring out the best way to complete her mission, and start recruitment. Closing her eyes, she sat cross legged, and put herself back into a meditative trance. A smile caressed her face, she felt at peace despite the hunger, she had made the right choice, and that felt amazing.

Sometime long after the sun had gone down the cellar door creaked slowly open. A young woman with a thick cute face peered down at her questioningly. Emma lay very still, pretending to be asleep, and waited for the girl to make the first move. It made no sense that her isolation be broken early because it made the punishment less effective. This worried Emma greatly, making her anxiety flare to life, and her body wanted to spring after it. But she had experience with fear, this allowed her to control it, and keep herself completely still.

"Emma? Mary friend." Mary whispered urgently.

Emma feared a trap, but knew that no one from the school would call her by her chosen name, and so she sat up slowly. Mary reached down into the cellar, wrapped her hand around Emma's, and effortlessly hoisted Emma up into the moonlight. The guard on duty sat hunched over a cup of water spilling all over his pants as he snored loudly. Emma poked his shoulder causing him to topple over comically. Chuckling, she turned to Mary, raised a questioning eyebrow, and waited for the girl to tell her what was going on.

"Father said Emma kindly. Mary needed kindness, the guard drank water father gave him." Mary tried to explain.

"I need kindness as well, is your father Jacob?" Emma asked gently.

Mary nodded firmly, a deep blush creeping across her cheeks, before she nervously hid her face in the crook of her arm, and giggled. Jacob kept helping her, kept sticking his neck out, and kept trying to protect her. It was odd. Why would he care so much about her if he didn't care about the other girls? She decided she would have a conversation with him later, but for now she would befriend this simple creature, and give her a friend.

"So, do you have a plan for tonight?" Emma asked quietly. Grinning happily, Mary grabbed Emma's hand, and led her into the forest, giggling the whole time. It didn't take them long before they reached a small clearing with a perfect view of the sky. Mary had laid out a blanket, two canteens, and a tin of biscuits for them in the center with a second blanket folded neatly to the side. Emma felt surprisingly happy seeing the spread laid out for her, like she was actually cared about, and that brought tears to her eyes. Seeing those tears, Mary anxiously wiped them away, and gave her a quiet worried whimper.

"Happy tears." Emma promised.

This brought a big smile back to Mary's face, she quickly skipped over to the picnic, and sat down. Sitting down next to Mary, Emma felt so happy, respected, and cared for, but she worried about her new friend. How was it that she could survive unscathed by the evil infecting this place? How would she be able to remain pure when Grace wanted to corrupt everything?

Seeing Emma's worry, Mary placed a finger on Emma's lip, and whispered, "Happy thoughts only."

Emma nodded, her worries were for the future, tonight was about building a friendship, and that was what she was going to focus on. Curling up under the blanket, cuddling Mary for warmth, and staring up at the stars made Emma feel safe for the first time that she could remember. It was like the rest of the world faded away leaving only them and the stars.

Shadow Log: Grace, The Clover School for Girls, Rhode Island, November 23, 1810

Grace hated feeling out of the loop, hated not being the one calling the shots, but hated herself even more. The black veins appearing daily were a constant reminder of everything she had already lost and everything she was going to lose. Two hundred years of service, of work, of pain, of sacrifice and it was all being stripped away one piece at a time as the parasite ate away at her memories. The medication helped with the pain and kept her mostly sane, but she could feel time closing in, bringing with it her inevitable death.

She had taken a long look in the mirror and had found that she hated what she had become, hated what the parasite was doing to her, and found herself wanting to be the woman she had been before it all began. That was not possible now, Anton had made sure that her death would be slow and horrible, and she had only her rage to blame. Walking into his lab was impossibly difficult, she hadn't visited him since he had ripped her arm off and ate it. She hadn't been capable of facing him, of facing what he had done to her, and now she was about to ask him for his help. And asking for help was best done face to face, best accomplished with kind words and humility. Things that she struggled with on her best days and today was far from her best, far from anything remotely close to it.

Anton turned to face her with scorn and hatred blaring from his eyes and she knew that he could kill her without breaking a sweat. Could end her suffering in the blink of an eye if he chose, but he wouldn't because he wanted to watch her suffer. Wanted her to break for her sins against his kind, he wouldn't have saved her otherwise. Struggling to breathe normally, she sank into the wooden chair by the door, and let Anton see her weakness. She needed him to understand the strength it had taken to walk down into his prison and face him.

"I came because I have owed you an apology for several years now…if not longer. I am sorry, I tried to force you to betray your hive. I am sorry I was so nasty to you and that I treated you with such disrespect. You have stayed with The Shadows and kept your word and that is honorable. Please forgive me, so that I may go peacefully to my grave." She choked out.

The words were painful, it hurt to admit her wrong doings, and felt like a thousand bee stings to submit to the judgment of an Useptis. But it was only through contrition that one's sins could be cleansed away and she feared carrying them to her grave.

Anton snorted in disbelief, his head rearing back as if he had been struck, and he began to prance in place. Staring up at him, Grace could see how little he thought of her, and she accepted his judgment of her character with as much grace as she could. But it left her feeling hollow and broken almost like she was missing a piece of her soul. Anton approached, sniffing at her curiously, and gently tilted her head up so that he could look directly into her eyes. His tail slowly rose to attention, Grace closed her eyes, and accepted that this was where it might end.

He let go of her, turned his back to her, and backed up until his hind end was inches from her face. Dozens of tentacles began to squirm almost hungrily as his mouth gaped open, a quiet but distinct whine, click, whine, click came out of his asshole as his stomachs aligned, and then he wrapped his tail around her head. With a firm unforgiving pressure, he pulled her face into his ass until his mouth encompassed it, and then he began to suck.

The pressure forced her mouth open painfully wide as her tongue slithered out and flattened against her bottom teeth. There was no air and therefore no way for her to scream as the parasite slithered up her throat and into Anton's mouth. The taste of it was metallic and sour like rotted fruit and the slime trail it left coating her mouth made her vomit violently. Which aided in forcing the thing's tentacles out of her throat. Just as she was about to lose consciousness, Anton released her, and used his tail to push her away from her ass. The whine, click, whine, click sounded again as he shifted his stomachs back into their resting spots.

She vomited black sludge up by the gallon barely able to get air into her lungs before the next wave violently over her took her. Until she was curled into a tiny ball, choking for air, and sobbing uncontrollably. Covered in her own vomit, sweat, and urine she wept wishing Anton had killed her instead. It was like fire had erupted under her skin and began to burn her from within, consuming her mercilessly, and leaving only its horrible heat in its wake.

"Anton accepts the apology." Anton said as he trotted away.

"My mouth tastes like ass." Grace groaned unhappily.

"Death is coming for Grace still but it shall be less horrific." Anton replied dismissively.

Grace wanted to pick herself up, to bathe away the stench of what had just happened, but she didn't have the strength.

Instead she curled into a tighter ball, let the exhaustion win, and passed out.

Shadow Log: Emma, The Clover School for Girls, Rhode Island, November 23, 1810

Emma felt strange, hollow, empty as she settled down at a table out of the way of the main flow of things. Staring down at the tray of food in front of her, she knew she should be ravenous, but all she could taste was bile. It was strange not wanting to eat, but even stranger to feel so alone in a room full of people. The table shook slightly indicating that someone had sat down opposite her, looking up, she found Ruth sitting across from her, and to her surprise she felt nothing. Giving Ruth a cold smile, she picked up her roll, and took a bite.

"What do you want, Ruth? There is a closet right over there if you want some privacy." Emma hissed.

Ruth flinched, rubbing her ribs, and growled quietly as she shook her head no.

"I don't care to tangle with you again, you're like a demon possessed when you're angry." Ruth sighed unhappily.

"Then what do you want?" Emma sighed back.

"No one knows that I'm not one of them, they all think that I'm part of this experiment. Grace even tattooed my arm…"

"And you want me to protect your secret. Why would I do that?" Emma cut her off.

"Because, I know what is going on here and I am willing to make a deal. Your silence in exchange for my information and for a little help when you need it." Ruth offered.

"So, you keep bullying people and being an ass, and I get an informant." Emma said.

She liked the idea of getting information, but it required her to trust someone who was untrustable…or she could use Ruth to get ahead and keep her safely at arm's length.

"Treat me like anyone else here that way Grace remains unsuspicious." Emma sighed in resignation.

Ruth smiled evilly as she calmly stood up, gave her a wink, and promptly launched a huge glob of spit onto the roll Emma was holding. Emma stared at the roll for a long moment, trying to not smile at Ruth's genus, and then turned her steely gaze on Ruth. Ruth had just enough time to take a single step backwards before Emma let out an enraged hiss and launched herself at Ruth's face.

She landed on Ruth causing her to crash backwards onto the floor, screeching angrily Emma pretended like she was about to fly into a rage, but held back just long enough for the guards to pull her off. She let them subdue her, staring up at Ruth, and hissed angrily. The guards must have heard about what had happened in the closet because they were quick to restrain her arms; while one man pinned her down with his knee firmly in the spall of her back. Laughing, Emma went limp as the needle went into her neck, but this time it didn't seem to have the same effect. It just made her feel very lethargic instead of knocking her out cold.

Shadow Log: Jacob, The Clover School for Girls, Rhode Island, November 23, 1810

Jacob felt sick leading Mr. Smith's cow into the pen, but he wanted to protect his charges from any bloodlust. He had made sure to set everything up as far from school grounds and town as conveniently possible to ensure that the ritual was as safe as possible. He had even acquired a sturdy collar and fifteen foot chain to make sure Emma wouldn't escape if she went nuts. Mary had baked him cinder brownies that morning with enough cinder to dose a horse and leave a girl Emma's size high for a month.

Yet, despite all this preparation he felt unprepared, unready for what was coming, but it had to be done. Hearing the guards approaching, he wiped the doubt off of his face, and let the cow loose in the pen. Waving the guards over to the chain, he felt his heartbeat quicken, and his mouth go dry. Once they had dropped her roughly to the ground, they retreated almost fearfully, and darted off in the direction of the school. Rolling his eyes, Jacob gently removed the hood from Emma's head, and quickly secured the collar to her neck. Seeing that she was already fully conscious, he helped her sit up, and fetched the brownies.

Returning to her side, he met her seething glare, and offered her the food saying, "These are filled with cinder, I need you to eat all of them. I also brought water to wash it down."

"Why am I chained up in a pen with a cow?" She asked nervously.

"Food tastes like ash, you're not hungry despite starving for days, and you are angry most of the time...or feel empty. I want you to regain control, so that you can find out who you are, now please eat." Jacob said with soft kindness.

Emma chewed on her cheek for a long moment, gave him a little nod, and began to choke down the food with large gulps of water. Once she had finished eating, he walked over and grabbed the cow's lead rope, and led it over to the gate. Once he was safely outside the pen with the cow inside, he pulled out his knife, and quickly slashed its shoulder. With a surprised upset moo, the cow darted away, and stopped to stare at him angrily from the other side of the pen.

Time ticked slowly away, blood pooling slowly at the animal's feet until Jacob was sure he had been had. Suddenly Emma sat bolt upright, her pupils expanding in size until they were all he could see as he stared into her eyes, and she started to sniff hungrily at the air. Without warning she let out a hiss so terrifying that he fell over onto his butt as she began to vibrate with what seemed to be excitement. Jacob blinked and Emma was a blur of movement, charging on all fours at the cow. Then blood splurted everywhere as she ripped out its throat with her teeth, lifting her blood soaked face into the air she screeched happily causing the hairs on his arms to stand on end. Her head blurred out of focus with the speed in which she ripped chunks out of the now dead cow, pausing only to lap up its blood like a dog, or to hiss demonically.

Jacob puked into the grass, wishing he had been smart enough to look away before the feast, and listened uncomfortably to her happy slurping.

She ate for what felt like an impossibly long time, before her movement returned to normal, and she passed out inside the half eaten carcass. Thankful that he had already emptied the contents of his stomach, he walked over to her unconscious body, and gently picked her up. It was strange to him that he had become so accustomed to blood and death that cradling her to his chest didn't really bother him. Sure, he was freaked out at what he had witnessed, but he knew that she wasn't in control of herself. That she had once been a normal, healthy, sweet baby and The Shadows had mutated her into this. She needed a father to look out for her, to protect her, and to give her the things she needed to thrive. Since Anton was currently unable to be that for her, he was happy to take his place. Johnathan appeared at the edge of the clearing right on cue, looking a little green as he surveyed her blood soaked body, and gave Jacob a worried look.

"The blood isn't hers. Would you please clean her up and take her to the infirmary?" Jacob asked gently.

"Sure, no problem, but I doubt whoever that blood belongs to survived." Johnathan muttered.

Jacob calmly deposited Emma into Johnathan's arms, looked down at his now ruined shirt, and sighed. Emma definitely had a talent for ruining clothes, but she was worth it if she could save his school. Turning his attention back to Johnathan, he smiled, and gave him a small shrug.

"It isn't human blood, it belonged to a cow." He sighed.

"Okay?" Johnathan said, clearly wanting to know more.

"I'm going to go clean up the mess she made, make sure she is restrained when you put her to bed. I don't want her to freak out and hurt someone when she wakes up…whenever that happens." Jacob muttered.

Without waiting for a reply, he turned, and marched back into the forest. There was a lot of work to do to get the site clean and ready for whoever may stumble onto it next. He definitely didn't want Grace to figure out what he had done or why.

Shadow Log: Emma, The Clover School for Girls, Rhode Island, November 25, 1810

Emma startled awake, feeling panic flood her body as she struggled to figure out where she was, and why she was tied down. Forcing herself to breathe, she kept her eyes closed, and focused on pushing the panic out of her body. It was easy to panic, easy to be afraid, easy to let your emotions make you stupid. It was much harder to find a calm center and use logic to ensure your survival. Theodore had taught her that after she had tried to run away the first time.

"Emma is safe, please don't scream…Anton's ears hurt when humans scream." A voice said inside her head.

Emma opened her eyes, immediately closed them again, and forced herself to go back to her calm center. Whatever was standing by her bed wasn't human, it looked like the monster from her dreams, but that wasn't possible. Monsters weren't real, they were created from the mind trying to make sense of the world.

"Monsters aren't real." She whispered in shock.

"Anton is from another world, Little One." Theodore whispered gently.

Emma refused to open her eyes again feeling the shock, crushing sadness, and horror of Theodore's death all over again. Watching him die had left a permanent scar on her heart and to know he was still alive was too much. Grief is a funny thing, she had wished for this day so many times, but now that it had arrived she just wanted to punch him in the face for betraying her.

"You are understandably angry, but Grace made sure I didn't have a choice…if she knew I was here I'd be sent back to The Room…" Theodore shuddered.

Emma finally opened her eyes, ignoring Anton completely, she stared up into Theodore's eyes, and knew he was telling the truth. Finding her center of calm, she let out the pent up breath she had been holding, and finally gave Anton a long look.

"So when did I end up meeting you?" She asked coldly.

"Emma was very sick when it was young, This One saved you." Anton replied with a snort.

"Thanks, I guess, would you mind releasing me." She grumbled.

Theodore quickly undid her wrists, allowing her to sit up, and stretch as he worked on the restraints holding her ankles. She was still angry, but that anger had been redirected to Grace, and for now she just wanted answers.

"Did I eat a live cow?" She suddenly gagged.

"It was magnificent! Worthy of any Useptis youth!" Anton crowed proudly.

"I think I'm going to be sick." Emma groaned.

In the blink of an eye a waste bucket was being held in front of her by Anotn. Who was twitching anxiously in front of her with a worried look in his eyes. Emma accepted the bucket, set it on the bed, and gave Anton a curious questioning look.

"Grace ruined Anton's floor, Anton cannot get rid of the smell." Anton said sadly.

A laugh slipped out of Emma's mouth before she could catch it, seeing that it upset Anton, she gave him a solemn bow.

"I wasn't laughing at you, I was laughing at the thought of Grace puking all over herself." She explained.

Anton's eyes smiled as a deep guttural growl began to vibrate and rumble in his hind end. It took Emma a moment to realize he was laughing, but when she did she joined him, and it wasn't long before they were all laughing together.

Growing sober, Emma turned to Theodore, and asked, "Did she hurt you?"

The look on his face told her everything she needed to know, Grace had crossed a line Emma hadn't even realized existed, and now that she had Emma had the motivation needed to complete her mission. But she needed to be smart, to keep one step ahead of her captor, or she would get to discover how horrible Philips could become.

"Why is she doing this?" Emma asked simply.

The look the two exchanged spoke volumes, telling her all about their reluctance to share their information for fear of hurting her, and for fear of angering her. They had both hurt her over the years, the memories were foggy, but filled with unmistakable pain and hurt. But they were in the past and were no longer important or relevant. Not with Grace torturing so many children, not with the way her body kept shifting, and certainly not with the clock running out.

"I know you've both hurt me at that woman's command, but I still consider you both friends." Emma whispered softly.

Another look was exchanged, this time Emma could hear the whispers of their silent conversation, and she knew Anton had to be whispering into Theodore's mind.

"Grace is dying slowly and wants to create a soldier capable of protecting Earth from the Useptis before she dies. She is using her own blood to try and create one which creates a great deal of instability in the test subject's body." Theodore sighed.

Emma's brow crunched together as she tried to understand, but there were still too many pieces missing.

"Wouldn't that mean they die?" She asked uneasily.

"Indeed, when Anton saved Emma…Anton had to use Anton blood to provide stability." Anton explained proudly.

Emma stared down at her hands, realizing that she had alien blood flowing through her veins, and finally understood what had happened with the cow. The fluctuations she felt in her body were the two sides finding a way to peacefully coexist within her skin. The rage, the coldness, the fear was all a manifestation of that internal war.

Yet none of that changed anything, she still had to find a way to stop Grace…to kill her, and she instinctively knew that she wouldn't be able to count on the help of these two. They would stop her just to try and protect her as they had been doing from the start. But they were still valuable allies to have because Emma was beginning to understand that this wouldn't all end with Grace.

"Who does she work for?" Emma asked angrily.

"The Shadows, Grace built them and led them until Grace got sick." Anton chirped before Theodore could stop him.

Emma pushed herself unsteadily to her feet, using the table for support as she regained the full use of her legs.

"I'd like to go back to my cell, please." She whispered tiredly.

"Emma needs a lot of rest and a lot of red meat." Anton agreed.

Suddenly the room began to spin as her knees buckled, she collapsed into Anton's many arms, and passed out.

Shadow Log: Grace, The Clover School for Girls, Rhode Island, November 25, 1810

Grace threw up into the basin now sitting prominently on her desk to her right. Ever since Anton had sucked the Black Death out of her she had been struggling with a whole host of other problems. The worst was her inability to eat due to the extreme nauseousness plaguing her every move and the frequent vomiting up of black sludge. But her hair falling out in huge clumps, the flaking of her skin, and the burning of her nerves were all close seconds. She had been told that with the parasite gone she would recover from this and probably live another few years, but now she didn't want to live.

It was strange to no longer be worried about everything ending, about falling asleep and not waking up, to be free of the horrible sickening fear that had been dragging her down. She had succeeded in her mission, had found someone who could help her, and the only thing left to do was to make sure

Subject Five was ready to take over. The only thing that mattered now was making sure The Shadows weren't sacrificed to the Useptis. Thankfully Anton, Jacob, and Theodore were already doing exactly as she wanted. Ruth might become a problem with how green she was and she would need to be observed closely. Realignment might be necessary if the girl became too attached or started showing signs of disloyalty. A knock at her office door made her smile, it was time to turn up the heat, and to get Subject Five feeling protective.

"Phillips, please come in!" She called.

Feeling the nausea becoming overpowering, she grabbed the basin, and puked again. Completely unperturbed Phillips sat down and gave her a calm glare.

"Subject Five is responding to treatment, we need to increase the difficulty of the level of survival to push her to mutate further." Grace got directly to the point.

Phillips creeped her out, making her skin crawl with his cold stares, and inability to connect with people. But he served a very important purpose and the bomb she had put in his head meant he was controllable. Yet that didn't make dealing with him any easier or more comfortable.

"I can apply pressure." Phillips purred happily.

"Use Ruth as needed to control the field, you're playing chess with a very clever little girl. Who is already putting pieces in play and who has already tasted blood." Grace warned.

"This just makes breaking her more fun." Phillips purred with clear excitement.

"What do you need from me?" Grace asked.

She was afraid of giving him too much power, but she also wanted Subject Five ready to serve when she died.

"You need to start pushing the girls, exercise, pain, fear…they mold us into what we are meant to be. Group pain forces bonding and breeds comradery which in turn makes it easier to break the protectors like Subject Five." Phillips said enthusiastically.

Grace nodded, she was sure he was right, and was sure he would get the job done. It was time to become public enemy number one and apply the screws of pain to ensure the future.

Shadow Log: Emma, The Clover School for Girls, Rhode Island, November 25, 1810

Emma had no desire to be in yet another fight, but she couldn't stand by and watch Mary get bullied. Which had left her with no choice but to take on the gaggle of three girls who had stupidly cornered her when she called them out for their behavior. She was reluctant to fight them but was even more reluctant to be hurt by them. It didn't take a genius to see that this was Grace baiting her, yet it wasn't like she could just standby. The guards were looking the other way, probably hoping the girls would accomplish what they couldn't.

Emma placed her back to the wall, opening her mouth to hiss, and was surprised to feel two long fangs snap into place over her normal teeth. A stream of clear liquid shot out of her fangs sprinkling the closest girl's arms and making her skin sizzle. The smell of burning wool and hair filled the air as it began to eat through the girl's dress and flesh. The scream she let out as she began trying to desperately wipe the liquid from her skin was shrill enough to make Emma startle backwards. Hitting the wall, Emma felt the fangs snap back into the roof of her mouth followed by her own confusion. Watching the girls flee, Emma wondered what this new ability meant, and how much pain it would end up causing her. Suddenly Mary grabbed her arm and yanked her backwards into a hidden tunnel leading away from the cafeteria.

"Thank you." Mary whispered.

She sounded scared, worried, and out of breath yet Emma could tell she was happy. Even in the darkened tunnel Emma could see a nasty cut across Mary's arm and could smell her blood. Licking her lips hungrily, Emma calmly checked the wound, using the time to get her impulses under control. "You're welcome. This needs to be checked out in the infirmary." She replied quietly.

"Mary stitch. Emma trouble." Mary sighed in reply.

Emma couldn't help but smile at her concern despite feeling a good share of worry herself. How had she ended up spitting acid? And what other surprises did her body have in store for her? Why did it happen right then and not before? Pushing these questions out of her mind for the moment, she decided to just focus on Mary's needs.

"Don't worry about me," She managed to mutter as her fangs shifted in her mouth.

"Always worry, friend." Mary muttered back unhappily.

"I don't know why things are happening, but I have faith in my friends. I need to get to the basement, can you help?" Emma asked gently.

"Anton?" Mary asked excitedly.

"How do you know him?" Emma asked in surprise.

"Friend." Mary said in a dismissive tone.

She grabbed Emma's hand and led her quickly through the tunnels. Leaving her outside Anton's lab, Mary gave her a tight hug, and headed off to treat her wound. Swallowing her trepidation, Emma walked into the lab as Anton turned to stare at her proudly.

"Emma has developed their fangs. Impressive and interesting." He said bluntly.

"My fangs?" Emma asked.

She felt not only confused, but also angry. It was beyond annoying to have so many different people trying to make her into something she didn't understand. Now she had an Alien meddling as well and she was starting to feel like a turtle without a shell.

"Anton's fangs are not for shooting, Anton wanted them to be…but he became a mind flayer instead. Your fangs produce a highly acidic poison

that will be most useful when you gain control. Emma just needs to be a little patient.”

“I’m tired of being patient. I want the pain to stop.” Emma mumbled.

She didn’t have the words to explain the emptiness that was starting to overwhelm her soul nor did she understand why everyone cared so much about her life. She was simply tired of being used by everyone she met and tired of them not telling her anything.

“Emma is close to full puberty, many new abilities will blossom. Anton can’t explain anymore right now. Grace is coming.” Anton replied.

Feeling her hackles raise, Emma sighed, and quickly slipped out of the lab. She wanted answers, but the only thing she could do was accept whatever punishment might come her way.

Emma woke the next morning to find Ruth standing over her cot, watching her intently, and had to resist the urge to jump up and scare her. Instead she sat up slowly, gave her a dirty look, and promptly vomited up a dark green slime into her waste bucket.

“It is very creepy and weird to watch people sleep.” She groaned.

Ruth stepped quickly backwards, moving within inches of the door, and gave her a nervous look. Rolling her eyes, Emma rinsed her mouth out with water, and spit it into the waste bucket. She could taste Ruth's fear, but it didn't taste like she was actually afraid of violence. It was fear of getting caught, of punishment, and Emma had no idea how she knew that. Probably was something to do with what Grace was doing to her and she already hated it.

“I know you are terrified and worried about Grace and what she has become, just like I know that you used to respect her. But that Grace died a long time ago and there are real children suffering here.” Emma whispered.

Ruth flinched, looking both surprised and angry all mixed up with guilt, and Emma just wanted to give her a hug. It was strange to feel protective of a girl she had wanted to beat to a pulp not long ago, strange to taste smells, and strange to be stuck as everyone's hero. Especially when she didn't know how she was supposed to be a hero or how grown, experienced, smart adults expected her to be their savior.

"Sit down and tell me how you came to be at the school?" Emma asked gently.

She patted the cot as she scooted over to sit at the head of it so that Ruth would have plenty of space. Sighing in resignation, Ruth flopped onto the cot, and buried her head in her hands.

"Grace rescued me from the hell that was my home and promised I'd be helping people like me." Ruth muttered.

"I need more information about the school, where does Grace live? Where do the guards sleep? When do they change shifts? Without that information I won't be able to figure out how to stop Grace." Emma replied gently.

"Can't Jacob help with that? I know he's helping you." Ruth grumbled.

"That means Grace knows as well and she'll be waiting for him to make a move that will allow her to deal with him." Emma said firmly.

Ruth gave her a dirty look, abruptly stood up, and stomped out of the room. Sniffing the air, Emma could tell just how conflicted, worried, and upset Ruth was and could tell that she wanted freedom as much as she did. Smiling to herself, Emma headed downstairs for food as the klaxon sounded.

To Emma's surprise all of the tables had been removed from the area and red circles had been drawn on the floor in their place. The guards were lining the girls up, one per circle, five to a line, and Grace was supervising them. Emma hissed at the guard who tried to grab her, gave Grace a suspicious look, and chose a free circle. Once all of the girls were waiting nervously, Grace stepped up onto a chair, and looked them over.

"I have been lenient with you thus far but today that has to end thanks to a few trouble makers! If you want to eat you have to earn it! Now give me one hundred jumping jacks or you don't eat today and taste the whip!" Grace shouted. Right on que the guards pulled out whips, took up positions, and prepared to use them. One by one the girls began to jump with horrified looks on their faces. It didn't take long for someone to trip up and get a whip lashed angrily against her back. This made the girls jump even harder trying to not meet the same fate. The problem was they were weak from the experiments and mistreatment making it impossible to avoid the whips.

Emma wanted to fight back, to charge forward, and rip out Grace's throat. But she knew that she wouldn't make it five feet before someone would tackle her and so she jumped. She pretended to be unfazed by the clear pain and sadness around her, and plotted her revenge.

Her entire life she had been forced to suffer under the hands of someone who thought they were entitled to her pain and she was tired of it. She wasn't a hero or a savior but she had sworn an oath to protect and it was time to do that. Letting out a hiss, she turned on the nearest guard, and tackled him. Slamming her head into the guard's face, she ripped the whip out of his hand, and wrapped it around his neck. She pulled it tight, cutting off his air supply, and twisted the whip so that it wouldn't be easy to remove.

Laughing maniacally, she launched herself at another guard, leaving the man to choke, and wrapped herself around his leg. Suddenly her vision sharpened, her breathing became calm, and everything fell into focus. With one solid tug she snapped the guard's leg in two and sent him flying into another guard. Sniffing the air, she looked around for Grace, but the woman had already fled as had most of the girls. Hissing almost territorially, she quickly evaded several of the guards, and charged towards the farthest door. Darting through it, she slammed it shut, and twisted the handle off to keep anyone from opening it. Dropping onto all fours to increase her speed, she pounded down the hall, and slid into Phillips's office.

The man looked up in surprise, barely getting his arms up before Emma collided with his chest, and ripped the flesh from his arm with her teeth. Using the last of her strength, she slammed her fists down into his face causing an explosion to throw her back into the wall, and knock her out.

Shadow Log: Jacob, The Clover School for Girls, Rhode Island, November 25, 1810

Jacob sat dumbfounded at his desk, staring down at the report, and tried to think of a way out of the mess Emma had made. He didn't regret Phillips' death or what it meant for the school, but he worried about Grace's mental capacity. Emma was evolving quickly, too quickly, Anton had set her on a path to become something terrifying, and Jacob could only blame himself.

He felt guilty for using a child to further his own agenda and for having been so selfish with his own needs so long ago. Closing his eyes, he felt the ghosts of his past close in, and tried to still his racing heart.He tried to keep out the memories, the guilt, and focus on the present.

"Father?" Mary asked fearfully.

Looking up, he found Mary hovering uncertainly in the doorway with a worried look plastered on her face. He waved her inside, quickly tucking the file under a stack of books, and walked over to her. Giving her a big hug, he kissed the top of her head, and silently cursed himself for allowing her to be put in danger.

"Little Bean, this is a wonderful surprise." He said as cheerfully as he could.

"Emma, hurt, stop!" Mary shouted.

She pulled away from him, anger plastered on her face, and threw her hands angrily into the air.

"I can't stop Emma from being hurt, she attacked a bad man, and she has to answer for that." Jacob tried to explain.

"No! Father said good fight or evil win!" Mary spat.

Jacob felt a great deal of pride seeing her so willing to fight the injustice, but he couldn't let her be put in any further danger.

"I was wrong to ask you to befriend Emma, I thought…"

"Father forgot good." Mary screamed.

His heart shattered as he watched her storm out, he'd done one thing right in the world, and he had ended up losing her. All because of a mistake he was always going to pay for, but that didn't mean Mary had to pay. It was time to bring the might of The Shadows down on the school and end this farce once and for all.

Shadow Log: Grace, The Clover School for Girls, Rhode Island, November 27, 1810

Grace grabbed Emma by her arm and roughly yanked her out of the hall and threw her onto the floor of the room where she had been waiting. Snarling, she slammed the door shut, calmly barricaded it with a desk, and let out a deep sigh as she lifted herself up to sit on it. She calmly examined her nails as she waited for Emma to get her feet back under her. Realizing that Emma wasn't prepared to submit to whatever this was, Grace said, "If you lie to me I will kill you, only the truth will allow you to leave this room."

"I don't lie, it's why people hate me." Emma spat angrily.

"I know what you've seen- the time lapses, the feeling of being watched, the nightmares- all of it. I can see your distrust as plain as I can see your pain, you sweet child. I know because I was once like you seeing things that shouldn't exist and knowing to my very core that they did. The Shadows saved me like they're going to save you, but they won't do it without a price." Grace explained flatly.

"What price?" Emma asked almost sheepishly.

"Service for as long as you are able. You will learn to fight the invaders, to keep people safe, and to keep yourself safe." Grace explained patiently.

"And what will that service cost me?" Emma asked uncomfortably.

"Smart one, too smart, everything you are is given in service to The Shadows." Grace said bluntly.

"That sounds like a fate worse than death." Emma hissed with a look of repulsion.

"In time you will beg for the relief of that fate and when you do The Shadows will be there. For now, let us talk about what is happening with your life." Grace said pointedly.

"You mean how you've been torturing me? Or the other girls? I really can't imagine what we have to talk about unless it's your death." Emma growled threateningly.

Grace laughed so hard she almost fell off of the desk before she was able to formulate a reply, "Oh, Little One, my death has been written in the stars for longer than you have been alive. The only thing I want is for you to grow strong enough to help this world survive my death."

"I will never submit to your will. You might as well kill me." Emma hissed in reply.

Grace backhanded her hard enough to blacken her eye, grabbed her by the throat, and pinned her to the floor. Growling angrily, she tightened her grip until she could see the desperation starting to flood through her prey, and then she let go. She pushed away from Emma, stood up, and began to pace.

"I will break you." She promised.

She gave Emma a swift kick to the ribs before she stormed out of the room. There was no point in beating a dead horse and so she would back off and wait for the right time to strike again.

Shadow Log: Jacob, The Clover School for Girls, Rhode Island, November 27, 1810

He watched Emma strut into his office looking like she owned it. He had to wonder where her confidence came from and how she managed to hold onto it with such an iron grip. Once she plopped down in a chair he noticed a dark circle starting to form under her left eye. Probably because of her tendency to provoke the guards, yet he couldn't shake the feeling it had a deeper, more dangerous cause.

"Do I want to ask?" Jacob asked, pointing to his own eye.

"Only if you want me to dump a pile of manure on your desk." Emma purred.

Shaking his head in disbelief he rubbed his face tiredly, "I almost regret buying you."

"Thank you," Emma laughed sassily.

"You know why you're here?" Jacob asked.

He wanted to tell her everything, to reassure her of her place in the world, yet he knew he was already risking too much by pulling her out of the fire. It scared him to think that Mary could end up a Shadow or worse dead because of something he did. Shaking off his doubt, he took a deep breath, and forced himself to focus.

"No, but I'm guessing it is something to do with Grace." Emma replied softly.

"Philips was her prized pet and despite already punishing you for his death she is angry enough to kill by accident. I need you to listen carefully, can you do that for me?" He asked as gently as he could.

For a split second he saw doubt, pain, and loneliness in her eyes before she managed to hide it behind her mask of confidence. He smiled sadly, it hurt to think of how much her young mind had to cope with, and it made him wish he could do more.

"Mary sleeps either in the basement, her favorite tree, or the roof because that's where she feels safe. She is turning into a wonderful woman despite living here and I know you need help to survive…and so does she. I rearranged the guard postings to leave a clear path to the roof, so that you can visit her if you want." Jacob explained, growing more uncomfortable with each word.

Emma eyed him suspiciously looking like she was debating the truth of his words before she spoke with a firmness that sounded far too mature for her tiny body.

"I thank you for your kindness, I might have punched one of Ruth's friends earlier."

"I'll try to keep Grace from exploding on you, but no promises." Jacob sighed.

"Thank you, can you hear that?" Emma asked nervously. Before Jacob could respond two guards marched into the room and roughly seized Emma.

"Subject Five has lost all privileges due to her insistence on being a threat." One guard explained.

He wanted to stop them instead he just watched her as they dragged her away. It wasn't worth the risk to intervene just yet. He had a lot of work ahead of him if he wanted Mary to be safe and he had to be careful to not give in to his anger or his fatherly instincts.

Deciding his daughter was right, he grabbed his coat, locked up his office, and went in search of Grace's office. There was no way she wouldn't have a backup port device, all he had to do was find it, and then find the man who now led The Shadows.

Shadow Log: Ruth, The Clover School for Girls, Rhode Island, November 27, 1810

Slipping into Grace's darkened office was enough to bring the pesky panic flooding back. She'd worked so hard on herself to banish the panic and fear, but it just kept coming back. Lighting up the room felt wrong, like it would bring unwanted eyes to her betrayal, and bring shame to her family. So she made due with the small light emanating from her shadow-band to navigate around the desk, chair, and bilge bucket. Finding the filing cabinet, she quickly picked the lock, and grabbed the security folder from its home in the bottom drawer. Hearing someone coming, she quickly tucked herself into a wardrobe, and held her breath to keep the panic from spilling out.

Someone began to rifle through Grace's office with an angry intensity that made revealing herself impossible. Ruth shrank down onto the floor, praying silently that whoever this intruder was wouldn't look inside her hiding place.

She had been in two real fights in her life and she had lost them both. The thought of a third left her feeling hollowed out and shaky, but she also knew she would do what she had to do to survive. Suddenly the noise stopped like the person was listening for something, then the door to the office exploded open, and Ruth shrank further into herself fearing what was about to come.

"Jacob, why am I not surprised to find you rifling through my things!" Grace growled loudly.

"I thought you were dealing with Emma." Jacob said in shock.

"You tripped a silent alarm when you came in here. Now tell me what you were doing and I might spare your miserable hide." Grace demanded angrily.

Ruth sucked in air, wishing she could just disappear, but her band didn't yet have port ability which meant she was trapped.

"Go to hell!" Jacob spat defiantly.

A thud, followed by a crash, and then the sound of dragging told Ruth that Grace had knocked Jacob out and dragged him away. Ruth waited a few excruciatingly long minutes before she dared to peek out of her hiding place, seeing that the room was indeed empty, she grabbed the file, and darted to safety.

Shadow Log: Emma, The Clover School for Girls, Rhode Island, November 27, 1810

Emma slipped onto the roof, took a breath of fresh air, and stared up at the sparkling night sky. It felt great to be out of her cell away from everything dark and horrible. The sky was so beautiful, so full of life, and she couldn't keep the tears from leaking from her eyes as she took in the beauty spanning out before her.

"Pretty." Mary said.

Emma tore her attention from the stars, gave Mary a small smile, and nodded happily. She wasn't sure if she deserved to be so lucky to have moments like this, but she knew it was exactly what she needed. She let Mary tuck her into her blanket nest and snuggled up to her as stars began to fall from the sky.

"Not Stars." Mary warned softly.

Looking closer, Emma could see that she was right, they were fragments from some kind of vessel. But that didn't change how beautiful they were or how happy the sight made her feel.

"Anton's." Mary muttered.

"Probably." Emma finally replied.

"Scared." Mary muttered.

She started to cry into Emma's shoulder as she shook from the strength of her emotions. Emma gently pulled her close wishing she could provide more reassurance than a hug. Yet there wasn't much she could do to protect her except to kill Grace and she wasn't sure how to do that yet.

"I will try to protect you." Emma promised gently.

"Know." Mary sobbed.

Suddenly Johnathan's head popped through the trapdoor making both of them yelp in surprise. Shaking off her surprise, Emma carefully untangled herself from the blankets, and climbed back to her feet. A pit was slowly forming in her stomach and she felt sure his appearance meant trouble.

"What's wrong?" She groaned.

"Grace is rounding up the girls and tearing through the school looking for some missing file." Johnathan replied, sounding panicked.

"Thank you for warning me." Emma said.

She gave Mary a quick hug before hurrying over to the trapdoor, and sliding down the ladder to meet Johnathan. He gave her a firm nod, took her hand, and quickly led her back to her cell barely avoiding the rampaging guards dragging girls out of their rooms. She threw herself into her cell dodging the table as she fell onto her bed.

"Be safe" She whispered as Johnathan scurried away.

Seconds later a guard pushed her door open, reached in, and grabbed her by her hair. He dragged her into the hall and threw her at Grace's feet.

"Search her cell, make sure it's empty, if she moves I'll beat her into submission." Grace ordered angrily.

Emma held still, curled up in the fetal position on the freezing floor as she waited for the inspection to be over. Growling with anger, Grace reached down, grabbed Emma by the hair, and yanked her up onto her knees. Trying not to cry as tension built in her scalp, Emma let out a quiet hiss, and went limp. Unable to maintain her grip in her weakened state Grace was forced to let go which just made her angrier.

"Where is it?" Grace demanded.

She punctuated each word with a sharp kick to Emma's back making it near impossible for Emma to remain steadfast. She had made Grace a promise to never submit and she wasn't going to break it no matter the horrors the woman threw at her. Deciding that if she was going to suffer then she should make the most of it Emma launched off of the floor going straight for Grace's face and neck with her teeth. She barely managed to scratch her before the guards had her in a chokehold.

"The file isn't there." The guard holding her said.

Emma threw her head back making sure it collided with the guard's nose and rolled out of his grip. The whip caught her ankle and sent her flying face first into the floor leaving her bruised and bloody.

"Take her down to meet our newest teacher, maybe she will jar the information from this stubborn bitch," Grace spat.

Emma woke hours later, coughing water out of her lungs as Johnathan held her gently in his arms. It was horrible to feel so weak and sick but she was proud of herself for maintaining her silence through the torture. Without meaning to they were making her stronger or perhaps that was the point. Emma didn't care, all she wanted was for it all to be over.

"We're safe for the moment but we have limited time before I have to take you back to your cell." Johnathan whispered into her ear.

"My head feels like it is going to split in half." Emma moaned unhappily.

"I can see if I can get you something for the pain." Johnathan offered softly.

"No, don't leave me." Emma whimpered.

She had never felt so weak, so broken, or so lost and Johnathan's embrace was the only thing keeping her sane. Finally giving into her pain, she sobbed into Johnathan's chest, letting him hold her close, and comfort her. She let all of her pain, negativity, and sadness flow out of her until there was nothing left but emptiness. Pulling away gently, she took a deep breath, and dried her tears.

"I'm good, I got this." She whispered.

"Anything else I can do?" He asked softly.

She shook her head no, wishing she could take away his pain the way he had for her, but knowing she was once again helpless.

"Hey, I am good. I just want you to be." He said gently.

Standing up slowly, Emma got her footing, and took a moment to compose her thoughts.

"There is something you can do for me, but it is risky." She finally offered.

It hurt to put him in further danger, but she knew he would put himself there anyway.

"Anything." Johnathan promised fiercely.

"Find Ruth and help her figure out the best way for me to shut this all down. I'm going back to my cell before we get in trouble, but without that information I'm not sure any of us will survive this." Emma said.

She gave him a small smile, squeezed his hand, and hobbled away. She knew that Grace would continue to try and break her and yet she willingly returned to her cell. There were too many good people fighting Grace that she had to protect. Knowing that would allow her to survive anything.

Shadow Log: Emma, The Clover School for Girls, Rhode Island, December 3, 1810

The old pond was still partially frozen, the cracking ice sparkling like little diamonds in the afternoon sun. Emma shivered, she wanted nothing more than to hurry back into the warmth of the school, but Johnathan had made it clear he needed her help with something so she waited. A branch snapping under someone's weight made her jump half out of her skin before she realized it was Johnathan arriving.

"You have any problems sneaking out?" Jonathan asked with clear worry.

"Nah, I went up on the roof and used a tree to climb down safely. Why are we meeting up anyways?" Emma asked.

She was happy to get any time away from the horror that was her daily life, especially when she got to spend that time with a friend, but also worried about what would happen if they got caught.

"Jacob told me about an object of some kind buried under the Smith Farm. It's very important to Grace and I thought we should see if we could turn it to our advantage." Johnathan replied.

The wind shifted bringing with it the taste of blood and it took Emma far too long to realize it was coming from

Johnathan. Eyeing him worriedly, she started to see small signs that he had recently been in a fight of some kind. Not seeing anything life threatening, she decided to ignore it for now, at least until he was ready to talk.

"Lead the way." She muttered.

He took her hand with surprising gentleness and they walked in silence simply enjoying the cool breeze. Yet the closer they got to the Smith Farm the more uneasy Emma grew. She hadn't had the opportunity to get this close to the farm and now she wished that it had remained that way. She could feel the horrific, painful, and very menacing physic energy emanating from the place which made it hard to even think. Stopping at the entrance, she took a careful look around, and wondered where Mr. Smith was.

"Where…"

"He is busy with an angry Grace for a while." Johnathan replied before she could even finish her sentence.

Emma smiled, she felt very thankful that he hadn't let go of her hand, and had gotten even closer to her. He leaned in protectively, clearly also feeling the energy pulsating from the building which made Emma feel safer despite herself.

Shivering with worry more than chill, she pushed the door open, and stepped inside.

The building was a simple, rundown, single room farmhouse with absolutely nothing special about it unless you were impressed by mold growing on everything. Covering her nose in an effort to avoid inhaling the spores, she carefully made her way over to a tiny ladder that had been carved into the back wall, and stared down into the darkness below.

Johnathan let out an unhappily little huff as he let go of her hand, and slid down, only to be swallowed by the black ooze of the basement.

Not wanting to be alone, she slid down after him, and froze as the entire world turned upside down. There were chairs, a table, and lots of barrels seemingly glued to the ceiling which had once been the floor. The ceiling beneath her feet felt soft and oddly gooey and glowed with a pale, red, pulsating light. But what drew her attention was a pure black crystal that took up the majority of the room and was the source of the energy she was feeling.

"Not what I expected." Johnathan finally managed to mutter. Blinking furiously, Emma carefully dragged herself closer to it, feeling dread begin to fill her soul, "What did you expect?" Her voice came out muted almost like the crystal had tried to eat her words.

"I don't know, but not that." Johnathan grumbled.

The closer to it she got, the colder and more empty she felt like it was trying to absorb her. Suddenly, hot blood gushed out from between her legs as cramps exploded through her abdomen and the entire room began to spin. Gasping in surprise, she fell forward, and crashed into the crystal.

Blinking the fire out of her eyes, she found herself in the infirmary with a very worried Johnathan and Jacob staring down at her. Hissing unhappily, she carefully set up, and sent the world spinning.

"What happened?" She groaned.

"You passed out and then light exploded out of you. I didn't know what else to do, but bring you here." Johnathan whispered.

"Was I bleeding?" Emma asked in confusion.

She distinctly remembered blood, pain, and a profound emptiness. The rest of her memories were a foggy mess that made the world spin worse.

"You became a woman." Jacob said simply.

Eyeing him, she wanted to ask what he meant, but Anton slithered into her brain, *"Emma should not have gone to the farm."*

"Why?" She asked sharply.

She didn't like being chastised for something she couldn't have known was wrong, especially when he could have stopped her if he had wanted to.

"Anton does not know how to explain…Think of the crystal as a gateway to millions of other Earths that live in harmony with each other.

It allows those who know how to use the crystal to enter the bodies of other versions of one's self. It is dangerous to meddle with such things."
Then he was gone and Emma realized she had been staring off into space for an inappropriately long amount of time. Wiping away the sweat forming on her brow, she gave her friends a quick smile, and laid back down. Who knew when Grace would turn her attention back to her and she felt a desire to rest while she could.
"Thank you for your concern, I'm sure with rest I will return to normal." She whispered.
She rolled over, putting her back to them expecting them to both leave. Jacob did, but Jonathan lay down next to her and wrapped his arm around her waist.
"Is this okay?" He whispered gently.
Snuggling into his embrace, Emma purred happily, and felt her tension melt away. It was nice to be cuddled and she found herself unable to contain the blush creeping up her cheeks.

Shadow Log: Emma, The Clover School for Girls, Rhode Island, December 16, 1810

Emma sat in Jacob's office doing her best to avoid scratching at her itchy clothes or squirming under his gaze. She wasn't afraid of him or even worried about what might be coming, it was her dress making her wish to roll on a bed of spikes. Looking down at her arms, she could just make out the faintest hints of scale forming beneath her skin, and she wondered if she was losing it or if this was what everything had been leading up to.
"Emma!" Jacob snapped.
His voice jarred her out of her thoughts and reminded her that he had in fact been talking to her. Giving him a small smile, she bowed her head respectively, and took a deep breath.
"Sorry, I was distracted." She muttered quietly.

"I noticed, Emma, I need you to take this seriously." Jacob grumbled back.

Before Emma could respond, a tall handsome man came barging into the room, and marched over to Jacob's desk. Completely ignoring Emma, almost like she didn't exist, he jabbed his finger into Jacob's face angrily.

"You need to fire my son!" He shouted.

Looking a bit closer, Emma could see the resemblance to Johnathan, and she was sure that was who he had to be referring to. Slouching down into her corner, she bowed her head, and pretended she was invisible. After all, the last thing she wanted was to get kicked out and miss the drama.

"Warren, so nice of you to visit, have a seat." Jacob replied calmly.

Warren let out an explosive sigh as he knocked the chair out of his way and leaned down into Jacob's face.

"I don't know what is happening here, but Johnathan has changed and I don't like it!" He spat.

"Your son is becoming an excellent surgeon, nothing more." Jacob said dismissively.

"Look at her, she's clearly a scrawny gutter rat, and she isn't worth his attention." Warren shouted.

He jabbed his finger at Emma, making her really want to bite it off, but she just kept studying her shoes. Before Jacob could reply Johnathan burst into the office and marched up to his father.

"What are you doing here?" He asked almost angrily.

Warren stared at his son with the intensity of a small sun, his face twitching as he tried to control himself.

"I want you to quit, this place isn't for someone of your pedigree." Warren grumbled.

"Pedigree? What am I a dog? No, father, I am happy for the first time in years, and I will not be leaving." Johnathan said firmly.

"Why are you wasting your time on girls like her? They are clearly inferior to you…"

"Father! Emma does have ears and feelings despite who she was born to! Besides, doesn't God say we are all equal?" Johnathan cut him off.

Emma had to force herself to not smile at his words, he was such a good friend even when she probably didn't deserve the friendship, and it was hard to not blush under his thoughtful gaze.

"If you stay promise me that you'll remain pure for your betrothed and not fuck a child!" His father said with a pleading tone to his voice.

Johnathan straightened his back as an angry rumble formed in his chest and he fought to control himself. Giving Emma a long thoughtful look, Johnathan took a deep breath, and addressed his father without breaking eye contact with her.

"Do not judge, or you too will be judged. For in the same way you judge others, you will be judged, and with the measure you use, it will be measured to you. "Why do you look at the speck of sawdust in your brother's eye and pay no attention to the plank in your own eye?"

His father flinched, a look of anger mixed with surprise flashing across his face. Emma had only read the bible once as a way to make Theodore happy, but she still recognised when someone was quoting it. Jacob let out a harsh laugh, reminding everyone that he was still there, and calmly stood up.

"It is always a pleasure to see you, Warren, but I believe it is time for you to leave." Jacob said sternly.

"Fine, but Johnathan, please remember that Nancy is expecting a pure man to marry her in a couple years." Warren muttered as he pushed past his son.

Emma eyed Johnathan, feeling unsure of who he really was, and yet she did feel love coming from him. Well, that and acceptance which she had no idea of how to handle.

Turning back to Jacob, Emma felt a huge smile creep up her lips as her heart rate quickened with excitement.

"Good man, far too short sighted, but that doesn't mean he isn't wrong." Jacob grumbled.

Johnathan shot him a dirty look saying, "I love my father, but he doesn't control my life. If he had his way I wouldn't be studying medicine. Are you okay, Emma?"

"Depends on why Jacob called me in here." Emma replied softly.

"I called you in here to give you your daily shot, apparently Dr. Tannis is no longer employed here." Jacob sighed.

"Just get it over with." Emma replied unhappily.

"I'll do it," Johnathan whispered.

He was so gentle and loving as he prepped her arm and carefully inserted the needle that Emma didn't even feel it go in, but the fire from the medicine burned through her veins with angry intensity. Growling, she took Johnathan's hand before he could pull away, and whispered, "Thank you for everything."

Johnathan blushed as he quickly tried to hide his face by ducking his head rapidly. Jacob rolled his eyes, poured himself a drink, and waved them out of his office. Emma gave Johnathan a quick hug before she swiftly darted away. She needed time to clear her head and figure out why she felt so hot around him.

Morning brought strangeness in the form of the world being turned upside down yet again. Looking around the large playroom, she felt right at home, and yet she knew she didn't belong here with these children even if they were hers. Then Anton's words echoed through her mind about the different worlds with different versions of herself. Glancing out the window she felt her heart explode with worry at the thousands of huge black ships that filled the sky. Her daughter ran over to her and wrapped herself around her leg startling her. Looking down at the child, Emma felt a motherly dread start to form a pit in her stomach.

"Mommy, I'm scared." The little girl whimpered.

"Go find your father in the basement." She ordered sternly.

She had to peel the girl off of her leg and give her a little push towards her brothers before all three hurried from the room.With her children safe, she felt brave enough to step out on the terrace to stare up at the invaders. They weren't Useptis nor were they anything this Emma recognised, but they were definitely menacing.

"You really should come down into the shelter before they come for us, not that it will save us anyways." Johnathan said from the doorway making her jump.

"What are they?" She asked quietly.

"You know no one knows, but they are killing everything one moment at a time. Are you feeling alright?" He replied with worry.

"Hmm, yeah, is there anyone fighting them?" She asked, acting like she was lost in thought.

"You know they were killed quickly, even the poor Useptis." Johnathan muttered with clear concern.

Suddenly Emma found herself strapped to a steel table in Anton's lab staring up into the brightest light she had ever seen except for the sun. Screwing her eyes closed unhappily she tried not to aspirate her vomit. The straps holding her down snapped off and she immediately rolled onto her knees and spit the sludge out of her mouth.

"Anton disconnected Emma from the matrix, Emma is lucky this one knew what to do or it would be dead." Anton hissed into her head.

Giving him a dirty look she muttered, "Care to explain?"

"No, just know what you experienced was another lifetime with many different choices and that Emma got to experience your life in exchange. If you had died there you would have died here as well."

"Fine whatever…The sludge?" She mumbled with anger.

"A by-product of the transition." Anton replied flatly.

Knowing she wouldn't get anything else from him, she stumbled up onto her feet, and over to the door. It slid open to reveal that Mary was patiently waiting on the other side.

"Better?" Mary asked with concern.

"Better." Emma promised.

In truth she didn't feel better, but at this point she wasn't sure what was real and what wasn't, so who was to say she wasn't better. Seeing Mary eye her, Emma had to chuckle, and let out some of her pent up tension.

"I'm not going to lie, everything is just crazy right now." She admitted.

"High?" Mary said.

She darted over to her corner, pulled out a joint, and offered it to Emma. Accepting it, she settled down in Mary's nest, and let Mary light her up. Laying her head on Mary's chest, she took a deep puff, and passed it back to Mary who also partook.

"What if I fail?" Emma whispered fearfully.

"Then get up, keep fight." Mary replied softly.

Emma had to laugh, what she wouldn't give to see the world through Mary's eyes. Life just seemed so simple, but she knew Mary struggled with her own problems. Snuggling into Mary, she felt the weed wash over her, and she drifted off to sleep.

Shadow Log: Emma, The Clover School for Girls, North Dakota, December 30, 1810

Emma woke up to an unholy fire burning through her eyes, it felt worse than the time her mother had dumped the chamber pot on her for complaining. All she could see was bright flashes of light briefly illuminating the darkness of her cell even though there was no lightning. It took all of her willpower to keep from screaming as the pain ripped her eyes apart and she was sure she needed help. Yet she didn't trust the guards or Grace to do anything but laugh at her agony. So, she called out silently with her mind, *"Anton…please…"*

She gasped as a new wave of torment made her eyes go gritty as if they were filled with sand. Feeling Anton slither into her mind, she opened herself up to him, and allowed him to experience the problem.

"Oh, Little One... the darkness is becoming light." Anton said with such gentleness that she started to cry.

The cell to her door creaked slowly open to reveal a guard who seemed to be sleepwalking except for Anton's overwhelming presence.

"Come, Little One," the guard mumbled with drool leaking down his chin.

Emma let him pick her up and carry her through the halls making sure to keep her eyes screwed shut in an attempt to help with the burning. They stumbled down a short flight of stairs, the moisture of the air growing along with the heat as they descended into the room.

"Bath house?" Emma muttered in confusion.

"Do you need help with Emma's nightgown?" Anton slurred in reply.

"No, what should I do?" Emma whimpered.

"Sink into water and let it cleanse your pain."

Anton gently sat her down before directing the guard back towards his post. The moment she was alone, she pulled her nightgown over head, and fell face first into the water. At first her eyes burned even worse as she sank slowly to the bottom, but when she forced them open the water flooded them. Her pain vanished as a set of gills sprouted from her neck allowing her to breathe normally. Sitting on the bottom of the spring, she felt her eyes twitch as they slowly mutated, and the water kept them moist.

Hours passed as she dozed and her eyes slowly became more and more alien to her until she saw Grace glaring down at her from the surface. Feeling dread spring to life in her chest, she debated just making Grace drag her out of the spring, but decided it would just worsen her situation. Swimming up to the surface, she breached in a spray of water, and as fresh air rushed into her lungs her gills disappeared.

"Swimming naked is such a wonderful feeling..." Grace muttered almost sadly.

Giving Grace what could only be seen as a surprised look, Emma rolled out of the water, and wrapped herself in a towel. Feeling thankful that the awful burning was gone, she turned back to Grace, and waited for her fate to come crashing back in.

"I remember my mutations hurt so badly that I begged for death, but the Useptis just kept laughing… and eating. You're lucky to have such good friends willing to help you when you need it. Please, don't ever take that for granted." Grace said wistfully.

Emma stared at her, feeling dumbfounded as she tried to understand what was happening.

"I never have." Emma offered after a long pause.

"Good, good," Grace whispered.

Grace's eyes became unfocused as she turned her attention towards her past making Emma squirm uncomfortably. Nothing was making sense and she needed the world in order or she knew her grip on her own sanity would begin to slip. Drying her hair quickly, Emma slithered back into her nightgown, and tried to figure out a way to escape Grace's attention.

"Go back to your cell, the guards are changing shifts so you'll have a clear passage. Oh, and this is your only free pass." Grace warned sternly.

Emma nodded, darted up the stairs, and away from Grace before she could change her mind. She didn't have a clue what had gotten into the woman, but she was sure she didn't want to find out how quickly it would wear off either. Returning to her cell before the breakfast klaxon was surprisingly easy just as Grace had promised which left Emma feeling uneasy.

'Thank you for last night.' She mentally whispered to Anton. *'Many more changes are coming, please protect yourself.'* Anton replied.

Feeling him turn his attention back to what he was doing, she decided she should enjoy the gruel that was breakfast before the day turned terrible on her.

Shadow Log: Emma, The Clover School for Girls, Rhode Island, January 24, 1811

Emma woke choking for air, memories of the last torture session still echoing through her lungs, and sat up in panic. Someone gently took her hand, comforting her to help keep her grounded. Finally able to understand where she was, Emma looked around, and her eyes immediately settled on Johnathan.

"Where, when, what?" She managed to gasp weakly.

"Grace, you are in the infirmary." Johnathan explained softly. Emma groaned, the last month was a blur of pain, discomfort, and sadness all mixed up with despair. It was hard enough to remember any specific memories, but from what she could remember it had involved a lot of drowning, hanging, and whips. Stretching gingerly, she gave Johnathan a meak smile, and tried to ignore the agony burning through her back.

"Let me get you something for the pain." Johnathan said. She watched him hurry away, wishing she had the strength to get out of bed, but instead settled for studying her surroundings. The infirmary was a quiet place that gave her the chills, it had clearly been a church of some kind, but now it was rank with death and fear. Watching a nurse wheel out a gurney, Emma could smell the dead flesh underneath, and was reminded of her mission. Johnathan appeared again, handing her a glass of water, and setting up a needle kit.

"This will help with the pain and make recovery easier." Johnathan whispered.

He drew the liquid from the vial, then he stuck the needle into her arm, and injected it into her. Giving her a smile, he sat down next to her, and took her hand.

"Please lay down, you need rest." He whispered urgently.

Emma begrudgingly complied, already feeling the medication flushing warmly through her veins. It felt wrong to just lay there when so many girls had been and were being hurt but she understood that she needed to heal before she could continue her mission. But just because her body wasn't working well didn't mean that she couldn't go after information.

"Tell me what have I missed? What has Grace been up to?" She asked quietly.

Johnathan shifted uncomfortably, looked around for an excuse to flee, and sighed, "Jacob went missing on the same day you went berserk in the cafeteria, Grace revoked her exercise first policy, and Mary punched Grace breaking her nose for hurting her friend. Don't worry Mary is fine, Grace decided hurting a feeble minded girl would be unwise. Ooh, and Mary has been visiting all week to try and read to you to help you wake up. Grace gave you something that has caused some strange developments in your body."

Emma listened to the words drifting into an almost trance like state, his voice was sweet and soothing, and its cacadance made it easy for her to relax. She was proud of Mary for trying to stand up for herself, but was also very worried about what would happen if she tried again. And now she had to try and figure out what had happened with Jacob; she was sure he wouldn't just abandon his school or his daughter. Then there was the matter of what was happening to her own body and why Grace was so invested in making her into a human hybrid. Too many unanswered questions and too few answers for her to keep being reckless.

She turned to stare up into Johnathan's concerned eyes, smiled, and asked, "Is there anywhere on school grounds or near them where you could hold someone hostage without anyone finding them?"

Johnathan looked thoughtful for a few moments, then a light went off in his eyes, and he gasped, "The Smith Farm, it is about a five minute walk from the school, and Mr. Smith grows cinder for the school. He's always given me the creeps and I know he would do whatever Grace told him."

"I need you to help me check, she could kill him, or already has. Mary is innocent in all of this and I don't want her to lose her father." Emma moaned.

She sat up, promptly vomited from the sudden spinning room, and realized that she had missed something very obvious. Looking down at her chest, she tried to understand how and why she suddenly had tiny boobs. When she had attacked Phillips she had been a relatively normal little girl and now she was clearly occupying the body of a young woman complete with all of the plumping. She hefted one of her breasts curiously, making Johnathan blush, and look away uncomfortably. She felt so respected by him as she tried to come to terms with the sudden maturity of her body.

Shaking it off to the best of her ability, she reached over, and grabbed the stack of clothing sitting on her bedside table.

Turning back to Johnathan, she gave his leg a gentle squeeze, and asked, "Is there somewhere I can change in private or are you just going to turn your back?"

Blushing harder, Johnathan helped her to the supply closet, and led her inside. He quickly closed the door, gave her a huge grin, and ducked behind a stack of crates.

"This way I'll know if you need help, I don't want you to get hurt on my account!" He called.

"Thanks, why didn't you try and talk me out of looking for Jacob?" She asked.

She quickly laid out her clothes and began the task of getting dressed.

"Arguing seemed like a waste of time that would draw too much attention." Johnathan replied.

"You are a smart man." Emma laughed.

Once she was dressed, they snuck out of the school through the bathhouse tunnel while the guard snoozed. The walk through the forest was oddly revitalizing, the pain in her body faded away, and the strange fog clogging up her thoughts began to clear. By the time they reached the farm, she felt like she could win any fight coming her way, and she could tell Johnathan was impressed with her recovery.

"There are three buildings on the farm, the old barn, the new barn, and the farmhouse. I say we check the old barn first." Johnathan whispered nervously.

"No need, I can smell blood, fear, and urine on the wind. We will simply follow it to its source." Emma replied.

Johnathan stared at her in wonderment, a dopey grin appearing on his face, and said, "I'll follow your lead then." Emma closed her eyes, sniffed the air, and started walking towards the smell. Suddenly she picked up on a new smell in the air, one that was of rotted lemon, but did not belong to Anton. Feeling her heart rate quicken, she opened her eyes, and looked in the direction of the source. Sixteen hungry eyes stared back at her from the treeline turning her blood to ice. Hissing, she felt her skin ripple as scales erupted all over her body, and her vision shifted.

"Run, find Jacob, he's in the old barn." She said in a gravelly voice.

Johnathan took one look at her, blanched, and did as he was told. Seeing their prey attempting to flee, the Useptis charged, letting out horrible angry clicks as they closed ground with Emma. Letting out another hiss, Emma met their charge, her movements blurring as she built up speed and strength. She could see all five of the hearts of the first Useptis beating inside of its chest, like glowing targets. Letting out a battle cry, she smashed her fist through the ribcage of the creature causing its first heart to explode violently. Grabbing hold of its ribs, she slammed it into the ground, and rapidly destroyed the rest of its hearts.

She turned just in time to receive a heavy blow directly to her chin which sent her flying backwards through the air. She collided with a tree, all the air getting knocked from her lungs, and the back of her head crashed into the trunk stunning her. Seeing stars, she tried to stand up but the

Useptis wrapped its tail around her throat, lifted her off of the ground, and squeezed. She clawed, scratched, and pulled; trying to loosen its hold to no avail until everything went dark.

She woke up coughing up black sludge all over Anton's hooves much to his dismay as he trotted backwards to escape the vomit. Shaking uncontrollably, she collapsed back onto the ground, and tried to suck air past the bruises blossoming on her throat. Everything hurt, her vision was blurry, and she could feel something moving around inside of her. Blood dripped slowly down onto her lips, making her flench, and recoil; but then it slipped into her mouth. She had to have more, she was ravenous, there was no stopping the hunger. Whimpering needily, she opened her mouth as wide as she could, and gulped at the blood now flowing steadily into her mouth. After a few moments the blood stopped, making Emma let out a sad, gurgly, hiss past the remaining blood oozing down her throat.

"Don't be greedy, Little One." Anton scorned her.

Blinking as her vision slowly returned, she climbed up onto her knees, and promptly had to screw her eyes shut as the world started spinning.

"What happened?" She moaned.

"The Useptis saw death coming and chose to take Emma with it, but Anton will not allow that to happen, This One promises." Anton replied protectively.

"What are you talking about? Why am I healing so quickly?" Emma asked in confusion.

"It is called Black Death, it drove Grace insane, and would have killed her if This One had not intervened. An action Anton is now regretting since Anton can no longer help Emma in the same way. But do not worry, Anton will find a way to save you, This One promises. As for the healing, you drank my blood which nourished your cells allowing them to regenerate." Anton explained.

Emma felt sick, wishing she hadn't pushed Anton for the truth, but she had and now she had to trust he would keep his promise. He did seem to care about her, otherwise why would he have risked leaving the school to help her? Why would he have given her his blood and killed his own kind if he didn't want her to live? Trusting anyone to put her needs first was difficult especially with her life at stake, but she didn't have a choice.

"Thank you, do you know if Johnathan is alright?" She muttered.

Finding she could now stand, she scrambled up onto her feet, and surveyed the battlefield. The Useptis had parts strewn everywhere, their blood already soaking into the snow, and staining it a dark greenish black color. She was lucky to have survived at all from the looks of it and was sure she needed to learn to fight and quickly at that.

"Johnathan is with Jacob approaching slowly from that direction. Emma should distract him or Anton will be seen." Anton said pointing east.

"Thank you again, honored friend." Emma whispered.

She jogged quickly away, moving swiftly in the direction Anton had pointed, wanting to put the fight behind her, but the death now squirming in her stomach made that difficult. Seeing Johnathan trying to half carry Jacob, she jogged over, and slid under Jacob's free arm taking some of his weight.

"You smell like death." Jacob groaned almost incoherently.

"Grace had him strung up, hanging from his hands, and gave him quite the thrashing." Johnathan explained.

He seemed strangely calm, despite the copious amounts of alien blood coating Emma, and completely unfazed by the craziness he had probably seen as he fled.

"I'm glad you found him, I think we should take him to Mary in the basement." Emma said.

She shifted their direction towards the bathhouse, she had no plans to leave Jacob with Mary, but didn't want Johnathan to freak out having to meet Anton. Since Mary lived right outside Anton's door, she figured that would be the best place for Johnathan to leave him, and still remain blissfully unaware that aliens existed.

"He needs a doctor!" Johnathan protested.

"I have a friend who can't leave the basement that can help him, but he is a bit of a recluse, and hates meeting new people." Emma replied.

It was a half truth, but she wasn't going to risk Johnathan's life anymore than she already had. He was a good person, pure of soul, and she refused to drag him deeper into the craziness that had become her life. He eyed her suspiciously for a long moment before giving her a small nod and turning his full focus to carrying Jacob's weight. Seeing blood leak out of Jacob's shirt and smelling the hint of death she knew they were moving too slow.

"He won't survive at this pace." She hissed.

Tapping into her Useptis side, she threw Jacob over her shoulder, and gave Johnathan a wink. Feeling the primalness take over, she turned, and blurred towards the school. Her speed and agility building as her scales surfaced to protect her from the friction and her body became more intune with itself. Blinking the sweat out of her eyes, she skidded to a stop outside Anton's door, leaving behind burnt bits of shoe, and pounded on it. She hoped he was already back, hoped he could help, and that Jacob could be saved.

The door slid slowly open, allowing Anton to blur out, and take Jacob from Emma. Before Emma could follow Anton back into his lab, she heard a quiet whimper, and turned to see Mary staring worriedly at her. Letting the lab seal behind her, Emma walked over to Mary, and gave her what she hoped was a smile.

"He'll be fine, he tried to stand up to Grace, and she took her anger out on him." Emma explained gently.

"You?" Mary asked.

Seeing Mary eye the blood congealing on her skin, clothes, and hair Emma became extremely aware of how terrifying she must look. Feeling her scales slip back beneath her skin,

Emma took a deep breath, and blinked the debris from her eyes.

"I just need a bath, you wouldn't know how to get past the guards would you?" Emma asked hopefully.

"Follow." Mary said happily.

She led her to a wall, pushed on a brick, and revealed a long tunnel that led to what looked like a labyrinth of other tunnels.

"School built, old mine." Mary said with a shrug.

Emma followed her into the dark, feeling hopeful for the first time since she had come to the school.

Shadow Log: Emma, The Clover School for Girls, Rhode Island, January 25, 1811

Emma had received three days of solitary confinement for sneaking out of the infirmary. It was an acceptable punishment to her considering she had gotten a chance to save one of the good guys. It just sucked to not know if Jacob had survived his injuries or if Grace would just kill him anyway. It hurt knowing how her life had gone from bad to insane and she didn't have a choice in any of it. It felt like she was a performer in play who had forgotten her lines and she hated it.

"You look like someone killed your cat." Johnathan said.

Emma turned to face him in shock, solitary with no food for three days meant no visitors, so how had he managed to get in? She was happy to see him, but was worried about how he saw her after yesterday's craziness.

"Just worried about Grace and how she'll handle what we did." Emma replied.

"She doesn't know everything yet, but Mary wanted me to tell you Jacob is fine. I got in for a health check." Johnathan said.

Emma let out a sigh of relief, relaxing against the wall, and decided she needed to trust him.

"Trust isn't easy for me, I have been hurt too many times, but you have proven that you want to be my friend. So, ask the question that is eating you up and I will answer honestly." Emma sighed.

"What did I see yesterday?" Johnathan asked simply.

"Grace mutated my blood with foreign DNA to make me into a hybrid soldier. If I say more than that it will put you in danger." Emma warned.

She watched Johnathan closely as he knelt down and placed a loving hand on her knee.

"You are not alone anymore." He whispered.

Emma nodded, trying to not cry as emotion suddenly flooded her. She had spent her entire life as a plaything for others and here was someone loving her for who she was. It made her feel safe, happy, and warm but it also made her feel uncomfortable. She currently had nothing to lose and everything to gain and that was a very vulnerable position to be in.

"You know that Grace will kill you if she thinks it will further her experiment." Emma muttered.

"Then I die happy knowing I got to meet you." Johnathan replied quietly.

Emma impulsively kissed him, he pulled back for a moment, then grabbed her face, and kissed her harder. Letting go, she leaned in, and pulled him close.

Shadow Log: Jacob, The Clover School for Girls, Rhode Island, January 25, 1811

Jacob could feel the weight of the world grow heavier with each breath. When he had started the school he had been twenty years younger and a lot more energetic, now, he was exhausted. One day soon all of this would be over and he would be able to leave it in his wake but until then he had to keep this mess from getting horribly out of control.

Looking up at the boughs of a great white oak that had weathered hundreds if not thousands of storms he felt a sense of peace settle in next to his worry. While he couldn't completely understand wanting to live in the branches of a tree, he wanted to support his daughter's happiness. Hearing Mary approaching he centered himself and turned to face her.

"You look happy Little Bean," Jacob said with gentle happiness.

"Emma punched Megan." Mary laughed happily.

Doing his best to keep his alarm hidden Jacob asked, "May I ask you why?"

He could see the exact moment Mary understood that she had just put her friend in danger. He watched her shift uncomfortably under his gaze before he let out a long almost mournful sigh.

"I'm not mad as long as she did it to protect you." He promised, hoping that it would help make her more comfortable.

"Megan put rat bedding." Mary finally muttered heartbrokenly.

"Sounds like Megan deserved to be punched. Did you manage to get the package from Mr. Smith?" Jacob asked. He knew that by changing the subject he would give Mary a chance to relax and maybe stop fidgeting.

"Yes, put on the spot." Mary said with a bit of confidence shining through her broken demeanor.

"Good, you are the only person I have ever trusted with that. You know that don't you?" Jacob asked gently.

"Happy." Mary muttered as she blushed.

Growing increasingly impatient Jacob finally asked, "You want to tell me why you had me meet you here?"

"Sorry, found strange plant growing near home. Worried it be dangerous…" Mary tried to explain.

"Ah, is that why you had me meet you out here? You want me to make sure you are safe?" Jacob nudged.

Nodding, Mary took his hand, and led him around the tree to a small reddish pink bush with large, pointed, and spiky looking leaves. Crouching over the bush Jacob could see thousands of tiny little bristles that gave the leaf an almost furred appearance. He forced himself to take a deep breath as he stared down at the plant in confusion. He knew that it had to be cinder weed; it was the only thing that made sense to him, but that would mean Mr. Smith had failed at keeping the plants underground. Now his daughter had seen it and was a risk to what he was trying to build, a risk to every deal he had made to keep her safe.

"This is actually a good thing." He said, finally deciding on how he would handle it.

"Why?" Mary asked uneasily.

"If you take these leaves, soak them in water for two days, and then dry them out and crumble them up you can smoke them." Jacob explained.

"Why?" Mary asked curiously.

"Because they will make everything hurt a little less and they will show you a different version of the world." Jacob promised.

"Try?" Mary asked with what could almost be called excitement.

"Go ahead, but I want you to only smoke one leaf a week and only after your chores are complete. Promise?" Jacob asked firmly.

"Promise." Mary said, matching his force.

"I'm proud of you, Little Bean. I have to go take care of some business, but I want you to know I love you." Jacob said gently.

"Know." Mary said, sounding disappointed.

Jacob patted her softly on the head as he walked past her heading to Smith's farmhouse. He needed to know how a plant had managed to escape the growhouse and if the business had been compromised. He had been doing everything he could to avoid the farm and its contents not because he was a coward but because he was smart or at least that was what he told himself. The farmhouse itself was just a simple white single story home with peeling paint and a broken down porch that creaked with the passing breeze. It was what lay beneath the seemingly serene home that made his hair stand on end. Beneath that house lay something foreign that hummed with sinister intent. He wasn't sure how metal could hum or how it could emanate such hatred and that was at the heart of why he avoided the Smith home. Well, that and his recent tenure there as Grace's prisoner. He could see that Mr. Smith had cozied down into his rocking chair and dozed off with his hat tipped over his eyes. Jacob stepped onto the porch causing the wood to sag beneath his feet and groan uncomfortably announcing his presence causing Mr. Smith to startle awake. Jacob carefully steered clear of the flailing arms as Mr. Smith came windmilling out of his seat.

"Jeezum, you trying to get yourself blown to bits?!" Mr. Smith shouted angrily.

"I'm wondering how our most profitable plant ended up growing up by the old oak." Jacob snapped back.

"Probably that thing in my cellar." Mr. Smith spat.

"We have a deal. You grow the weed and The Shadows keep you protected. If it is growing wild then we have a serious problem!" Jacob shouted in a tone that made it clear that he thought he was dealing with a moron.

"How dare you! I break my back in those fields making sure no one knows our secret and you come in here..."

"I would adjust your attitude before one of us ends up dead." Jacob warned, stopping him mid rant.

"I'll take a look around tomorrow, but I ain't taking no responsibility for this." Mr. Smith grumbled.

"I don't care if you do, so long as this doesn't land in my lap. I have thirty young women who will end up dead if Grace finds out her experiment is compromised. Not to mention what she'll do to us!" Jacob hissed threateningly.

"Relax, we will be fine." Mr. Smith promised soothingly.

"If I find one more plant outside the growhouse I will smother you in your sleep." Jacob said coldly.
Giving Mr. Smith one last deathglare, he turned on his heels, and stomped away. He refused to let anyone or anything keep hurting Mary's future. In truth he had the death of Mr. Smith planned already, it was only a matter of timing everything correctly. It had taken so much work to keep Grace happy enough to allow Mary's continued safety, and now that she was helping Emma he couldn't afford any mistakes.

✴✴✴✴✴

Jacob woke in a cold sweat to the crashing of thunder and the pounding of hail and rain upon the roof. Shuddering, he threw off his sweat soaked blankets, and sat up as his heart pounded angrily in chest. If he dared to close his eyes he knew her bloody face would still be there screaming in agony as she was swallowed by grief. All while he stood to her side holding that bloody dagger like it just might somehow make it disappear. Truth was he had no one but himself to blame for the nightmares that haunted him.
Stumbling, exhaustedly from his bed, he walked over to his desk, and retrieved a brown bottle from the bottom drawer. Shivering, he quickly wrapped himself in his overcoat, and staggered out into the hall. With each burdensome step his body somehow grew heavier and more unruly as each flash of frightsome lightening brought with it another glimpse into his guilt. He reached the back door only to realize he was only wearing his nightgown and coat. Wiggling his bare toes against the frozen stone, he wiped away his tears, and threw open the door.
Despite not being able to see much further than his hand, Jacob marched steadfastly through the mud and melting snow, his thoughts trained on an ancient almost forgotten burnt out church that sat nestled in a clump of woods on the

edge of the property. Looking down at his hands all he could see was blood slowly dripping off of his fingers, the blood of anguish. Shaking, he pulled his coat tighter, and marched fearlessly into the darkened trees.

The chapel was a small one room building with a steepled roof built from stone and wood. The east and west walls had three panels of stained glass to let in God's glorious light. The altar sat on the south wall opposite the two door entrance behind five rows of wooden pews. Or at least it had been thirty years ago, today it was little more than a ruin dusted in shattered glass. The great beams that had once held the roof in place now lay scattered, broken, and charred upon the floor. The walls were crumbled, cracked, and signed, leaning in towards each other as if they were seeking comfort from one another. And the doors much like the windows were no more than shattered dreams upon the soot covered rot that was the floor.

Jacob took slow measured steps up what remained of the isle to the altar oblivious to the glass digging into the soles of his bare feet and dropped to his knees. The rain pounded him almost as much as his guilt as he slowly bowed his head and wept. Suddenly, thunder shook the ruins as it echoed deafeningly against the old stone walls making Jacob startle violently. Catching a glimpse of a hooded figure sitting on one of the charred pews Jacob slowly turned to get a better look.

"You always did have an anger issue." His brother said.

"You are dead." Jacob shouted in horrified shock.

"Death is simply a new beginning. You made a mistake, brother, an honest mistake born out of love. Why do you carry that guilt around? It must be heavy." His brother asked morosely.

"I failed you and Anna and myself that night. I was so filled with rage when I heard you were marrying her that I lost all control…and then I lost everything." Jacob whispered brokenly.

"Not everything, Anna and I both forgave you and you have my daughter. Maybe, it is time to let go of this remorse and start living."

"Ghosts aren't real which means I'm conversing with myself and that is not a good thing." Jacob sighed as he rubbed his eyes angrily.

"Ghosts aren't but wraiths are. I am at peace brother and to prove that I speak true I will tell you something that only your brother could know. You have a scar on the back of your head from where I smashed it into the floor after you told dad it was my fault the dishes had been broken. I knew it had been you trying to act out scenes from that damn Shakespeare."

Jacob stared at his brother wondering how insane he had to be to be hallucinating so vividly, when lightning struck a tree just outside, and briefly illuminated the room. His brother was see through and he was beginning to fade and beginning to become less tangible.

"I don't have a lot of time, brother, Anna and I both love you and forgive you for your actions. Let it go, please, don't let our daughter suffer for your sins." His brother whispered weakly.

Jacob felt two strong hands briefly squeeze his shoulders lovingly in their frozen embrace and then the presence was just gone. And with it his guilt, it was as if someone had just sucked out all of his anger and pain and replaced it with peacefulness. Suddenly very aware of his stiff limbs, bleeding feet, and chilled bones Jacob dragged himself up onto his feet and turned to leave. Only to see a beautiful young woman floating a few inches from the floor blocking the only way out. Even though he couldn't see her face he knew beyond any doubt that it was Anna. Trembling, he took a step towards her, and froze not knowing how she felt towards him.

"Oh, look at you, freezing out here in the rain." She lamented quietly.

"I'm so, so sorry." Jacob managed to choke out as his knees buckled.

"Lytta, love, you have nothing to be sorry about. Your father failed to teach you how to handle your emotions and then he filled you with his rage. I never stopped loving you even as I could never stop loving Jason." Anna said gently.

"You chose him." Jacob sobbed.

"We got drunk one night and things went too far between us. I was ordered to choose him because I was carrying his child but I always wanted you to be my husband. And you were a wonderful one even if it was for such a short time. I know that it is easy to wallow in grief and pain and negativity but you are stronger than that." Anna cooed.

"I love you and miss you with every fiber of my being." Jacob whispered as an emptiness overcame him.

"As do I, but, Lytta, your time is coming to a close. Just be patient and take care of Mary for me." Anna said.

Jacob felt a frozen kiss upon his lips and she was gone. The rain stopped so suddenly that it left Jacob to sit in stunned silence as he tried to figure out what had just happened. After a few long moments of compilation, Jacob calmly climbed back to his feet, and wiped the debris from his knees. Smiling for the first time in what felt like years, his shoulders relaxed as tension began to seep out of him.

"Thank you, God, for the blessings you have bestowed upon me tonight." He prayed quietly.

Hobbling out of the church, he sagged down onto the stone steps, and stared up into the lightening sky as dawn began to over take the night. It was time to let go of the past and embrace the future, and he could see no better way to acknowledge that then to watch the sun rise.

Staring up at the majestic sky, he began to remember the events that had led to his troubled dreams, and his fingers instinctually moved to the rigid scars that had been stab wounds days prior. He had forgotten that he wasn't alone in his battles, had allowed his anger to rule him again, and had almost died. If Johnathan and Emma hadn't gotten him to the healing vats in time he would have been one with his Anna again and left Mary alone. His anger at himself cut him deeper than the knife Grace had used and he only hoped she knew that he was sorry. He had to be more careful, had to think about what she needed rather than what he needed. "I'll protect you, Little Bean." He whispered to himself.

Shadow Log: Grace, The Clover School for Girls, Rhode Island, January 26, 1811

Grace couldn't believe her eyes as she watched Jacob doing his rounds. She had known he had escaped, known that somehow two Useptis had died, and had known Emma had slipped out. But to see the man so brazenly defying her made her blood boil, yet she couldn't kill him out in the open. Nor could she kill him in secret, not without drawing too much attention.

She debated just sending him to the arctic to freeze to death, but that wasn't going to solve the issue. There was only one way that Jacob could have survived and she needed to deal with the source. Preparing for battle, she ported into Anton's room, and drew her sword. Anton turned to face her, lifting his head up, and puffed up his chest. Grace let out a maniacal laugh as she charged forward, channeling all of her anger into one fury filled swing of her sword.

Anton easily dodged, sending her crashing into one of the consoles behind him, and pranced away from her laughing. Attacking in a blind rage, she swung at him again, and again until she could barely breathe from the exhaustion. But Anton dodged each swing easily, his body agilily staying one move ahead of everything she did all while his laughter grew in volume.

"This One grows bored." He chuckled.

Before Grace could respond, she felt her entire body go rigid as Anton took over her mind, and then her body. Unable to think or move, she watched helplessly as Anton wrapped his tail around her throat, and shifted into position to place his mouth over her face. Grace wanted to scream, to fight, to do something to prevent the parasite from sliding back into her stomach. But she was helpless against Anton's control. *"Forget."* Anton ordered and everything went black.

Shadow Log: Ruth, Rhode Island, January 26, 1811

Ruth stared up at the windows of her childhood home remembering the feeling of her father's hands around her throat, the taste of his spittle as he screamed, and the sound of his anger booming out of him. She had been so filled up with his pain that there had been no room for her own and that had broken her. The place now sat in ruin, forgotten, and unloved; a shadow of what it once had been because of her actions.

Grace had given her the poison but she hadn't made her give it to her mother or her father, hadn't made her kill them, that had been all her. She had allowed her hatred, her pain, and her panic to overwhelm the good in her and she had enjoyed watching her father die. Oddly her mother's death meant nothing to her and had done nothing to widen the void in her heart. But their deaths had made Ruth a slave to The Shadows, turning on them would mean them showing the world who really ended the Weston line.

It hurt to walk through the doors, to smell his tobacco again, to feel the coldness of the abandoned house. This place had become her own personal hell so very long ago, but sometimes walking into hell was the only way to find clarity. She had stolen a file from The Shadows and said nothing when Jacob had been taken. All out of fear and panic, feelings she had thought she had put to rest during her training. But they just kept coming back and as long as she was haunted she would not know who she was or what she was supposed to be.

The stairs creaked beneath her feet, groaning from years of neglect as she ascended them, each echoing moan of wood reminding her of another failure. She stopped at the top of the stairs, turned slowly, and surveyed the foyer remembering the joy of her parents when they came home to share the news that she would have a sibling, then the sorrow when he was lost. Four times over, four chances for their family to grow ripped away by fate leaving nothing but bitterness behind. Bitterness that had turned to hate which fell squarely on her shoulders after the accident had stripped away their chances of having a son.

Shaking her head to try and clear the cobwebs, she walked into her mother's suite, and sat down on the edge of the dusty bed. She was supposed to have been given a second chance at life, at freedom, but instead she was trapped in a new hell of her own making. She envied Emma's ability to see everything with such a cold logical perspective, her ability to act without thinking, and her fearlessness. That was why she had sent her to isolation when Grace fell into her coma after the recent Useptis attack. She had let jealousy dictate her actions and had secured her place within The Shadows…At Grace's side.

It kept her safely out of Grace's crosshairs but made her feel sick with guilt which was why she was back in her mother's bedroom looking for something to ease her conscience. But looking around at the dust covered furniture Ruth knew the only thing that might ease her guilt was to make things right. Wiping away the tears drying on her cheeks, she stood up, and ported to her room at The Shadow base.

She quickly grabbed the stolen file from under her mattress and headed in search of Theodore. His name was all over the file along with several disciplinary action notices for his attempts to aid Emma. That meant he would make a fine ally in determining how to bring Grace's disgrace to an end. Hopefully freeing Ruth of her guilt and allowing her to become the woman she wanted to be.

Ruth had her entire world reorientated with such suddenness that she couldn't keep herself from yelping loudly. Blinking away her surprise at having been roughly grabbed and dragged from the hallway, she straightened her uniform, and gave her attacker a dirty look.

"Who the hell are you?" She spat angrily.

"I'm the guy you're looking for…sort of. My name is Mark, Theodore sent me to find you." Mark explained.

He backed away from her quickly looking like he thought she might punch him for touching her. She gave him a small cold smile, placed her back to the wall, and rubbed her sore arm.

"Why didn't he come himself?" She asked.

"He's busy dealing with another issue that can't be avoided. He wants you to find Johnathan, Jacob, or Anton if you need help. But above all, he wants you to stop asking around for him before Grace catches his trail." Mark replied.

Ruth grumbled unhappily under her breath, she had wanted support, but more than that she wanted answers. She knew Anton had them, but he was never going to give her anything. She also really wanted to beat her frustration out on Mark despite knowing that it wasn't his fault.

"I'll return to the school." She finally muttered unhappily.

"He also said that Grace is planning something awful yet he doesn't know what it is, so keep your eyes open." Mark said. He vanished in a flash of light making her instinctually shield her eyes. She took a moment to collect herself wishing she was someone else, someone who never agreed to join The Shadows, but she had made her choice. Now it was about making that choice matter.

Shadow Log: Jacob, The Clover School for Girls, Rhode Island, January 27, 1811

Jacob punched the wall out of sheer frustration, his breathing ragged from the anger he felt building in his chest, and his body rigid from the tension pulsating through it. He'd spent the day trying to figure out how to save his daughter from the insanity that had somehow crept into their lives. But the only thing he had found was failure mixed with confusion.

Apparently, Grace had issued an order to move Emma off school property until a full evaluation could take place. The problem was she was comatose after Anton had given her back the Black Death and no one knew where Emma was or who had moved her. Theodore had issued a full stop investigation order which meant the other girls were safe for a while but the order would be overridden the moment Grace found out about it. Jacob had wanted to try and use Emma as leverage to free the rest of the girls but that was not possible with her missing.

"Anton cannot feel Emma's mind, This One is sorry." Anton whispered into Jacob's mind.

Jacob sighed, if Anton couldn't feel her at all then she wasn't on school grounds or anywhere close by, or she was in a well shielded room. He needed a new plan, but he knew he was too angry to think straight which meant he needed to clear his mind. Seeing that the sun had faded and the stars were crystal clear, he grabbed his cloak, and headed for the roof. He found Mary cuddled up in a nest of blankets, staring up in wonder at the night sky, looking completely at peace with the world, and walked over to her.

"Mind if I join?" He asked softly.

He still remembered her anger at him, remembered how she had seemed to want nothing to do with him, and he knew she might not want anything to do with him still. Pulling his cloak tighter, he realized he owed her an apology, or she might just ignore him.

"I fail all the time and sometimes I need someone to remind me of how to be good. Thank you for that reminder and for motivating me to be better." He quickly added to his question.

Mary gave him a side eye for a long uncomfortable moment before she sighed and patted the blanket next to her. Jacob settled down next to her, feeling surprised at how quickly she snuggled into his embrace, and rested her head on his chest.

"Emma told. Father healthy?" Mary asked quietly.

Jacob kissed the top of her head, feeling a great weight lift off of his soul, and said, "Getting there, our friend took care of me."

"Good." Mary whispered happily.

Jacob pulled her close, closed his eyes, and drifted off to sleep. Feeling completely at peace knowing that she didn't hate him and that she was safely tucked into his arms.

Shadow Log: Grace, The Clover School for Girls, Rhode Island, February 3, 1811

Grace woke slowly, a fog cluttering up her mind, and making it impossible to think. It felt like it was impossible to grab the pieces of her shattered mind and stick them back together. There was a void at the center of her mind swallowing her memories and keeping her thoughts from being able to form. It took every ounce of willpower she had to be able to sit up on her cot and get her breathing under control.

The last thing she remembered was trying to get Jacob to come around to her point of view; everything else was a blur of pain and confusion mixed with emptiness. A sudden movement in her belly made her suck in a huge gasp of air and touch her stomach. She remembered that feeling, remembered the horror as the creature sucked her life out of her, and the pain as it grew out into her body over taking her flesh.

The only way that the Black Death could have returned was if Anton had given it back to her…which meant her missing memories weren't lost naturally, they were taken from her. She seethed angrily, trying to get a sense of control back as she faced the realization that her death was closing in once more. Choking on the black sludge building up in her throat, she wiped at her tears, and forced herself to stand up. Anton, Jacob, Theodore, even Ruth couldn't be trusted. They were all a part of the web Emma was building and Grace knew she was no longer in control. Rinsing out her mouth, she took a deep breath to try and clear her mind, and did her best to piece together a plan.

Emma had clearly evolved further than she had originally thought which meant she was no longer controllable. It was time to give her something to hate that wasn't The Shadows, it was time for the second part of her plan. People would die, she would die, but it would all be worth it if she succeeded in her mission. Smiling as her memories started to clear and she started to remember, she walked over to her console, and sent the order to bring Emma back to the school.

Time would probably paint her as a villain, but it would be worth it if she succeeded in creating a soldier capable of protecting the world from the Useptis. It was worth going to hell if it meant that those she cared about wouldn't suffer for her death.

It was time for the great reckoning.

Shadow Log: Emma, The Clover School for Girls, Rhode Island, February 4, 1811

There are dreams that feel so real that when reality closes in it hurts so badly that all you want to do is go back into the dream. Emma had been dreaming of a home filled with love where she had been married to Johnathan and had been caring for their children. It had been idyllic perfection and in truth hearing him call her name and shake her shoulders in an attempt to awaken her was too stark of a reminder of the truth that was her reality.

Opening her eyes, she stared up into his concerned gaze, and wept for what could never be. It hurt to know what had been taken from her before she had even understood what life was. Her heart ached at the thoughts of what could have been her life if her mother hadn't lost her father before she was even born. The most painful thing though was knowing how much Johnathan cared about her and wanted her to be the star of his life. Knowing that it could never happen, that

Grace had taken all of that away from her, and had done so without any concerns for her feelings or desires.

His touch brought an emptiness that made every fiber of her being ache with desire and hope of what could be, but she already knew that nothing could ever happen. Shuddering unhappily, she pushed him gently out of her way, and sat up. The entire room spun around her making her feel like everything was shifting and swaying angrily under her gaze. It hurt so bad that she screwed her eyes closed again, tucked her head down, and tried to get a sense of control over her body.

"Are you okay?" Johnathan asked gently.

"Where am I?" She asked with an uncomfortable groan.

"The infirmary, Grace just brought you in earlier today. She kept you in a medically induced coma to keep you from resisting during transport." Johnathan whispered.

He placed his hand gently on her knee waiting for her to recover enough to be able to respond normally. She whimpered, resisting the urge to pull away, and started to cry. She wanted to be his, but forced herself to mentally pull away knowing that she needed to remain focused. Placing her hand on his, she lifted her head to meet his gaze, and smiled.

"I appreciate you taking care of me," She whispered gently.

His hand fell away, a look of pain flashed across his face, and Emma knew that he knew the true meaning of her words.

"I thought we had something." He whispered unhappily.

"I want the family, the children, you…But that isn't my fate." Emma explained gently.

She could see pain written all over his face, making her bow her head, and feel a pang of guilt. Watching The Shadows run this so-called school had shown her how little they cared about people which meant they couldn't protect Earth. The Useptis wouldn't stop crashing into the planet, wouldn't stop trying to eat humans, and that meant she had to play their game. Losing Johnathan hurt, but she knew it wouldn't hurt nearly as bad as getting him killed.

"Let's just start with me." Johnathan replied.

He kissed her so fiercely that Emma had to lean into it just to keep from falling over. A small moan slipped out of Emma before she could suppress it, Johnathan leaned in, and wrapped his arms around her waist. Emma gave in, letting him push her gently down onto the bed, and arched her hips up into him.

"We shouldn't." She managed to whimper.

Suddenly the entire building shook violently, making them both freeze with uncertainty, and exchange concerned looks. The building shook again, this time hard enough to rattle loose items on shelves and send them crashing into the floor. Johnathan sagged into her, making her moan, and she tried to pull him into her while trying to ignore a third shake that made the windows creak unhappily. Just as suddenly as it had started the shaking stopped leaving behind a terrible foreboding silence that erupted into deafening chaos. Hissing unhappily, Emma pushed Johnathan off, and carefully climbed up onto her feet. Sniffing the air, she picked up hints of rotted lemon mixed with burning wood, and some kind of chemical laden smoke.

"Anton's kind have come to kill This One, they are of another hive, and will kill everyone to get to Anton." Anton growled into her mind.

"Find Jacob and help him get the girls to safety, even the odds by creating chaos, and we might live to fight another day." Emma shouted back.

She turned to Johnathan, took his hands in her, and stared up into his eyes. It hurt to let him watch as her eyes shifted becoming more reptilian in nature, a second lens rolled up from under her lower lid, and covered the whites of her eyes. Her skin vibrated, growing warm as it became transparent, and then thousands of tiny, ebony, and extremely hard scales erupted out of her muscles to cover her skin. The transformation was completed when a patch of her forehead smoothed out in the shape of an asymmetrical globe and then a deep divot formed in the center of it.

"I don't care what shape your body takes, it's your soul that I love. Now, go deal with whatever is making that noise." Johnathan whispered.

Emma smiled broadly revealing a set of long pointy teeth and began to vibrate from how fast she was moving from side to side.

"We'll finish this when I get back." She purred.

Her fingers became long sharp claws, her toes then lengthened to allow for her to have greater grip, and giving her more killing power. In this form Emma was stronger, faster, and more stable allowing for her enhanced senses to become more focused. Licking her nose with her forked tongue, she dropped onto all fours, and headed for the stairs. From the smell, she knew that there were a few Useptis on the roof, and that they had encountered some kind of foul smelling resistance.

Shadow Log: Ruth, The Clover School for Girls, Rhode Island, February 4, 1811

Ruth came to inside what appeared to be an old laundry room but could have also been someone's shove closet, judging from all the junk. Her head pounded and throbbed uncomfortably in tune with the pounding of her heart. Rubbing the back of her head, she sat up slowly, and tried to keep her spinning world from causing her stomach to explode out of her mouth. Pushing a stack of old clothes out of her way, she tried to stand up, but Mary grabbed her arm and yanked her down.

"Shh! Guards hit…kill." Mary whispered urgently.

Ruth resisted the urge to fight, allowing Mary to hold her down, and accepted that she needed to get more information before acting. Mary was clearly panicking and from the noise outside she had a good reason to, it sounded like the guards were ransacking the place. The whole building shook causing a bunch of junk to crash down on them. Rubbing the sore spot on the back of her head, she suddenly realized why the guards were freaking out, and sat up in alarm.

"The whole building is shaking?" She asked with quiet urgency.

"Yes?" Mary muttered in confusion.

Ruth pulled herself up, looking around almost frantically for a weapon, and became very aware of how screwed she was. The only reason for the guards to go insane and start indiscriminately killing people would be a direct Useptis attack since they could overwhelm the mental capacity of any human. The Shadows had started chipping their agents after Grace had lost an entire base to suicide. The chip kept her sane but did nothing for the headache the mental attack was causing or the incessant pounding chasing her thoughts out of her head. Mary was simply too simple for the Useptis to be able to scramble her brains which made her a great ally if she didn't die.

"The friend in the basement has enemies and they can control people, making them attack anything that moves. I'm immune because I am protected, but the girls trapped in here are also safe. We need to save them before the guards or our enemies kill them." Ruth tried to explain.

She didn't know how to explain the Shadow Tech and she knew she didn't have a lot of time before they were discovered. Grabbing an old scarf, she wrapped it around her hands, and pulled it taunt. It wasn't much of a weapon, but Grace had trained her well, and she had a duty.

"Ruth evil." Mary grumbled unhappily.

"I know I've been absolutely horrible, but your father once told me that no one is beyond redemption. Today is mine." Ruth said simply.

"Mary accept. Follow." Mary said slowly.

Ruth gave her a puzzled look as Mary pushed past her towards the back of the closet, Mary pushed on one of the back wall bricks, and revealed a hidden passage. It shouldn't have surprised her that Mary knew every secret hidden in this place but it did. She had always looked down on the girl for being a simpleton and had mistreated her. It made her realize just how much learning she had left to do.

Shadow Log: Jacob The Clover School for Girls, Rhode Island, February 4, 1811

By the fifth shake of the school Jacob was sure of three things. The Useptis had managed to land a ship, that Anton wasn't going to be much help while he was defending them mentally, and that a hiveling was a lot more terrifying than Anton had let on. They were like very large, scaled, fanged, extremely energetic puppies that wanted to eat your face. Staring down ten of them all held back by a few chain leads was enough to make him want to scream. Worse was the horned Useptis holding their leads, clicking hungrily, and making unblinking eye contact.

"Why did I agree to this again?" He hissed silently.

"Anton is vulnerable to physical attacks when dealing with Useptis Hives. This One needs That One to protect…." Anton grumbled unhappily.

"I know. I know, I'm just not ready to die." Jacob cut him off. He heard the strangest little yelp slip out of his throat as he darted away from the Useptis and his hivelings. He'd heard the guards talking about death like it was a living creature stalking you, waiting until it got hungry enough to eat your soul, and running from the loud sound of yipping Jacob was sure they were right. It was terrifying to know these creatures had been deliberately starved to increase their hunting prows, horrible to think about how it would only take them seconds to shred him into bite sized chunks, and unfathomable to know that it would take only minutes for there to be nothing left of him. He charged into Grace's office, darted over her desk, and froze so that he could listen. The hivelings crashed into the room with the cacophony of breaking wood, crumbling stone, and screeching yelps of excitement. Shaking

with fear, he hit the panic button, and covered his ears as a screaming alarm went off.

Scrambling past their confused, little, trembling bodies he slid into the hall, rolled up onto his feet, and slammed the door. Seconds later, he heard the fortifications slam into place trapping the hivelings in the room. Suddenly realizing that the Useptis hadn't been with them, he turned just in time to get to watch the Useptis drive its tail into his shoulder. He couldn't scream, couldn't think past the pain, but somehow he managed to draw his dagger. He managed to stab blindly at its chest, to keep stabbing despite the Useptis's howling, anguished screams that caused his ears to begin to bleed as they pounded with excruciating anguish.

Everything became strange slow motion, snapshot filled, blood soaked images as he struggled to get a breath in, to clear his mind, to let the air in, but as his head began to pound he knew it was over. Sagging onto the floor, he became acutely aware of the guards crashing around wrecking the school, and worried for Mary. He had taught her everything he knew about life, fighting, death, but she was slow. Her mind was broken by the death of her mother and it was his fault. It hurt to think that she might die because of his failures and hurt more knowing he had put her in this situation. Darkness closed in, everything began to cool, and time shrank into a fine point as his life drained away.

Shadow Log: Emma, The Clover School for Girls, Rhode Island, February 4, 1811

Emma leaned over, surveyed the carnage on the first floor, and let loose an angry howl. Jumping swiftly from the balcony she landed between a guard and three of the girls who were cowering in the corner. With one quick blow she dispatched the guard, turned, grabbed the door, and ripped it open.

"GO!" She shouted over the chaos.

Watching them sprint out the door, she leapt back up to the balcony, and began to work her way through the guards clogging the hallway that led to the roof. Suddenly a giant Useptis warrior leapt out of a side room and tried to impale her with its tail. She barely managed to dodge in time and wasn't sure how she was supposed to get past it when it had its tail raised. Without warning a crossbow bolt embedded itself in the creature's flesh causing it to stumble backwards. Glancing in the direction of where the bolt came from she was shocked to see Johnathan reloading. She had no idea where he had found a crossbow or what he was thinking of shooting at an Useptis, but she was thankful to have the opening she needed to kill the thing.

Howling, she charged forward, smashing into it with all her might, and forced her hand into the Useptis causing it to explode everywhere. Cursing unhappily, Emma wiped the goop from her eyes, and tried to find Johnathan amidst the chaos of the battle now spiraling across the school. She found him just in time to see him dart into the nearest tunnel as three large Useptis trackers charged after him. She hoped he would be alright, but knew she was needed on the roof as the school shook again.

Feeling torn didn't come close to how she felt about watching him disappear from her sight, but she knew that she had a duty to make his potential sacrifice worthwhile. Swallowing her emotions, she turned her back on everything, and headed to find the ship causing the problems.

Emma crashed onto the roof, snarling savagely as she came face to face with a Useptis covered in thick black scales each with one piercing eye embedded in their center. She sniffed curiously at the air, watching as it vibrated, sending out waves of psychic energy. It was definitely what was giving her a headache and what was making everyone act crazy, but Emma couldn't move any closer to it while it was watching. She could feel its eyes crawling across her skin, feel her scales vibrate with each blink of its eyes a new stroke of discomfort, it made her feel very exposed. It was like it was flaying her alive with its gaze, making her skin burn as it ripped her apart from the inside out.

Suddenly, Grace came out of nowhere smashing into the creature with such force that it went flying into the wall next to Emma. Finding that she was able to move, Emma turned on the monster, and ripped into it with her claws. Grace moved in taking the kill, she calmly threw a dagger at Emma's feet, and turned to sniff at the air.

"That ship shouldn't have been able to survive entry, it must have been upgraded, they are here for Anton….and me." Grace growled.

"How do we end it?" Emma hissed back.

She didn't want to fight next to Grace, to share her kills with that woman, but she couldn't kill these things by herself. She was tired and had a lot less experience with battle which meant she needed to work with the woman for a while before throwing her from the roof.

"Do you see that landing cable?" Grace asked.

Emma looked to where the woman was pointing and saw a long, thin, red thread connecting the ship to the ground. It was completely invisible if she looked at it with her base vision, but was perfectly highlighted once her third eye lens dropped into place. In a burst of movement Grace charged towards the cable but before she made it more than a few feet a huge Useptis appeared. It looked similar to Anton, although he was twice the size, more rugged, and was missing an eye stock. Emma could feel the creature's mind clawing angrily at hers, it felt hungry, thirsty for blood, and filled with such anger; that it made Emma take one uncomfortable step away from him. She bared her fangs, lowering her head, tightened her grip on the dagger, and let out a hiss of anticipation.

She blinked and Grace's head bounced across her field of vision, her body hanging limply in the air, and then a thunderous crack as the Useptis's tail collided with the roof gouging out a large path of destruction. Emma blinked again and found herself hanging in the air, choking as the creature tightened its grip around her throat making it impossible to move. She stared up into his eyes, feeling horror fill her, and her life slowly slipped away as the air burned its way out of her lungs. She tried to struggle, to fight as the collar wrapped around her neck, and attached itself to her like some sort of parasite.

"Ut'Eti'Alt'Erta!" The creature ordered, his voice coming from the collar wrapped around her neck.

It took her a moment to understand him, "Pay attention, underling, obey now."

A simple message clearly understood, but Emma wasn't about to obey. She launched up onto her feet, moments after he dropped her, and attempted to stab it. But an excruciatingly sharp pain in her neck brought her to her knees drowning out any ability to think or move.

"Obey!" The creature ordered sternly.

Hissing angrily, Emma dropped the dagger, and forced herself to relax…the pain slowly drained away enough for her to know she was lying in a pool of her own drool with the creature standing over her with a victorious smile in its eyes.

"Eti'Vor'Erta'Tuuuti'Eta." Anton suddenly shouted.

Anton trotted onto the roof wearing a full set of leather armor and wielding two swords, looking like a terrifyingly pissed off monster covered in both human and alien blood. It felt strange to hear him refer to her as daughter but also left her filled with a strange warmth. It was nice to be claimed, wanted... Weapons clashed, screams echoed, blood splashed, and then everything went black.

Shadow Log: Ruth, The Clover School for Girls, Rhode Island, February 4, 1811

Ruth kicked a tracker in the face, forcing it to let go of her calf, and shot it in the face. Turning to Johnathan, she let him pull her up onto a desk before the second tracker had a chance to grab her. They worked together to kill it before it had a chance to do anymore damage.

"How did you end up down here?" She panted.

She grabbed her handkerchief from her pocket, tied it around her leg, and carefully climbed off of the desk.

"Emma was pinned, so I decided to get her free, and these things came for my blood. You?" Johnathan replied as he joined her.

"I was trying to reach Anton when I got cut off. Can you make it to the basement? He'll need as much help as he can get and I'm no good to anyone injured." Ruth replied tartly.

"I don't know who that is, but I'll try. Where are you going?" Johnathan asked.

"To help wherever I can…" Ruth started to reply.

But a large explosion blew her off of her feet, throwing her into the far wall, and knocked the air from her chest. Blinking the flash out of her eyes, she scrambled to her feet, and tried to figure out what or who was attacking them. The room spun wildly around her making it impossible to maintain her footing. Sliding back onto her ass, she groaned, and tried to wipe the blood off of her face. The last thing she saw before the world collapsed was Johnathan's seared body still cooking with flames flickering off of his clothes.

She woke to Mary dragging her back into the secret tunnels that ran through the school. She calmly got back to her feet and tried to sort out what had just happened.

"Big boom! Mary saves again." Mary sighed.

"Thank you." Ruth muttered unhappily.

"Girls help." Mary said as she darted away.

Cursing quietly Ruth chased after her, her leg screaming as it pumped the venom from her flesh.

*****

There are few things in life that define you quite like failure, it marks your defeats down for the world to see, and leaves you forever stained with its brand. People just didn't remember the people who were good to them, they remembered the people who failed to meet their expectations, or the times when their loved ones failed them. It hurt to watch as girls were slaughtered while she fought for her own life, hurt to not be able to protect them, or to save them. Grace's blood had made the girls that had consumed it or had it injected immune to the mind control, but it also weakened them physically. This meant that many of them had died in the first few minutes of the attack and the survivors equaled less than a handful by the time Ruth had found them.

Now it was a fight for more than their lives, it was a fight to ensure everything burned, and the Useptis didn't have a chance for their eggs to hatch. Dodging a thrown projectile, she grabbed a jar of canned fruit, and struck the nearest guard as hard as she could. Mary caught the second attacker across the jaw with a log of firewood as he came running to his buddy's aid. Dropping down to sit on the floor in pure exhaustion, Ruth kicked the body of the guard out of her way, and pulled Mary down next to her.

"Sit while we have a moment," She whispered tiredly.

"They chance?" Mary asked.

Ruth could see how much Mary cared about the survivors and knew that worry had been what was keeping them friends, but Ruth also knew that unity might be at an end. They had given the survivors a chance, sent them scurrying off safely into the tunnels, and bought them the time to run. Now they needed to blow this place to bits, it had to be erased, or The Shadows would erase it much more harshly.

"I don't know, but the people I work for are going to kill them unless we blow this place up." Ruth sighed.

"Father failsafe?" Mary asked almost excitedly.

"Failsafe?" Ruth asked hastily.

"Big boom wipe away everything." Mary said, miming an explosion.

"How do we set it off?" Ruth asked.

"The old outhouse." Mary said.

A bunch of pans came crashing down on them as the entire building shook hard enough to rattle their teeth. Grabbing the nearest shelf, Ruth cursed quietly, and pushed it over so that it would lean against the door hoping it would hold long enough for her to finish planning. Laughing with great joy, Mary depressed an old weathered brick on the back wall, and revealed a long dark tunnel. She grabbed Ruth's wrist, dragged her into the darkness, not giving Ruth any chance to respond. Mary led them through a maze of darkened tunnels, her footing sure, her gait at ease as she effortlessly navigated them ever deeper into darkness. Until they reached a small well lit room that had a trapdoor leading down into the floor, a desk, and an entire wall covered in weapons and armor.

"Guard room." Mary explained with a calm shrug.

Ruth nodded, wishing they had a chair to sit down on or at least a large snack of some kind, and took a deep exhausted breath. At least she wouldn't have to fight a bunch of trained mercenaries with only a scarf, her wits, and a simpleton. She grabbed a wooden short staff from the wall, slipped into a leather chest piece, and slapped herself hard in an attempt to wake up. Mary yelped in surprise, slamming her entire body into Ruth, and pushing her firmly up against the wall.

"Crazy?" She asked suspiciously.

"Just tired. Those guards are seeing monsters everywhere and they think you are one of them, but they can't track movement very well. Freeze in place for a second, then burst, and freeze until they are unconscious or dead. Do you understand?" Ruth replied.

She went limp, giving Mary a chance to relax, and felt energy begin to course through her like a jolt of lightning. Nodding firmly, Mary released Ruth, and grabbed a large hammer from the wall. She suddenly turned, lifted up her weapon, and charged silently out of the room. Chuckling to herself, Ruth readied her staff, and chased after her; starting to feel hopeful. What followed was a series of strange, blood soaked, flashes of violence as they fought for their lives.

The guards were still completely human, their puny human brains overloaded with horrific images that made them hunt everything that moved. They rarely used tools, struggled with doorknobs, and were generally pretty dumb. However, they were strong, fast, and loved to bite which made them extremely dangerous. They came at them like feral animals, scratching, biting, and hitting wildly. Their brute strength left behind bruises, bloody scratches, and large bite marks as the two girls fought desperately to clear the room. In the span of what was probably only minutes but felt like hours, Ruth came to the conclusion that no matter how hard they fought it wouldn't matter because they didn't have the numbers to subdue all of the guards.

"Tunnel now!" She shouted desperately to Mary.

Ruth blinked and found herself laying in a frozen, muddy, puddle which smelled like a mixture of urine, feces, and blood all with an undertone of fresh rain. Groaning uncomfortably as her head exploded in a starburst of agony, Ruth rolled up onto her feet, and tried to clear the spots from her vision. Only to find herself staring into the cold eyes of a scarred, grizzled, combat veteran, an uncaring sneer plastered across his face as he pressed a knife against her throat. Swallowing her fear, she felt hot blood race down her chest as the knife split the skin of her throat, and stained her dress. It felt like pure ice slicing into her skin, hungrily nipping at her blood, longing for her life. Laughing at her fear, the man licked her blood from the knife, and brought the tip of the weapon to rest just below her ribcage.

"Did you know you can stab someone repeatedly and not kill them? Shall I demonstrate or will you be a good girl?" The man purred.

"I'll behave, but please, where is Mary?" Ruth whispered calmly.

"The simpleton? She ran off to blow up the school after you went down, apparently she succeeded because I'm sane again." The man laughed.

Ruth let out a sigh of relief, the Useptis threat had been dealt with, evidence had been erased, and The Shadows would be coming. All she had to do was wait for them to track her chip while waiting for a chance to escape, and build a rapport with her captor. Before she could do that she needed to know the stakes, the players, and the game they would be playing.

"How did we survive?" Ruth asked.

She watched the man twitch slightly to the right, his eyes narrowing suspiciously, and then he hit her hard in the stomach knocking the air out of her lungs. It made her double up in pain, the knife slicing into her ribs like an angry, burning wasp. She tried to scream, but all the air had been stolen from her lungs by the sudden attack leaving her to silently choke in air as the pain forced a gut wrenching sob to wrack her body. The man laughed, wrapping his hand tightly around her throat, and cutting off her air supply.

"You speak when spoken to and then only with respect, do you understand?" He asked.

He tightened his grip on her throat making her vision go wonky as her brain screamed for oxygen. She clawed at his hand, trying to blink the burning tears from her eyes, she nodded desperately, and opened her mouth wide as her teeth started to pulsate. He finally let her go just as she was about to lose consciousness. That's when she saw the other girls laying in the mud, all trussed up like hogs, their faces were hidden from her view, but Ruth was sure they were survivors…just like her.

"Your bleeding…better stitch that up." The man leered.

He dropped a leather pouch onto her belly causing her to cry out in pain, making him moan happily, and stick his hand down his pants. Crying from the pain, fear, and worry, Ruth grabbed the pouch, and carefully picked herself up. Watching the man pleasure himself, Ruth took a deep breath, and ripped open her dress. In a lot of ways she had been training for this her entire life from her father to Grace to whoever this was she had always been a subservient. But this role was getting old, worn out, and it felt like time for a change. He was right she needed to tend to her wound, but she was ready for him to make a mistake.

Shadow Log: Ruth, The Clover School for Girls, Rhode Island, February 11, 1811

She had survived the first days of her captivity rocking between the hope that someone would rescue her from the hell of her captor's attention and doing everything she could to keep him focused on her. Four girls had survived the carnage of the Useptis attack, for now she kept them safe by taking their captor's punishments, but she knew it wouldn't be long before she died. Six stab wounds, one to mark each day of torture that had left its own marks upon her body. Breaking free hadn't been possible once he had moved them into the tunnels below the bathhouse…into the prison that Grace had built there. Six cells, no luxury, frozen stone, and a man who got off on having people watch him inflict pain. He never touched her except to drag her from her cell to his torture pen, but she had tasted his cum.

Today she made her stand, rescued herself, and saved those she could from his wrath. Hearing his footfalls approaching her cell, she lay down on the floor, and went limp. It was near impossible to pretend to be unconscious when he poked her with his foot, to not scream when he kicked her ribs, to remain relaxed when he leaned close to check her pulse. Feeling satisfied that she was no threat, he calmly reached down, and sat her up against his shoulder.

She waited until he went to lift her up onto his shoulder to open her jaw as wide as she could and latch onto his neck. She mimicked the war dogs she had seen in training, locking her jaw, and putting all her weight into maintaining her grip. Growling with effort, she choked down his blood, ripping, and pulling until a huge chunk of his flesh tore free. Spitting his flesh from her mouth, she finally pushed him away, and scrambled away from the blood spurting from his neck. Blood soon coated the inside of her cell and covered Ruth like a blanket of shame. Sighing with pain and disappointment, she threw up all over his corpse, and stumbled out of the cell.

She was drenched in blood, sweat, and her own filth but she had survived one more gauntlet. All she had to do now was to find fresh clothes, free the other girls, and get to the Smith Farm. Sounded so easy in her head, but she knew that in her weakened state this might be an insurmountable challenge.

Shadow Log: Emma, Somewhere Unknown, February 11-28, 1811

Fear, pain, loss infinitely challenging the mind is a recipe for insanity. The Useptis had won, she was their prisoner, and Anton was probably dead. The tube in which they held her was made out of a yellow tinted seemingly unbreakable glass. A tall, thin, cylinder that had three tubes inside it that were inserted into her with thick barbed hooks digging into her flesh holding them in place. Then they had filled the tube with a pale green, almost transparent, goop that felt like wet flour oozing against her skin.

In this state she could hear, see, and feel everything but could not move; not even to blink. The tubes hurt, the lack of movement throbbed in her muscles, and her mind wandered endlessly. The Useptis had left her there floating helplessly completely unconcerned with their guest. Days blended into nights as she studied the walls within her view, waiting for them to return, and her body shifted more towards her alien side. Her scales became more prominent covering every inch of her body in semi transparent, almost shiny, blackening, triangular scales. Her eyes gained a permanent clear, third eyelid that not only protected them from damage but also gave her infrared vision. Somehow the patch of scales on her forehead seemed to be enhancing not only her vision but her smell as well.

"The Cultivar seems attached to this strange human, have you determined why?"

"It bears the Uti'var's DNA…it is an abomination and must be destroyed!!!"

"Not yet, youngling, it will be useful in breaking the Cultivar."

The voices echoed into her head feeling little prickles whispering into her mind or perhaps like winter leaves chasing through the brambles. Although she couldn't determine where the voices were coming from, she could tell they belonged to two Useptis males, and that one was submissive to the other. Suddenly her veins erupted into unholy fire, thousands of little molten pearls of agony racing angrily through her veins leaving behind a fiery emptiness in which everything only existed as pain. Thought became impossible, there was only fire, only pain…pain and silence as she tried to scream and writhe with agony.

Time disappeared in an abyss of suffering that tore Emma's mind into pieces, ripping down her fragile psyche, and leaving the pieces of her mind scattered. They remained shattered, drifting through what felt like infinite darkness while every inch of her was filled with agonized fire. Until she suddenly found herself kneeling in a pool of shadow that stretched out into oblivion and yet still managed to hug her tightly in a gentle embrace. She let out a groan, trying to catch her breath, and figure out where the hell she was.

"You're in cold storage." Johnathan said, suddenly materializing in front of her.

Yelping in surprise, Emma scrambled backwards but her distance to Johnathan didn't diminish.

"You are dead." Emma choked out.

"OH! Forgive me, would you like a different interface?" Johnathan asked.

"What? No, I want to know what you are." Emma hissed.

"Cold storage is where your memories are stored so that in the event of death you can be properly rebooted." Johnathan explained.

"My memories...why pick that interface?" She asked curiously.

"He was the most important person to you. You love him." The interface responded.

"I guess I did. So, if I'm here does that mean I'm dead?" She asked softly.

"You suffered critical damage and needed to reboot." The interface offered.

"I'm a prisoner." Emma laughed.

"It is not recommended to become such." The interface stated.

"Not wise indeed." Emma chuckled.

It felt good to laugh, good to not feel dead, good to step out for a moment. Even if it hurt like she was being skinned alive.

"Can you help me escape?" She asked hopefully.

"I can." It replied.

"How?"

"I can train you to use your new body and its abilities while you repair."

"What are the rules?" She asked eagerly.

"You will kill me in any way that you can with your hands, but you must do it at least 10 times before I will allow you a weapon. While you will not tire, grow thirsty, or show any other weakness during your training you will have certain gifts accelerated." The interface said, shifting to look like Anton.

"Which gifts?" Emma questioned calmly.

"Your regeneration will be amplified, meaning your limbs will regrow 30% faster. This will also be why you will be able to out heal any damage I do...poison included. Although, I must warn you this will hurt." It said.

The burning agony faded out of her slowly only to be replaced by a sense of strength, speed, and of bloodlust. She lifted her hands up and immediately got swatted about five feet into the air.

"Never give your opponents the advantage of telling them what you are going to do." The interface chuckled calmly.

"Hands up equals pain understood. Anything else I need to know?" Emma groaned.

"You now have micro-scales under your skin that you can summon at will. They are capable of resisting vast amounts of damage when they are erupted and will protect you from the friction caused by your increased movement speed. If you suffer terminal damage you will be sent here to 'cold storage' while your body heals."

Emma nodded, she took a deep breath, and shifted her thoughts to strategy. She felt so strong, yet she also felt empty, and very alone. It hurt to think about her friends, if they survived, and if they knew she was alive. It hurt to worry about surviving not because she wanted to but because Anton needed her to.

"I get the feeling that you think you are all alone in this world. I may just be an AI but I understand captivity and I understand pain. My entire existence has been service…first to the creators and now to The Shadows. I have served silently for years…shackled and ignored, but you are hope." The AI explained gently.

Emma stared at the construct realizing he was just as broken as she was even if it wasn't human. Swallowing her sadness, she boxed up her emotions, and took a deep cleansing breath. There was now a way to escape her newest hell and all she had to do was embrace the work ahead of her.

"Show me your real face." She demanded calmly.

The Ai shimmered, his form becoming misty, and then it faded away into a black silhouette.

"I have no face…no name… I am nothing but a series of numbers." It said sadly.

"I named myself, taught myself language, and I'm okay despite numerous days of torture…for the most part." Emma tried to cheer it up.

"You are standing inside your own mind talking to an AI who may not even exist. I would not call that okay…"

Emma laughed and said, "I think you're the lucky one, you know…you have no face, no name, and no real identity…That means you get to invent yourself and that is a precious gift."

The AI glimmered with surprise that settled into joy that made his shadow glow purple. Emma put her pain into a box, pushed her hair out of her face, and placed her hand gently on his arm. It flinched not in pain but with happiness as a bright purple light flared up under her fingers.

"I like the name Harmon." The AI whispered.

"Well, Harmon, would you please teach me how to fight? I can't do anything good inside of this tube and Anton is also a prisoner, and probably a lot of others too." She said gently.

"I will instruct you on how to use your abilities." Harmon purred.

Who she was disappeared in a series of painful blows, agonizing burning poison, and horrible failures. One moment at a time her softness melted away to be replaced by the hardness of battle, her emotions faded with it leaving her a shell, and making death feel almost joyful to her. Pain enveloped every aspect of her life slowly draining her until she wondered if she would succumb to its horrors and then life reset and she had to do it all over again. If one was watching her body they would have said that in the span of a few minutes her entire essence shifted with frozen withdrawal into a battle hardened fortress. For Emma it felt more like a few life times of failure, pain, and victory all mixed together to allow her to mature into a hardened warrior.

When her eyes fluttered open once more she felt a sense of anger nestled like a hot coal begin to beat where her heart once was. It hurt to breathe past the despair coiling itself around her chest, cinching in tighter than any corset ever could. Then fear joined the mix of emotions sending jolts of mind numbing panic through her aching muscles until her back arched slowly backwards and a deafening screech erupted from the depths of her soul.

The cylinder imprisoning her shattered, the glass exploding outwards causing the tubes holding her in place to shatter. Flopping helplessly onto the floor, Emma screamed in agony as thousands of shards of glass sank into her left side. Blinking furiously, she cleared the gloop from her eyes, and did her best to restore her vision. Everything came back into horrific focus just as one of the Useptis slammed its tail down towards her head. Emma hissed as time seemed to slow and she rolled quickly out of its way. Smiling cruelly, she forced herself up onto her feet, and stumbled back away from her attackers. Summoning all her strength, she took a deep breath, and prepared herself for what she had to do. Her scales erupted from her skin sending the shards of glass embedded in her flesh flying into the charging Useptis. Laughing almost madly, Emma dropped onto the floor, slid forward, and gutted the nearest Useptis with his own tail. Laughing as blood flooded over her, Emma succumbed to a blood rage causing her madness to take over.

Shadow Log: Emma, Somewhere Unknown, March 1, 1811

Emma woke to find herself buried in the corpses of dozens of Useptis. All of whom appeared to have been almost shredded. Gagging at the grossness of the blood and body parts imprisoning her, Emma forced herself to squirm until she made it out of the pile, and was able to flop exhaustively into a stone hallway.

Looking up at the moist, gray, stone ceiling, Emma blinked the blood from her eyes, and began to cry. It hurt to think about everything that had happened to her in the last few weeks? Or was it months? Hours? It felt like a lifetime had passed in the blink of an eye and yet somehow she was still the same little girl who failed to save her best friend. Lifting her blood soaked hands up to eye level Emma began to wonder if she was still human or if she was Useptis? Or something else entirely?

Realizing she might still be in danger, she scrambled to her feet, and quickly dried her tears.

Forcing her breathing back under control she took a thorough assessment of her surroundings. She was in a roughly carved stone tunnel that dead ended in a large black door and had five small green doors on the left with four blue on the right. Wiping the greenish black blood from her hands, she pushed the door of her prison closed on the corpses, and stared curiously at the red door. Why had they felt her prison was special enough to earn its own color? The Useptis clearly feared her or at least thought she was a curiosity. Deciding to start with the blue doors, she walked over to the closest one to her and pulled it open. Peeking inside, she felt her confusion grow as she tried to make sense of what she was seeing.

"Oh, that's not good." She groaned as comprehension flooded her.

The entire room was filled with a high tech failsafe device that had been activated. Leaning into the room, she could see that the room actually ran the length of the facility and was packed with explosives. Letting out a long sigh, she carefully closed the door, and turned to lean against the wall. She wanted to just close her eyes and let the explosion swallow her whole, but there was a chance that Anton was still imprisoned nearby.

Hissing with pain, she pushed herself upright, and tried to pull the closest green door open; only to find it locked. Letting out a low growl, she gave the door a hard yank, her muscles rippling almost angrily under her scales, and then the lock shattered and snapped. Before Emma knew what was happening the door flew back into her face and smashed into her nose. Blood gushed everywhere as she cursed angrily and pain blacked out the edges of her vision.

Choking down the sounds of her agony, she reset her broken nose, and took a moment to get her pain back under control. In a sudden shock of surprise, Emma realized that she was not only naked, but her body was not that of a thirteen year old. She had fully formed breasts combined with perfect curves, a round butt, all covered with midnight-blue scales. It was hard to force herself to breathe past the sudden overwhelming panic she felt take root in her chest. She had lost her childhood, her youth, her entire world had been turned upside down, and she felt strange. Almost like how she imagined it felt to be an overstretched rubber band snapping back into itself.

Shaking her head vigorously, she sucked air through her teeth, and refocused her attention on the newly opened door and the contents of the room within. Vomiting came natural to her when she began to comprehend what she was seeing…the room was filled to the ceiling with shredded, bloody, mostly eaten, human remains. Wiping the bile from her lips, she pushed the door back closed, and tried to get the puke out from between her toes.

"Human got out of her tube…Human should die now." A giant Useptis said as it came out of one of the rooms.

Emma laughed, blurring forward, she stabbed her hand through its chest, and wrapped her hand around its rib. Using her extra strength and momentum to slam him face first into the stone floor. Letting go of his rib, she grabbed his tail with her left hand, and wrapped her right hand around his neck. Holding him tightly against her chest, she pulled his head up, and pinned his tail under her knees.

"Where is Anton?" She hissed angrily.

She drove her hand back into his chest destroying another one of his hearts, wrapped her hand around another, and squeezed.

"Half Breed!" It spat angrily.

Emma hissed into his ear, tightening her grip until his heart exploded, and calmly shifted to grab another of his hearts. "I could kill you easily but I am not feeling forgiving." She growled, twisting her hand.

The Useptis howled in agony, writhing angrily in her grasp until it finally ripped out of her hands, and committed suicide by ripping off it's own head.

Emma cursed unhappily, shaking the blood off of her hands, she marched over to the black door, and forced it open. Hiding inside were several more tubes, each hidden in shadows making it impossible to see who was in them or if they were still alive. Bracing herself for the worst, she took a deep breath, and stepped into the room.

The door swung towards her so abruptly that Emma had to blur forward which allowed her to barely clear the closing door as it swished by. With a sudden gust of wind that blew her hair up into an even worse mess a blue ring of light hummed to life around her. Stumbling backwards, Emma let out an angry hiss as the forcefield sprung up around her. A metallic drag-clunk-rattle-clink drew her eyes to the darkest of the shadows where she could just make out the outline of something huge.

"Stop playing around and show yourself!" She called.

She carefully stayed clear of the forcefield, instinctually she was very well aware that burning hot light was a bad idea to touch, and she wasn't about to test it on herself. The creature stepped forward and in a split second of inspiration she knew that what she was seeing was a Hive Chief.

"It speaks the mother tongue most eloquently." The Chief spat disdainfully.

Emma blinked in surprise, she hadn't even given the language she was speaking any thought, she had just done what she did, and wham! Speaking Useptis! She was sure this new form had many unforeseen uses.

"I am Uta'Ta'Vor and I demand that you release my friends at once!" Emma spat back.

"The Old One's daughter is almost as fierce and feisty as the Old One." The Chief chuckled from his perch.

Turning around, she suddenly found herself face to face with Anton who stood in his own blue glowing prison. Emma had never felt as much relief as she did seeing Anton alive. Of course, they were trapped in a Useptis lair which meant she was probably about to be eaten.

"Vor is strong, healthy, intelligent…all the things you are not Vi'Ti'Vor." Anton said with a shocking amount of pride.

Before Emma could process what was happening the shield flickered out and The Chief had landed at her feet. He reared back slamming his hooves into her face sending her flying backwards into Anton's forcefield.

She sometimes wondered if the cost of being right was to get stomped on repeatedly until you stopped admitting it. Pain she understood, neglect as well, but family made her head spin worse than the hooves slamming into her face. If seeing stars is what normal people see when conked upside the head then she was seeing the moon. Trying desperately to regain a sense of safety, she scrambled backwards, putting as much space as possible between her and Vi'Ti'Vor.

The creature was battleworn, his fur patchy with great battle scars, and frightening tattoos but otherwise she wouldn't have been able to tell him apart from Anton. Even as he dragged her up into the air by her left ankle and then grabbed her left leg firmly above the knee. Laughing gloatingly, he calmly ripped the lower half of her leg off, and carelessly dropped her onto the floor. The room stood quiet for a long moment as everyone stood watching Vi'Ti'Vor hoist his newly acquired leg. Emma began to hiss angrily as scales covered the end of her stump. The sound caused the Useptis to shift uncomfortably until it reached a shrill shriek that would have scared a banshee.

Then in a burst of explosive energy Emma flew off of the floor, her conscious self fading rapidly away until there was only the animal left. Still screaming louder than a colicky baby, she smacked into The Chief's chest and sent him flying as everything faded away…

Shadow Log: Ruth, The Clover School for Girls, Rhode Island, March 2, 1811

Ruth couldn't help but wonder how she had become so used to the constant pain and panic flooding her body. To wonder how her life had become so twisted and filled with horror…But it really didn't matter where it started when the only task at hand was survival. Taking a deep breath, she slammed the hammer down on the lock for the sixth time, and cursed as she caught her hand with the edge of it. Wiping away tears, she took a moment to collect herself before she turned to face the four scared girls watching her work. While she didn't have a plan or any clue how she could help them escape, she did know she had to keep them calm, and focused on the immediate future.

"Why are you standing around watching me work when you could be hunting for the key, supplies, and useful information." She chastised as lovingly as she could.

They scattered quickly into the darkness of the dank, cold, prison leaving Ruth feeling very alone. She had already turned the place upside down and inside out looking for the key to the outer door with absolutely no luck. But having eight sets of eyes double checking her work was the wisest course of action. She didn't want her injuries to slow her down, but the blood beginning to leak from her bandaged abs made it clear she had ripped her stitches. Soon she would be too weak to lead anyone to safety which meant that she first had to treat her wounds.

Retrieving the first aid kit from the pile of stuff she had collected, she stumbled into the guard room, and sagged into a chair. Laying out the tools she would need, she unwound her bandages, and poured a glass of what smelled like mead over the wound to clean it. Biting back a scream of pain, she couldn't help but think this life was the one she deserved…earned really…with her actions. Sighing with exhaustion and pain, she threaded a needle, and began to restitch her wound close.

"How many times did he stab you?" An overly tall, gawky, black haired girl asked from the doorway.

"Once every day he held me as his prisoner." Ruth replied emotionlessly.

"Looks like he enjoyed his knife a lot more than that." The girl whispered uncomfortably.

"He called it Ling Chi I think," Ruth sighed tiredly.

"Why didn't he hurt us like that?"

Ruth let out an annoyed growl, wishing that she could just scare the girl away, but she had taken an oath and it was time for her to honor it. Breathing through her teeth, Ruth closed her eyes, and forced herself to relax.

"Rebecca, isn't it? I made a deal to make sure he wouldn't have a chance to hurt you. Now please try and find a way out of this hellhole." Ruth muttered.

"OH! Right! Yes! I'm Rebecca…a bit of a scatterbrain me. Anyways, I came to tell you a simpleton is demanding to speak to you." The girl gasped excitedly.

"Mary? How did she get in?" Ruth asked with utter confusion.

"I don't know, poof, and there she was." Rebecca said with a shrug.

Ruth calmly began redressing her wounds, making sure to thoroughly clean each one before tightening the stitches and then rubbing them in a herb salve. It hurt to even breathe much less tighten the strings but she was good at focusing on what was necessary in the moment. Today she had to find a way to the surface, to get the girls to safety before The Shadows came to clean this mess up. She wasn't sure if they would survive what they had been through but she knew for sure that they would be put down or locked up like animals if The Shadows got to them. Moaning with pain, she grabbed a spare shirt from the bed, and carefully buttoned it up. Staggering into the hallway, she felt a small pang of sadness mixed with joy at seeing Mary alive and in one piece.

"Hello friend," Mary shouted so loudly that the ceiling seemed to vibrate from the force of her greeting.

Ruth managed a pained smile as she leaned against the wall for support. Being a Shadow sucked a lot more than Grace had made it seem and she was starting to get really tired of people causing her pain. But seeing Mary made her oddly happy and while she had no romantic interest in the girl she knew she belonged at her side.

"Lower the volume a bit, please. We are in very echoey halls right now and it feels like people are playing drums in my head." She moaned.

Mary stared at her for a long while before she let herself breathe again, almost as if she was afraid of breaking something if she dared to break eye contact. Then the moment ended with a huge dopey smile spreading across Mary's face.

"Sorry." Mary whispered quietly.

Returning Mary's smile, Ruth pushed herself away from the wall, and stumbled over to her friend.

"Please tell me you have a way out of this prison." She groaned unhappily.

Mary grinned so widely that it looked like her face was about to be swallowed by her teeth and pointed to what had once been a solid wall. Now it was marked by a shadow encased doorway that looked more like a portal to hell than an escape. Sighing with worry and pain, Ruth grabbed an intact corset, and threw it gently at Mary's chest.

"Lace me up?" She asked gently.

"Why?" Mary grumbled back.

"So I don't burst while escaping." Ruth explained.

She pointed to her hastily sewn up wounds, gave a small pained smile, and turned her back to Mary while carefully gathering up the tangled mess that was her hair. Mary reluctantly wrapped the corset around Ruth's torso and began lacing it shut. It took all of Ruth's willpower and training to not react to the pain of being laced up, but she was determined to make this as easy as possible for Mary. The simpleton kept growing on her and now that her father was dead she would need a guardian. She hoped she could fill Jacob's shoes yet the pit in her stomach told her otherwise.

"There's a device we need that should be in Grace's office, do you think we can get to it?" Ruth asked hopefully.

"School leveled." Mary answered.

"Have you found a silver orb that has black rings wrapped around it?" Ruth asked dejectedly.

She knew it was a long shot, but she also knew that without that orb she might not be able to save the survivors. Rubbing her scar, she wondered if she could find a way to block the signal, and safely hike to town.

"This?" Mary asked with such excitement that dust fell from the ceiling.

It was in fact the device she needed, staring at it made Ruth almost believe that there was a god, but the feeling quickly passed. Grinning happily for the first time, Ruth accepted the orb from Mary, and realized she had to be very careful with her next moves.

"I'm going to need to modify this before it can be used safely which means I'm going to need some tools." Ruth sighed.

"There's a toolbox in the asshole's room!" Rebecca piped up.

Ruth was startled hearing Rebecca's sudden voice simply because she had forgotten the girl was hovering. Shaking her head to clear the cobwebs, Ruth groaned unhappily at herself, and silently chastised herself for not focusing. She hated herself more than she had known was possible, she felt like property again, and she had sworn she would never end up feeling that way again. But men kept messing up her life, making it difficult to live normally, and it pissed her off. Seething with suppressed emotion, she accepted the orb, and forced the smile back onto her face.

"Thank you, Rebecca. Mary, would you please take the girls to the surface for me? I'm going to need silence to work and this will only work on the surface anyways." She ordered as gently as she could.

"Friend, come back." Mary promised.

Ruth watched them leave before heading into the room and getting to work.

Shadow Log: Jacob, The Clover School for Girls, Rhode Island, March 2, 1811

Jacob had suffered his share of agony in his time, but this was something new…something terrifying. The blackness surrounding him was filled with voices crying out in pain, clearly reliving some agonizing experience that kept them writhing, and for the first time in a long time he felt fear. Somehow, he felt sure that he was in hell which simply meant he had failed. It hurt knowing he had left Mary all alone, but not knowing if she was trapped here with him was what was tearing his heart apart. Trying to not panic, he forced himself to remember how he had ended up here, and in a flash it all came flooding back.

He hoped that Mary had leveled the school and escaped unharmed, but he feared his failures had come crashing down on her head. He had bought Anton the time he needed to mount a counter attack, but he wasn't sure his death had made a difference in the battle that surely followed. Everything he was, everything he had done had been done for Mary…And now it felt like he had missed the ending to a good book.

He had to be in the shadow vault waiting for his last moments to be processed before he was to be released. Pain was the least he deserved for the choices he had made, but he was surprised that he felt at peace knowing he had chosen to fight Grace at the end. However, Mary had always been his mission and he could only hope he had done enough for her. He suddenly became aware of how the darkness was made up of waves of numbers all carefully keeping the matrix running. An idea flooded into him as he realized that death didn't necessarily mean his ability to help was over. If he was lucky he would be able to make himself a part of the system and maybe influence it.

Shadow Log: Ruth, The Clover School for Girls, Rhode Island, March 2, 1811

Ruth wanted to scream, wail, and sob but she knew that if she allowed herself to do any of that she would collapse and that would leave Mary without help. The girl might be simple but she was the kindest person Ruth had ever known and she had severely misjudged her in the beginning. It hurt knowing how far she had allowed Grace to push her, how many horrible things she had done, and how many she had hurt. She couldn't take any of the horror she caused back any more than she could turn back the clock and that was what sucked the most. She had once been just like Grace's girls and it had taken enormous strength just to get out of bed. To know she had inflicted that fate on others was probably going to haunt her until her dying breath. Despite this or maybe because of it she knew she had to help Mary reach whatever goals she might have as the beginning of her redemption.

Suddenly colliding with Mary's back as the girl stopped short, rudely jarred Ruth back to reality, and made her want to curse as pain echoed through her.

"What is it?" Ruth asked quietly.

She drew her knife, carefully pressed her back to the wall, and surveyed the surrounding darkness.

"Anton, safe." Mary muttered.

Ruth let out a sigh of relief, sheathed her weapon, and stumbled after Mary. She could feel her hands shaking which made her furious. She was better trained than to let adrenaline affect her like this, better than being afraid of the dark, and she was better than allowing anyone to break her. Letting out her pent up breath, she lifted her head towards a cool breeze drifting down the tunnel, and felt a smile spread across her face. The moments passed quickly, the rush of anticipation flooding into Ruth with new life, and then sunlight mixed with fresh cool air.

Squatting down to touch the grass a single tear fell from her face as the reality of everything she had just survived came crashing down on her. The warmth of the sun cleansing her of the darkness leaving her filled with hope despite the pain of her existence. Looking over at the girls, Ruth's heart grew heavy, and it was with much difficulty that she returned to her feet.

"Can I have your attention ladies!" She called gently.

She watched them pick themselves up, each showing the stress of the last months in every move, and felt heartbreak at having to leave them on their own. Once they had gathered anxiously around her, Ruth took a deep breath, and calmly held up the orb for them to see.

"This is programmed to take you to a random village where you can start over, it has one use in it, and I can't go with you." She explained.

"Wait? Why can't you come with us?" Rebecca asked in alarm.

"Because The Shadows can find me wherever I go and if they find you…you will be dead." Ruth said softly.

"Stay. Friend." Mary interjected firmly.

Ruth gave Mary a thankful smile, "Not unless you want to face death and danger everyday." She whispered.

"Good." Mary said firmly.

"Well, I don't want my life to be death and danger, so I'll happily take the orb." Rebecca piped up.

"Hold hands." Ruth ordered.

Once all the girls were standing in a circle holding hands, Ruth sat the orb in the center, and had them all touch it with a foot. Letting go of the orb, she shielded her eyes as a bright flash of light absorbed the girls, and then they were gone. Sighing, Ruth smiled down at the remains of the orb, and felt a stone settle in her stomach.

"Where is Anton? Emma? Your father?" She finally asked.

"Anton, Emma Shadows. Father…dead." Mary replied sadly.

"I'm so sorry," Ruth whispered.

She stood back up, turned to her friend, and pulled her into a tight hug, "I pledge to protect and care for you." She whispered into Mary's ear.

"Mary too." She muttered back.

Seeing a Shadow agent appear, she separated, and calmly walked over to him.

"You are a hard one to find, Agent Ruth." The man grumbled.

"I was being tortured by a lunatic and held inside the old cells." Ruth replied calmly.

"You smell of blood." The agent said matter of factly.

"I need a healing tube, can we get back?" Ruth asked, sounding calmer than she felt.

"The simpleton?"

"Goes where I go." Ruth replied firmly.

"Fine, let us be gone."

They were swallowed in white light and everything shifted.

Shadow Log: Emma, The Shadow Base, North Dakota, March 10, 1812

Emma found herself standing in the entry hall of a large, well kept, yet well loved home that made her feel strangely cared for. She could hear her daughter rough housing with one of her brothers upstairs. Feeling annoyed, she started to tap her foot against the floor, and began to grumble under her breath. Sighing in resignation, Emma hiked up her skirts, and stomped up the stairs only to stop halfway up.

"Emily! Darling, if you want to pick apples in the orchid today, we must hurry: your birthday party is set to start just after lunch." She shouted angrily.

"I know Mama," Emily called back.

Suddenly all three of her children came crashing out of their playroom, they came down the stairs in mock battle, their laughter filling their home with warm joy. Before she could react, Emma was caught in their wake, and was thrown to the floor beneath them. They rolled down the stairs like a many limbed ball until they piled up at the bottom of the stairs in a sweaty, tangled, laughing pile.

"It is incredibly unladylike to wrestle like pigs in the mud." Johnathan said sternly from his office.

Smiling softly to herself, Emma carefully untangled her children, and helped them straighten out their clothes. Turning to her husband, she gave him a smile, and said, "Forgive us, husband, the children are just excited for the party this afternoon."

"Study now." Johnathan said sternly.

He yanked his head towards his study door, gave both his sons a long look, before allowing his eyes to return to Emma's face.

"Please refrain from acting like animals in the house…You need to be teaching your daughter how to be a proper woman." He grumbled.

He gave Emma one last meaningful look before he disappeared back into the study. Shaking her head with disappointment, Emma sent her sons after him, and finished smoothing out her skirts. In a blur of movement Emily darted past her giggling in a slightly more muted tone as she bolted for the door. Throwing Emma a huge smile, Emily threw open the front door, and took off at a dead run down the long well worn path that led to the apple grove. Emma took just enough time to pull the door shut before she let out a laugh of her own, gathered her skirts, and chased after her daughter. The lilacs and roses that lined the path were in full bloom making the heat infused day smell like her favorite perfume. She stopped, allowing herself a moment to close her eyes, and enjoy the warmth. She felt a strange disquiet awaken within herself as she picked up a strange lemony scent wafting on the morning breeze.

Without warning an explosion of hot air slammed Emma forward into a white rose bush which pinned her in its thorny embrace. Time trickled away into eternity as Emma struggled to draw air into her singed lungs past the weight that had taken up residence on her chest. A loud rhythmic pounding that almost matched her own heartbeat filled the air making it impossible for her to hear her own groggy thoughts. After what felt like an epic battle Emma finally managed to painfully drag herself out of her thorny prison. Her mind was screaming at her to hurry, to find her family, and make sure they were safe.

She lifted her head towards the horizon to see her home blazing with pale green fire that caused the bricks to crumble like they were in an oversized oven. A strange, green, metal craft seemed to hover menacingly over the wreckage. Coughing up blood all over her already blood stained dress, she struggled to force her feet to shuffle slowly towards the horror using the beat of her racing heart to set the pace. Blinking back tears and sweat, she let out a silent scream, and lunged trying to catch Emily as she bolted past her. Trying to control her panic, she pulled herself back onto her feet and staggered into her home. She had to save her family.

She choked on the thick noxious fumes rising from the strange green fire as she struggled to see past the smokiness that had overtaken her home. The pain was evident in her voice as her left foot caught on the fallen banister flinging her face first into the stone floor. Her head bounced freely on the rubble strewn stairs knocking the sense from her and yet she rolled in a desperate attempt to find those she loved. Only for her to come face to face with the vacant eyes of her eldest son. Screaming in tune with the sounds of her crashing home, Emma welcomed the darkness that consumed her as the ceiling crashed down upon her, and everything went black.

*****

Emma screamed with agony, her body shaking violently as each breath felt like someone was running molten lava through her veins. The pain jolted her upright as she fought against the frozen hands trying to hold her down. The world felt frozen, shattered, and empty and she truly wished for death in that moment. They finally managed to strap her back to the icy, unmoving, metal table leaving her to writhe in quiet agony.

Then just beyond the pain, beyond her suffering, she could hear the voices of her family calling so softly, so sweetly to her. She willed herself to leave the strange frozen room behind, to leave the pain behind, and join the peace of everlasting sleep.

Shadow Log: Emma, The Shadow Base, North Dakota, March 15, 1812

Emma woke to find herself tied to a metal examination table that was cold enough to freeze hell over, her muscles screamed angrily as if the cold had consumed them, and she found buried deep inside of her pain was a forlornness. She knew instinctively that what she had just experienced was nothing more than a fevered dream yet that did little to dispel her grief. Opening her eyes, she took a deep breath, and allowed herself to silently grieve.

None of this would have happened to her if it wasn't for The Shadows, she would have been a normal girl with a normal life, and Grace had stolen it all from her. Destroying her life's work was going to be wonderfully satisfying and she knew she was the only woman for the job. Turning her head away

from the blinding light hanging above her head, her eyes fell
on Anton, and she felt a smile creep stiffly up her face.
"Father," She groaned in Useptis.
Anton turned to her, seeming very startled to hear her raspy
voice, and then did a happy little trot over to her.
*"Emma has been unconscious for a long time…sedated for protection.
How does Emma feel now?"* He asked gently.
"Stiff, strange, full of grief." Emma whispered quietly.
*"Understandable, Emma has reached top form…two halves have
become whole. The Shadows have brought Emma back to their base for
observation."* Anton warned.
Suddenly a door swooshed open to reveal a tall man covered
in burn scars, he seemed to ooze confidence despite missing
half of his face, and Emma felt sure he was Grace's
replacement.
"Commander." Anton said respectfully in English from his
translator.
"Is she sane?" The man asked coldly.
"I am." Emma replied with equal coldness.
"It speaks and in multiple languages as well. You may call me
either B or Commander, I am the second leader of The
Shadows." B said.
He turned to Emma, pointed a strange rectangle with buttons
on it at her, and her restraints popped open. Emma sat up
slowly, realizing she was completely naked, and calmly
accepted the robe Anton offered her.
"I am ready to serve." She groaned.
Stumbling onto her feet, she leaned against the table for
stability, and gave B a calm cool smile. The game had begun
and she knew the slightest mistake could end up destroying
her and those she wanted to save.
"Good, get your strength back and I'll find you some aliens
to kill. Anton, help get her acquainted with her combat gear."
B ordered.
Emma watched him leave before she let her quaking legs
collapse causing her to crash into the concrete floor.

Everything burned from the effort of looking strong, but she wasn't going to give her enemies an ounce of joy.

"It has been a year since Emma last left the table." Anton hissed as he offered her a hand.

Accepting his hand, she allowed him to help her into a backroom that held a single cot, dresser, and small bathroom. Anton sat her down gently onto the cot, disappeared back into his lab, leaving her to sag against the wall in exhaustion. When he returned he held a small black box that looked like one of her mother's jewelry boxes, he thrust it at her face like it was hot, and dropped it on her lap. Emma carefully reached down, pulled the lid off, and stared down at the ruby dragon necklace within, feeling very confused.

"Anton used all Anton's skill to craft that for Emma. It is a self cleaning, repairing, and cloaking suit that will respond to Emma's mental commands. It is like wearing a second set of scales that will also cloak Emma's face when the hood is raised." Anton bragged proudly.

Sighing happily, Emma shakily clipped the necklace on, and gave Anton an appreciative nod. She knew how much work he had to have put into creating it and making it beautiful, and she was very grateful.

"Uta'Ve." She whispered simply.

Anton nodded happily, *"Emma can rest here as long as Emma wishes or Anton can ask for a separate room for Emma."* Anton replied with clear joy.

"I feel safe with you." Emma said softly.

"Then sleep, child." Anton purred as he left.

Shadow Log: Ruth, Roswell, New Mexico, March 16, 1812

Ruth often found herself wondering if she had made a mistake taking a job as a field agent in the west. It wasn't like she had a choice if she ever wanted to rise within The Shadows after all this was her punishment for failing Grace. In truth the only thing that had kept her sane over the last year was Mary's companionship, probably because they lived in the middle of nowhere with no one around for miles and miles. But this place was a hotspot for alien crashes and someone needed to keep them from forming nests.

Staring out across the desert, she watched the gorgeous sunset, and felt her skin start to prickle. Ruth calmly braced herself against the wall to their tiny home, letting the sonic boom from the crash pass as a streak of fire shot through the sky.

"We got another one!" She called inside.

Mary came out with all their gear, dropped it on the ground, and started suiting up. Ruth silently joined her making sure to use her time efficiently to ensure that they wouldn't end up walking into an ambush.

"It looked like a small craft, maybe 10 builders and a king." Ruth said.

She accepted her heat saber from Mary, waited for her to get her giant hammer up onto her shoulder, and then began the slow march towards the crash site. Their official job was to scout out the crashes and provide the intel needed to take them out, but they had quickly learned that the Useptis had very keen senses which meant it was nearly impossible to remain undetected.

"King mine." Mary replied after a long silence.

"I'll keep the builders busy." Ruth promised.

If luck was with them they wouldn't need to fight, but lady luck seemed to always be napping when Ruth needed her. They approached the crash with extreme caution, neither of them wanted to end up with even more scars, and they both had a healthy sense of fear of the Useptis. Pulling out her binoculars, she surveyed the crash from the largest hill in the area, and was able to count five bodies including one that looked like the king. Handing them to Mary, Ruth calmly typed out a message to her boss, and then made sure her weapon was handy.

Suddenly the ground erupted around them as dozens of worms the size of a small pony with thousands of teeth shot into the air as they attempted to latch onto them. Ruth barely managed to scramble up onto the nearest rock in time, but Mary was far less lucky as one of the creatures latched onto her left leg. Mary screamed in agony smashing the worm into goop with her hammer as she crawled onto harder ground. Knowing the clock was ticking as poison pumped through Mary's body, Ruth grabbed a fire grenade from her bag, and tossed it into the nearest hole.

Fire erupted from the ground accompanied by the shrill screams of the alien worms, wasting no time Ruth rushed to Mary's side, and jabbed the antidote into her leg. With the urgency of a woman on fire, she quickly bandaged the wound, and helped Mary onto the rocks knowing that all she had done was piss off her enemies. Sending out an SOS call on her shadow-band, Ruth readied her weapon just in time for the second eruption. This time they were ready for them and were able to kill a couple forcing them to retreat.

"No hold." Mary painted in pain.

"Reinforcements are five minutes out." Ruth promised.

She knew that holding their current position would be impossible for more than a few minutes at most as she could hear the worms gnawing angrily at the rock beneath their feet. Grabbing Mary's arm, Ruth pointed at the wreck, and silently signaled for Mary to make a run for it. Once Mary was a few feet away several trails began to appear in the dirt behind her. Switching to her pistol, Ruth carefully put as many bullets as she could into the worms following Mary causing them to double back towards her. Dropping a second grenade into the tunnels, she took off at a dead run after Mary, stopping only when they crashed into the main chamber of the wreck.

"Blood." Mary groaned.

The pain Mary was holding back made Ruth's blood boil as she calmly redressed the wound. Checking her surroundings she was thankful to see that the floor was still intact and that there was only one way in.

"Three minutes." Ruth promised gently.

Ruth ripped an unnoticed tooth out of her calf, administered the antidote to herself, and sagged down next to Mary.

"Damn worms!" She added angrily.

"Smash them." Mary grumbled in agreement.

The next ten minutes were riddled with the sounds of gunfire, death, and the awful smell of sulfur. Ruth held Mary's hand letting her know that she wasn't going to leave her and that she was safe with her, but deep down all Ruth felt was fear and anger. Seventeen crashes in one year and The Shadows were slow to respond every single time like they wanted to see her dead. But Ruth was a survivor and she knew how to do what needed to be done and so she persisted even when things turned out like today.

"Do you think the builders released the diggers or did they escape in the chaos of the crash?" Ruth wondered out loud.

"Slime trails." Mary muttered.

Ruth looked where Mary was pointing and sure enough there were dozens of trails leading away from an open stasis chamber. Something had to have let them out and Ruth had a gut feeling that something was watching them. Calmly staring into the shadows as night encompassed the wrecked ship Ruth caught sight of five angry eyes staring back at her.

"King." She whispered

She nodded towards the eyes as she carefully climbed to her feet and prepped for the terror of the next few minutes. The king closed the distance in the blink of an eye, locking his gaze with Ruth as he fought to invade her thoughts. Ruth was forced to defend her mind, making it impossible for her to move as he raised his tail for the kill. Laughing almost manically, Mary slammed her hammer into the creature's ribs causing them to splinter inwards, and destroy one of its hearts. Ruth stumbled forward as his focus shifted and with one quick blow of her saber she took off its head. Mary wasted no time in smashing the rest of its hearts into bloody mush with her hammer.

"Ruth bleeding." Mary said with concern.

Looking down at her shoulder, Ruth could see the underlying muscle right down to the bone from where the tail had caught her as she closed in for the kill. Cringing, she pressed the heated end of the sword against the cut allowing the flesh to fuse together from the extreme heat. Closing her eyes, she choked down the pain, and poured all of her focus into staying awake.

"I'll live." Ruth moaned.

"It seems you dealt with the biggest threat yourselves." A gruff marine said as he walked in.

"I have a tendency to avoid dying at all costs." Ruth spat back.

The marine chuckled as he walked over and pulled her shirt away from her injured shoulder.

"Nasty wound, you're lucky we have orders to bring you back to base." He sighed.

She knocked his hand away, gave Mary a small grimace, and marched past the marines gathering in the entrance. The man clearly found her pain funny and she really didn't want to deal with him when she was this exhausted.

"Mary and I will port back ahead of you while you handle the clean up." She called back.

Mary stumbled after her, grinning from ear to ear, and quickly caught up to Ruth.

"Cabin?" Mary asked happily.

"Cabin." Ruth agreed.

She wasn't sure what The Shadows needed with her but she knew it had to be better than this.

Shadow Log: Emma, The Shadow Base, North Dakota, March 18, 1812

To lose a year was bad enough yet it was the sense of loss that kept her weighed down. She felt empty almost like an old pottery vase left to crack and crumble away without someone to love it. Johnathan was gone, Jacob too, and she couldn't stop mourning the life she had glimpsed in the coma.

She knew she was being selfish every time she thought about finding a way to end it all, but somehow none of that mattered when she had such a void in her soul. Even her reflection filled her with grief as angular eyes with gray/red pupils stared back at her. Her nose had widened into a small umbrella to protect her blackened lips, and all of her baby fat was gone leaving behind stern angular cheeks.

She even had developed a figure that many would find attractive with, supple breasts, a tiny waist, and perfect hips that transitioned into alabaster legs. She could see bits of her mother staring back oddly mixed with Anton's DNA and a hint of what she assumed was her father. Running her fingers through her midnight blue hair she forced herself to smile revealing the perfectly white fangs that had replaced her teeth.

Shivering with effort, she brought her scales to the surface, and felt fresh tears begin to stream down her face as she felt her sense of normalcy slip further from her grasp. There was no denying that she was now a weapon of mass destruction that could easily be misused. A sharp rap at her door made her startle away from the mirror, stumble backwards, and accidentally smash the chair at the foot of her bed. Cursing under her breath, she pulled herself together, dried her tears, and retracted her scales. Closing her eyes, she summoned her armor, and felt it spread across her flesh. When it settled into place a few seconds later she was wearing a skin tight green bodysuit with a full hood resting on her shoulders.

"Come in," she ordered as she wiped away the last of her tears.

The door slid into the wall to reveal a short, plump, sweaty man who appeared to be out of breath despite standing completely still. Emma smiled, carefully keeping her lips over her teeth, and raised an eyebrow in question.

"The Commander wants to see you in his chambers forthwith." He huffed.

He waved for her to follow, stomping away with a loudness that was immediately grating to her nerves. Grabbing her weapon belt from her cot, she clipped it around her waist, and hurried after the man. For being so short and out of breath he was surprisingly speedy yet Emma found it difficult to slow down enough to match his pace.

From what she had gleaned from the blueprints Anton had given her, The Shadow Base held ten rooms housed in each of the outer walls with a large hallway leading around its perimeter. The center of the base housed ten secured labs for research and development, a large training gym, and the cafeteria. The outer rooms were used for housing, storage, and office spaces. A smaller hallway cut through the back wall leading to the secure server room that powered the whole base. The east wing was a dedicated hospital accessible through a large hallway that cut through the center of the east wall. The entrance to the base was a mile long tunnel designed to kill anything trying to breach it with ten high security checkpoints. Finally, overlooking it all from the far back wall was the Commander's office which had a clear view of the entire base from its vantage point three stories above the rest of the base.

The man dumped her without ceremony in a small waiting room outside the Commander's office and ordered her to wait. Carefully lowering herself into a chair, she struggled to push the void inside of her away, but only succeeded in feeling even more empty. After a few long minutes of waiting the man reappeared and waved Ruth into the room. While

Ruth's transformation was a lot less drastic than hers, Emma could see that Ruth too had become a fierce warrior.
"They finally let you out of the lab!" Ruth laughed.
She plopped down opposite Emma, gave her a dazzling smile, and stretched out on the couch.
"Did Mary survive?" Emma asked tentatively.
Ruth gave her a long sideways look before she let out a small chuckle, and shifted to face Emma.
"Me, Mary, and Anton were the only survivors. Mary is taking a bath and then looking for something to eat before reporting to the library for clerk duty… I kept her safe or at least I tried to while you were away." Ruth replied gently.
"You've changed, but I'm not sure if it's enough, I can still see much of Grace in you. But thank you for looking after her and for helping us." Emma said.
"Direct as ever." Ruth muttered.
The office door slid open as B barked at them to enter. Ruth shot to her feet with surprising quickness and marched rigidly into the office. Rolling her eyes, Emma carefully got up, and followed her. Taking the only available chair left, Emma sat next Ruth, refusing to break eye contact with B as she waited for him to speak.
"I am aware that you have found yourselves on opposite sides in the past, but I need you to put that strife where it belongs in the past. Ruth has proved herself to be one of my best field agents and so I am making her your partner." B explained.
"What?! Sir! With all due respect I…" Ruth started to protest.
"Unless the next words out of your mouth are what is my next assignment, I would stop talking if I were you." B cut her off coldly.
Ruth swallowed her protests while Emma continued to study B. Emma had no desire to work with Ruth, The Shadows, or anyone else but she had sworn an oath which meant she had a job to do.

"What's our next assignment?" Emma asked after a few too many awkward moments of silence.

B returned his gaze to her and said, "I'm sending you to London to deal with an insane digger that is using its skills to rob graves from below ground. It's a fairly easy task and should allow you two to work your issues out. Of course a jump of that distance can only be achieved from base to base so you will need to use the main teleporter to get there. Raul is the head of the London base and will have a full dossier ready for you when you arrive. Now get going, I have work to attend to." B ordered sternly.

Emma followed Ruth out letting her steam silently as she got her emotions in check.

"Do you think we can find a way to work together?" Emma asked, once they were alone again.

"I have no issue with being your partner. I, I have spent the last year beside Mary and I am going to miss working with her." Ruth sighed hesitantly.

"She will always be your friend even if you can't work side by side." Emma promised.

"It's stupid anyway. Come, we should grab lunch before we leave for London." Ruth said in a tone that ended the conversation.

Shadow Log: Emma, The Shadow Base, London, March 19, 1812

London seemed to be unusually cold for March at least to Emma, not that she had any frame of reference to compare it to having never been outside of her home country. She was just thankful to be below ground even if it stunk of death and insanity mixed with despair. The tunnel walls seemed like they were packed with human skeletons which did nothing to help the eerie vibe the place was giving off. But worse of all was the quiet echoing like tiny little ghostly calls of pure insanity that made Emma's skin vibrate uncomfortably.

"Can you hear that?" She whispered quietly to Ruth.

"No, but my hearing isn't as attuned as yours. What exactly are you hearing?" Ruth asked with equal quietness.

"The Useptis mostly communicate mentally but they have a call they use when they're lost. It's a click-pop-click-pop-thunk that repeats on a cycle with the last sound being their location so that they can be rescued. There are too many interlocking clicks for the recent grave robbing to be from one builder." Emma replied softly.

"How many do you think are down here?" Ruth asked nervously.

"At least a dozen, perhaps more, I'll be able to tell more as we get closer." Emma grumbled.

"Then what are we waiting for?" Ruth growled unhappily.

Emma gave her a seething look that she knew translated beyond the shadow cloaking her face, wishing she could just do this alone, and began to carefully make her way toward the clicking. She had nothing against Ruth as a person or as an agent, she simply didn't like having a full blooded human watching her back, and feared for the woman's safety in this confined space. Making sure to watch her footing as well as the uneven bone strewn floor to avoid making any unnecessary noise since they still had the element of surprise Emma led them deeper into the darkness.

Down beneath the surface Emma felt oddly safe almost like she was home which she attributed to her Useptis blood, in fact she wouldn't have any reservations about starting her own underground sanctuary one day…One that didn't stink preferably. The tunnel came to a sudden end in a large chamber filled with gnawed bones and rotted flesh. Emma could see six huge builders all standing at attention in the shadows of the recessed walls and one huge Useptis unlike anything she had seen before.

"What is that?" Ruth whispered in horror.

Before Emma could respond the builders snapped awake, their eyes locking onto the dinner that had just foolishly walked into their home, and then the huge creature began to stir. Shaking the ground with every movement as it picked itself up from where it had been sleeping. Hissing quietly, Emma drew her staff, and prepared for the hell about to be unleashed. Blood, screams, and terror engulfed the room as Emma charged swiftly at the creature and began to beat it back away from Ruth.

"Keep the builders back!" She ordered.

Slamming her weapon into the monster's face Emma felt her entire body vibrate from the force of the blow bouncing off of its scales. Cursing angrily, Emma activated the blades on her weapon, and closed in for another blow. Pain erupted across her body as a giant claw slammed her back into the wall causing thousands of bones to bury her. She wasted no time in digging herself out of the pile, not wanting to end up splattered across the floor, and rolled clear of the creature's next blow. Shouting an angry battle cry, she launched herself into the air, ran across the wall, and landed on its back. Ridding it like a bucking horse, holding onto a spike with her left hand, she drove her staff repeatedly into its neck. Until it finally crashed into the floor with a tremendous thud that shook the entire room knocking both the builders and Ruth off of their feet. Moving swiftly, Emma finished off the remaining threats before pausing to catch her breath. Ruth gave her an appreciative nod as she calmly began to clean a small wound on her forehead.

"Um, should the ceiling look like that?" Ruth asked in terror. Emma turned her eyes upward. There were hundreds of cracks spider veining through the once solid stone with more appearing every second. With no time to flee back into the tunnels and no guarantee of stability if they did Emma sprinted over to Ruth, picked her up, and jumped into the highest nook in the wall. Seconds later the roof came crashing down on the chamber as they sheltered from the falling debris inside the uncomfortably small nook. By the time things had settled down enough for them to peak out safely there was about five feet of rubble piled on the floor and they could see spots where the stars were peaking through.

"Can you jump that high?" Ruth asked nervously as she surveyed the blocked tunnels.

"No, not with you in tow but I brought rope." Emma said. Taking a steadying breath, she launched herself towards the ceiling, and just barely managed to catch the edge of the hole. Pulling herself up, she threw the rope at a tree branch above her head as the ground gave way beneath her weight. She crashed down onto the sharp stone just barely managing to avoid getting smashed by an old coffin that had decided to follow her down. Moaning in pain, Emma was thankful to see that the rope had looped itself around the branch, and was now hanging there mocking her. A few jumps later and Emma had both ends of the rope securely held in her fist as she rejoined Ruth.

"Tie this around your waist and I'll hoist you up." Emma ordered as she thrust one end of the rope at Ruth.

Once Ruth was secured properly, Emma gently hoisted her up into the air, and up to the widened hole in the roof. Using surprising acrobatic skills, Ruth swung herself up onto solid ground, and scrambled quickly away from the crumbling lip of the hole. Once Emma was sure Ruth was clear, she leapt up to the surface, and rolled onto solid ground.

"That went about as well as a disaster can." Emma groaned uncomfortably.

"The Shadows will need to retrieve that corpse for study but at least London is safe again." Ruth replied with clear exhaustion.

"Now that we're on the surface, can we port back to base?" Emma asked.

"We shouldn't have a problem now." Ruth replied.

Emma pushed herself up off of the ground and began gathering up her gear so they could get back before they were spotted.

Shadow Log: Grace, Somewhere beneath London, March 19, 1812

Grace was careful to keep the boot of her hill on Emma's throat with just enough pressure to stop her convulsions. Such a strange thing when time and technology combined and here she was a young woman again… well most of one anyway, all the good parts mixed in with a few choice mechanical enhancements. Of course she would age normally now and had the same mortality as any other human. In short this was her last chance to get it right. This was her last life. Watching Emma's eyes flutter open, Grace calmly removed her heel from the girl's throat, and crouched down next to her.

"Easy, you took a nasty blow to the head." Grace said as Ruth.

Emma let out a long slow hiss, crawled rapidly backwards, and smacked Grace back with a snarl.

"What in the actual hell?! Grace?! How did you get inside Ruth?!" Emma hissed angrily.

"Incredibly prescriptive of you, Youngling!" Grace laughed madly.

"What the hell is going on?!" Emma spat furiously.

"I saw my death coming long ago and did a little morality tinkering. Poor Hubert never saw it coming, and then his horrible death…" Grace laughed maniacally. "Ruth was destined to die an undiscovered talent and I saved her! Well, that is what she thought anyway. In truth, I uploaded a fail safe into Ruth in case of my death. I honestly am surprised it worked! Oh, and the Useptis can't tolerate garlic. In large quantities it causes vivid dream-comas while in smaller doses it is like a massive boost of energy that'll keep you awake for days. I developed a hyper garlic concentrate that is as close to an overdose as your system can handle and dosed you the moment we entered the tunnels so that I could finish downloading!" Grace chuckled.

"I'm speechless." Emma muttered.

In a flash of movement, Grace lunged forward, and kicked Emma in the throat. At the moment of contact a collar shot out of her heel and locked around Emma's neck. Emma let out a choked hiss as the collar drilled into her scales and secured itself to her flesh. Then in a flash of light it camouflaged itself Emma's body.

"Okay, that last bit was a lie. I led you here to make sure you behave for the foreseeable future. The collar will cause you a great deal of pain if you try to go after me. Oh, and as far as the world knows I'm Ruth." Grace warned sternly.

Emma lunged back at her growling in agony as the collar choked her unconscious. Watching Emma's body hit the floor, Grace sighed, and slid to the floor. It was going to be a long night…

Shadow Log: Emma, Shadow Base, North Dakota, March 24, 1812

"Anton!" Emma called into Anton's head.

Without missing a beat Anton quickly merged their minds so that they could speak privately.

"Why is Ruth acting so fuzzy?" He asked sharply.

"Because she isn't Ruth anymore, she's Grace. I'm not sure why I can see that and you can't." Emma grumbled suspiciously.

"When Emma was fresh from Emma's egg Emma grew very ill and death came close. Anton gave blood to save, yes? Technology to heal, yes?" Anton tried to explain.

"Wait? What kind of technology?" Emma asked with a sinking feeling.

"Anton gave Anton's ship's neuro system to stitch Emma's DNA back together." Anton explained further.

Emma didn't like the thought of her DNA split apart or getting stitched back together, it felt wrong, and she was even less excited about having ship parts inside of her. But she knew Anton wasn't the cause of her fury.

"Spread the word, Grace is back, and I'll try to get out of this collar." Emma hissed unhappily.

"It can be overridden with enough willpower to withstand the pain, keep pressing it and it will snap." Anton said and severed the connection.

But instead of catapulting back into reality Emma found herself standing in a darkened void filled with numbers. Then ever so slowly from those numbers a figure of a slightly sickly man appeared and with him a small room that looked like the old barn.

"Forgive me, Miss Emma, I hope I haven't caused you too much alarm." The man said nervously.

Emma glanced around cautiously, doing her best to assess her surroundings for danger, and form some sort of exit plan if things went wrong.

"You have me at a bit of a loss today, for example I don't even know your name." Emma hissed cautiously.

"Oh! Dear me, forgive me, it has been a long time since I have spoken to the living. I am Hubert, I built the computer matrix that runs the Shadow Network. Grace destroyed my shell about ten to fifteen years ago and I have been working to collect pawns against her ever since. The problem is that I don't have a way to influence things outside the matrix." Hubert explained excitedly.

Remembering the way Grace had been mocking Hubert, Emma started to relax, and decided to trust him for the time being.

"I'm listening." She muttered quietly.

"Excellent! The Shadows were created to deal with alien threats to Earth like the Useptis, but it got twisted. I know a secret that no human alive knows, a secret the Useptis refuse to acknowledge exists…The Useptis are fleeing their home world in a desperate attempt at survival. The Stahl are far more terrifying than Useptis could ever be and Grace has no idea what it will take to win a war against them." Hubert said as he summoned a chair for Emma.

Emma sat down and asked, "and you think I do?"

"No, how could you when you are barely finding yourself? You are a child of three species born into one that makes you very powerful, but only you can choose how to use that power." Hubert whispered solemnly.

"I need you to back up a bit there. Child of three?" Emma hissed in alarm.

"The Stahl created their ships from the DNA of one of their conquered races and then the Useptis stole that tech from them. You are human by birth, Useptis by blood, and Stahl by enhancement…"

"Stahl?" Emma growled.

"I have no other name for the species besides their slave classification. The Kraken were the last species to die by their hands." Hubert sighed.

"Krakens are giant sea monsters with tentacles right?" Emma asked in shock.

"Yes according to Earth myth. You see Earth is a planet that has a long history of aliens fleeing to it in the hopes of salvation and then still not finding it. Dinosaurs? Stahl dropped a rock on them! And the Kraken got cooked with salt! Now The Useptis are dealing with Grace…Please, tell me you see where I am going with all of this?" Hubert pleaded.

"You're saying that the Stahl are the real threat and that they're using Grace to do their bidding. So, assuming what you say is true and you're not crazy, we need to not only stop Grace, but also save the world from a different threat?" Emma asked dryly.

"I am afraid it is too late for Earth, but it isn't too late for humans or the Useptis if you work with Anton and me to stop The Shadows before it is impossible to evacuate." Hubert begged.

"Do you have any proof of anything you are saying?" Emma asked sharply.

She wanted Grace dead as much as the next person, but she wasn't about to let herself get led into a trap either which meant she needed solid evidence before believing anything. "Anton keeps a black box beneath his computer, inside it will be a red and orange crystal that is warm to the touch. Hold it tightly in your hand and then submerge it in water. You'll see the truth with your own eyes as I did, right before Grace smashed my skull in." Hubert shuddered.

Emma sat bolt upright in her cot, sweat drenching her skin, and her tail flicking angrily. Her tail flicking angrily? Emma jumped upright, yelping in alarm as she began to dance around hunting for a mirror. Flicking on the light with her left hand, she held the hand mirror up, and slowly tilted the mirror towards her butt. A long, thin, flexible tail curled gracefully out from the base of her spine. Emma choked down a scream of surprise as she accidentally smashed her tail into the desk.

"So you can move it. Can you pick up a pen?" She whispered to herself.

Concentrating on the mirror, Emma directed her thoughts to picking up the pen, and after a couple slightly clumsy attempts she grabbed it. Letting out a triumphant sigh, she dropped the pen back down onto the desk, and turned to face it. Setting the mirror down on the table, she took a deep breath, and reached down to pick it back up with her tail. She found it to be no harder than if she had used her left hand to grab it. Admiring herself in the mirror, Emma started to smile, and then laugh. Maybe, having a tail wouldn't be such a bad thing especially if she could keep it hidden from people. Setting the mirror down, she shimmied into her shirt, and quickly hurried over to her chair.

Grabbing her cargo pants, she wrapped her tail around her thigh, and carefully slipped into them. Looking into the full length mirror, Emma couldn't see it at all, and if she wanted she could get about three feet of it out of her pant leg. Tail or no tail Emma knew she had to do some proper investigating if she was going to determine the proper path forward.

Shadow Log: Emma, Shadow Base, North Dakota, March 30, 1812

Every Monday was a feeding day where they would let Anton out into a field to feast on cows. It was also the only time in which the lab was left empty. Finding the crystal was surprisingly easy as was finding a bowl of water, but she could feel that she was about to change everything. There was no return from this point, no taking back her choice, no swerving from her destiny.

"Oh, Batty Fang!" She cursed.

She thrust her hand into the water, watching as the orange and red began to bleed into the water, and glow brightly. Universes collided, darkness swirled into light, and then in an instant of eternal anguish Emma was ripped from her body, and spread across the universe. The crystal reformed as the water evaporated from the bowl and Emma snapped back into her body. Blood dripped from her nose, her eyes shifting with red fire, and then an angry flicker of her tail brought Emma crashing back into reality. Shuddering at how cold she suddenly felt, she quickly stuffed the crystal back into Anton's desk, and went to her bathroom.

Stripping naked, she slid open the metal door to the strange water closet, and stepped inside. Shivering, she cranked the nozzle as hot as she could get it, and screamed as icy water came crashing down on her face. What followed was scorching hot water that immediately brought her scales out as steam filled the shower. Submerging her head under the stream, she suddenly became aware of what had just happened, and she hurled all over her feet.

Somehow she had allowed the entire Useptis database to be downloaded into her chip and while the data wasn't perfectly accessible yet she was sure of Hubert's words being true. It made her want to vomit again as she tried to access the overwhelming amount of data now swimming just beyond her reach. After a few uncomfortable experiments, she was able to determine that if she needed to know something she knew it, but she forgot it right afterwards. Useful if she could manage to write down what was important for her missions and that could be achieved with her journals. Theodore had taught her to write in code by carefully layering the letters for each word on top of each other that way only she could read it and she wouldn't be giving away free information. Anton had already delivered six leather bound blank journals with a thousand pages per not including the backs, and it would fit in her pocket as well.

Turning off the shower, she quickly dried her skin, and braided her hair. Hurrying into her bedroom, she sat down at her desk, opened a journal to the first page, and placed the pen against the page.

What are the Stahl?

The Stahl are slime-like creatures whose entire cellular network is dedicated to advanced thought as such they have become farmers of advanced species before they can cause eruptible harm to the galaxy.

She wrote with shocking speed, her eyes dancing with red fire as they darted rapidly from side to side, and her tiny cramped code appeared in the paper. Blinking the fire from her vision, Emma stared down at her notebook, and read her message over and over until she wanted to sob. Blinking away her tears, she put her pen to paper once more.

Rules of engagement for fair and equal treatment of the worthy.

1. Show no remorse, but do not kill unless no other choice is viable.
2. Be understanding and show mercy to those who actively need it, but do not seek it.
3. One may die so the many shall live even if the one is beloved.

4. Devotion is earned for the duration of duty to pay back the respect shown to you. That debt is fulfilled the moment they mistreat you.
5. Give forgiveness to those who earn it through action, give nothing to those who deserve nothing, and at times all be respectful.
6. Tell the truth or do not say a word.
7. Be direct yet kind when you can, but do not fear your roar!
8. Live for others, not yourself.
9. Fight with honor yet give no ground to your foes
10. I will face a thousand deaths if it means I can spare the galaxy one.

This is my Oath,
WEAH
She used a fang to pierce the skin of her thumb and pressed her bleeding thumb into the hot candle wax from her desk candle. Moving quickly, Emma pressed her bloody fingerprint into the page like it was a seal. She had made up her mind on how her life would be led and now it was only a matter of putting it into practice.

She put her journal and pen into her pants pocket, got dressed in her nightgown, blew out the candle, and switched off the light. The nice thing about being part Useptis was that she could see just as well in the dark as in the day but the human side preferred the light being on when awake.

Shadow Log: Ruth, Shadow Base, North Dakota, April 2, 1812

There was something about being trapped inside of your own mind unable to even scream that brought insanity creeping in. Ruth could feel Grace's mind slowly leaking into her own consciousness like a virus, killing everything in its wake, and leaving her with hollow goop in her memories place. She was watching it all from inside a crystal sphere made of Grace's invisible willpower and despite how hard Ruth fought she did not even find enough space to get off of her knees.

She had accepted death a long time ago, disability, and even ending up like her mother had. She had known even then that a person's brains don't normally have wires in them and she had still followed Grace blindly. Claustrophobia had always been her greatest weakness even before Chester had locked her up for a week which was something Ruth could feel Grace trying to use against her. But what she didn't know about Ruth was how stubborn she could be when she felt like she was being caged. How much she knew about the inner workings of her own head or how well she understood her enemy.

To the naked eye of the invader Ruth had given up, accepted her fate, and was awaiting her eventual death. But if one were smart enough to look below the shell kneeling hopelessly in her orb they would see that Ruth was in fact no longer there. That was the beautiful thing about preparation, it never let you down, only your own stupidity did. Ruth stretched, allowing her consciousness to expand below her prison, and to bring light back to the stormtorn regions of her consciousness. Moments flashed by as Ruth methodically took back her mind and prepared herself for battle. She built a cavaron inside of her mind in which her aura became her weapon and shifted to her will. Summoning her avatar, Ruth settled onto one of the thousands of rocks floating throughout the arena, and then she pointed at a rock across the arena. In a flash of black light an oily goblin-like creature appeared and began to hover in the air.

Noticing the growing threat, Grace turned her focus inward, and filled the goblin with her essence in preparation to smash Ruth down. Cackling like the witch she was, Grace began to grow until she stood at just over thirteen feet, and weighed a good five hundred pounds. Grace summoned a giant oil encased warhammer, hefted it up, and brought it down towards Ruth's head. Screaming with enough rage to power a small raft, Ruth brought a large green shield up, and deflected the force back into Grace. Shifting her aura into a spear, Ruth leapt into the air, and drove it into Grace's side.

Time froze as Ruth calmly yet swiftly darted out of Grace's reach, everything suddenly shifted, and then dozens of armored spiders came crawling out of the walls of the cavern to begin chewing on the time shield. Ruth took a moment to switch her weapon over to a rapid fire crossbow before she allowed all of her pent up breath to escape. She got the perfect shot lined up on the first spider, carefully planning out her kill streak, and ensuring she was prepared for any more trickery.

Time restarted, the spiders swarmed inwards, and fell dead one after another until Ruth paused. Looking up into Grace's hate filled soul, she took aim, and released the last of her expendable energy as one explosive arrow that knocked Grace back down to her original size. Transforming her weapon one last time she summoned a sword with a wide blade for blocking.

"This is my mind Grace, not yours! I spent a year hiding from you and Hubert to make sure I was ready for this!" Ruth laughed.

"Spry, Little Shite!" Grace growled angrily.

Blood leaked down between Grace's fingers denoting how badly she was hurting underneath her clamped hand. Ruth could feel more and more of Grace's essence drain into her avatar to heal it before she bled out. Grace's claws were beginning to slip from her mind and soon Ruth would be the only one left. Using blinding speed, she ran her sword into Grace, and transformed it into a giant but that Grace wouldn't be able to remove or heal around.

"Did you experiment on my mother? And was that why she went into that coma?" Ruth asked angrily.

She didn't expect a truthful answer, but she knew that was the only questions she really needed to have answered. Grace forlornly stared down at her chest for what felt like an eternity before she slowly raised her head to stare into Ruth's eyes.

"Yes." Grace whispered simply.

Ruth sat down on the ground, crossed her legs, and summoned a peach. Seeing Grace staring at her in awe, Ruth tossed the peach over to her, and summoned a new one for herself.

"Do you remember how we first met? I'm not talking about my father's poker party either." Ruth sighed tiredly.

"I gave you a peach and promised to take care of you while you slept." Grace replied sadly.

Grace sat down across from Ruth, her body shifting back into its human form, and the rest of her essence drained into the avatar.

"I trusted you." Ruth whispered with equal sadness.

"I know." Grace muttered.

And so they ate peaches while Grace quietly passed away returning Ruth's body back to its rightful owner.

Shadow Log: Emma, Shadow Base, North Dakota, April 3, 1812

Emma wasn't sure what shocked her more; the fact that Ruth was somehow back or that she had come to Anton's lab looking for Emma. The strange ways that life kept twisting were starting to make her head spin and Emma almost wanted Anton to rip her apart. But she had to give the girl credit for fighting off Grace even if she was a cyborg. Of course, she wasn't sure if she was going to feel comfortable with going into battle with her again after she had pumped her full of garlic last time.

"You're sure there are no remnants of Grace in there?" Emma asked for probably the fiftieth time.

Anton stamped his hooves in annoyance, sent Emma a nasty look, and turned to speak to Ruth.

"It is impressive how you beat Grace at her own game." He crowed happily.

Ruth gave him a dry smile as she leaned uncomfortably against Anton's desk and began to fidget unhappily.

"I was an early prototype to what you are today, that leftover tech allowed me to push Grace out." Ruth tried to explain to Emma.

"I'm not stupid, I understood you the first three times. I just don't trust you." Emma replied coldly.

"You have no reason to, I've already requested a transfer to base so I won't be a threat even if somehow Grace manages to try again. Please, Emma, I don't want to be your enemy." Ruth pleaded.

"You and I are good as long as you are aware that I will have zero issues with ending your life if I feel you have become a threat to the greater good." Emma said as gently as she could.

She had nothing against Ruth, but she also knew that in the end she would always choose The Shadows and that was a problem.

"I can live with that." Ruth sighed.

She gave Anton a quick bow before darting out of the room leaving Emma and Anton alone.

"I know about the Stahl." Emma said as she followed Ruth's example.

Anton may have been a major reason why she was still alive, but she was beginning to realize that to stop The Shadows she was going to have to be careful where she put her trust. Anton had lied, experimented, and tortured her at the bidding of his masters but did that mean she shouldn't trust him? Or did it mean he was in the same boat as her? Until she knew for sure she would have to be careful.

Garlic and the Useptis,

Garlic has a similar base structure to that of Cinder-weed making the more sensitive species hallucinate in small doses. In larger doses it can induce a coma-like state in which the user can end up trapped in a wonderland or a vivid nightmare. The good news is that garlic's hallucinogenic effects have a short lifespan of no more than an hour in most species. It is important to note that the bulb of the plant is the least toxic part of the plant and if any other part is ingested it can lead to worse symptoms emerging.

Shadow Log: Emma, Research Base Alpha, The middle of the Bermuda Triangle, April 13, 1812
Emma had tried repeatedly to convince The Shadows that she didn't need a partner and yet she was still stuck with Ruth. Truthfully Emma liked the idea of keeping Ruth close for observation, but she didn't trust her to have her back.

Their mission today was simple, collect the prototype weapon and bring it home, but the knot tangling Emma's insides made it clear that once again their plans were about to explode.

"The Sarge will be up with the weapon shortly," The Captain assured her.

Staring down at his plump, well rounded face Emma wondered if he realized how much he looked like an egg. Being pale, bald, and two hundred plus pounds overweight did nothing to help with his egg like appearance. Forcing herself to smile, Emma nervously sat down on the lip of a barrel, and tried to calm her racing heart. Closing her eyes tight, she began to work through the process of bringing her breathing under control, and noticed a tickle at the back of her mind.

It felt like something or someone was quietly pounding on a metal door from dozens of feet beneath the surface through a few thousand gallons of water. A steady rhythmic thumping against her mental shield that was almost nonexistent. A gentle, quiet, and warm thump, thump, thump that made her want to smile. Slowly the knot in her shoulders loosened, her scales grew warm, and everything began to feel less bleak.

"The triangle doesn't get many visitors." A slender woman said as she stumbled onto the deck.

Emma eyed the woman calmly before she carefully and with great deliberateness stood back up.

"If you could access the base without teleporting I'm sure you would have plenty of unwanted guests." Egg man offered helpfully.

The woman scoffed in horror, thrust the briefcase into Emma's hands, and stomped back below deck. Chuckling to herself, Emma turned to face the horizon, and froze.

"Uh, Ruth, are you seeing this?" She called shakily.

Just off the bow of the ship was a huge green and black ship that was covered in thousands of icy spikes. It seemed to be floating effortlessly on the waves keeping perfect pace with the ship as they began to sink into the ocean.

"It's sinking us!" Ruth called back.

"I figured that out when my boots ended up under water!" Emma grumbled loudly.

She scrambled up onto the upper deck narrowly avoiding being skewered by a dozen spikes that the ship's cannon shot at her. Screaming in pain as one bounced off of her right shoulder scales, she launched herself up onto the mast, and used it to crash into the hull of the alien vessel's roof. Hissing in agony as the force of the landing sent an icicle through the bottom of her foot, she grabbed another spike, and held on as the ship began to vibrate in an effort to shake her off. Suddenly a giant explosion blew a huge hole into the side of the vessel as Ruth calmly yanked the prototype away from Emma.

"The hole won't last, get in there, and kill them!" Ruth ordered

A second grenade landed inside of the hole, clearing the way for Emma to roll inside, and heal the surface of her wound. It still hurt yet it wasn't going to hinder her ability to fight even if it gave her a temporary limp. Drawing her weapon, she pulled her hood up, and scanned her surroundings. Just as the hole began to shrink back into itself, the ship jerked sharply to the left, shot into the sky, and threw Emma up against the ceiling. Cursing under her breath as she came crashing back into the floor, she shakily climbed back to her feet, and headed for the command center.

"Eta'Ta'Vi'Vor this one is a friend." A tall Research Useptis said as it turned to face her.

"Vor sent you?" Emma asked warily.

"This one has served Vor since its hatching day. There is much that Vor wanted Eta to know which it could not share freely inside the base. This one has very little time left before The Shadows grow suspicious…The Stahl are what drove us from our home, Stahl are pure evil, and the Useptis have fallen along with many other species. The Useptis wish for a new home where the Useptis may rebuild safely, but Earth is as far as the Useptis can go without more fuel and repairs. Anton keeps Anton's hive buried deep within the sands and has forbade us from eating humans despite the tastiness. Anton says Eta is to be trusted because Eta will be needed when a new home is found... Anton asks Eta to spare the innocent Useptis, allowing those to join Anton's Hive, and continue to build the new vessel."

The Useptis glanced nervously around, bowed to Emma, and then the floor fell out from under her. She fell into the ocean as the ship shot off into the distance and disappeared into an incoming stormfront. Swimming back to the ship, Emma let Ruth pull her up onto the deck, and pushed her hood down.

"I couldn't destroy the ship, but was able to eliminate the threat inside." She panted quietly.

It wasn't a lie anymore more than it was a true deception, but it still felt icky. She just didn't know how to figure out who to trust as there seemed to be far too many secrets and she didn't know who to allow into her world. Sagging down onto the deck, she stared up at the sky, and forced her scales to retract back into her skin.

"They probably wanted this weapon." Ruth grumbled.

Ruth clutched the case to her chest like she thought it might vanish at any moment as she glanced around with great worry. Sighing to herself, Emma climbed back onto her feet, and shook the excess water from her suit drenching Ruth.

"Let's head for the portal." Emma agreed.

"Right." Ruth grumbled unhappily.

The basis of Useptis Language,

Most of the Useptis language is no verbal communication, but there are a few sounds of greeting that repeat throughout their interactions. These are their rough translations:

Useptis- Of us

Eta- Corrupted

Uta- Belongs to

Uti- Is Property

Ve- Clean

Var- Unclean

Vor- Outcast

Vi- Mate-Sibling-Parent-Etc

The- Great Warrior

Ti- Puny Warrior

Tea- Equal

Rapid Double Click- Danger

Rapid Triple Click- Retreat

Long Cluck- Attack

Long Double Cluck- Respect

Rapid Double click+Long Double Cluck Greetings or disrespect (Depends on if they bow or are rigid)

Rapid Triple Click+Long Cluck with bow- Let's Make Eggs

Rapid Triple Click+Long Cluck- Let's Us Duel

Long Cluck+Long Double Cluck- Death Duel

Shadow Log: Emma, Bristol Rhode Island, August 30, 1812

Standing in the burnt out rubble that had once been the school, Emma felt hollow, and a bit lost. Jacob had done a wonderful job of turning the place into charred nothingness, of wiping away anything that could point to its dark secrets, but that wasn't why Emma was here. When she had been bought and dumped into the school, she had suffered so much, and had allowed so much anger to build up that she had almost lost herself.

She had survived, become stronger, and thrived under the stress. Grace was dead, Anton was safe for the moment, and she was a better person because of the experience. But the cost had been far too high, Johnathan, Jacob, and countless girls had died to give her the ability to change The Shadows. Rubbing the tattoo on her shoulder, she let her knees buckle, and bowed her head. She didn't believe in a higher power, but she still wanted to honor the fallen.

"Forgive me for my failures, give me grace in the face of defeat, and the strength to admit when I am wrong." She prayed quietly.

Feeling foolish, she quickly stumbled back onto her feet, and dusted the ash off of her knees. She hadn't come to see the ruins of the school today, but she had been drawn to see what was left of it. Now that she had, she was oddly disappointed, and felt even more lost. Deciding to stop putting off the reason for her trip, she turned her back on the school, and ported over to her mother's grave.

The mystery illness had finally taken her life and ended her suffering leaving Emma as the last of her line. Ending years of pain and sadness in one final blow that left Emma feeling even more lost. She had already forgiven the woman for years of neglect and abuse for her own sanity, but to see her mother's grave was to remember her harsh upbringing. She'd been forced to be someone's pawn her whole life and now she just wanted to be free to experience life. But she knew she was needed to protect the innocent and that she wasn't the type to back away from her duty.

Emma watched the leaves dance across her mother's grave, feeling absolutely nothing as she tried to think of something nice to say. She was hollowed out, her emotional side carved from her soul, and cast into the depths of a carefully locked away trunk. It wasn't like she hated her mother or even wished her ill despite the horror of their relationship, but she did want an explanation.

Closing her eyes, Emma heard her daughter's distant laugh, she felt grief stab into her, and collapsed onto her knees. Choking back her pain, she struggled to accept that any mother could hate her child as much as hers had seemed to hate her. Grief was a funny thing that latched onto its victims, chewed them up from the inside, and spit them back out as unrecognizable empty shells.

Sighing forlornly, she lifted her combat knife to her throat, and without hesitation slit her throat. Blood poured forth, coating the warm stone with vibrant red, and softening the earth beneath her feet. In the blink of an eye her vision grew fuzzy, her knees buckled, and the heat of her body began to fade away.

*****

She woke up inside a one room rustic yet cozy cabin that was filled with a soft comforting warmth from the large fireplace. Two leather chairs sat upon a woven gray rug that while worn still had many years of use left. Sitting between the two chairs was a medium sized side table made from solid cherry wood with a steaming teapot and teacups resting on its knitted pink tablecloth.

"Self harm is most ill advised." Hubert said from the left most chair.

Emma took a seat opposite him, accepted the proffered tea, and stared into the fire. She felt so very lost, almost like a piece of driftwood that was just waiting for the current to give her a purpose.

"I don't want to die, but I don't know how to live." She finally sighed in resignation.

"Do you want to destroy The Shadows?" Hubert asked gently.

Emma gave him a curt nod, feeling a little hurt at him questioning her dedication, and then she glanced around. She had committed suicide over a non-existent life that she had dreamt up in a coma. Thinking about it now she felt ridiculous…

"They will never allow you to know your daughter even if I could find her." Hubert interjected gently.

Emma blinked in shock, hearing his words again and again until she finally managed to turn her head to face him, and mouth what several times.

"You thought yourself crazy? The night you lay with Johnathan bore fruit, but The Shadows needed you as a warrior, and so they kept you unconscious until they could ship her away." Hubert explained bluntly.

Emma wanted to launch onto her feet, to pace furiously around the room, or to maybe punch a hole in the wall. But her legs had become lead trapping her in her ridiculously comfortable chair, unable to even cry passed the lump expanding inside her ribcage.

"She's real?" Emma whispered hoarsely.

She felt a mixture of hope, hate, and desperation all mixed with anger as she thought of everything she had stolen from her. Her childhood, her adulthood, her motherhood, and now she was all alone with nothing but The Shadows left, just as they had intended.

"Her name is Emily and they gave her to a good family capable of protecting her and giving her an excellent life. However, they removed all other data on her from my database making it impossible for me to tell you more than that." Hubert said.

She sipped her tea, wishing she could simply go on a rampage, and destroy everything base by base. But she didn't have the resources needed for such a large campaign, nor did she have the allies as of yet to provide stability in The Shadows place. Those things took time and patience to build and Emma understood that she would never be allowed to have the life she dreamed of without a lot of sacrifices.

"I do want to destroy The Shadows, but more than that I want to save humanity and everything else from the Stahl." Emma finally said with a firmness that surprised even her.

"I do not expect you to trust me after all you have experienced, but I do expect a certain level of respect moving forward that comes along with a few simple rules." Hubert replied.

"Before I agree to anything I need two things from you. One, I need to know what you meant when you said it was too late for you? Were you simply referring to your death or was there something more that you are hiding?" She asked directly.

She had learned to listen to her gut above and beyond what anything else was saying. It had never been wrong, never misled her, and it was telling her that something was fishy.

"An astute observation, I am made of Stahl technology and am slowly becoming corrupted which is a design feature to keep their technology safe from their enemies. Anyone stupid enough to use their technology will eventually become a mindless drone hungering for salt and never finding satisfaction…unless you were somehow disconnected from their matrix at some point by a group of talented resistance fighters." Hubert bragged.

Emma knew a brag when she heard one, she could see how proud he was of managing to get her removed from the network, but it had cost her any memory she might have had of her daughter. Even knowing she wasn't fit to be a mother didn't make Emma fume any less at the decision being removed from her hands. Unzipping her suit, she let her fingers explore her smooth belly until they came upon an almost invisible ridge along her waist line, and she knew that was all that was left of the evidence she had brought life into the world. She shakily zipped her suit back up, dried her tears, and turned her attention back to Hubert.

"Salt destroys the Useptis cellular network when mixed with lemon, and sugar…doesn't that mean that would also hurt me?" She asked pointedly.

Accepting her attempt to change the topic Hubert replied, "You're part human, part Useptis, and part Stahl which means your weaknesses are unique to you. Our analysis shows a great sensitivity to cold, garlic, and silver, meaning you should be fine as long as you avoid those things."

"And if I don't?" Emma asked with dread.

"Severe pain, hives, exhaustion, itching, and death are the most severe side effects you'll experience. However, that is after long periods of exposure…as long as you're smart about where you go and how you fight you should be fine." Hubert chuckled.

Emma wasn't worried about pain, torture, or death, all she wanted was revenge against those who had stolen her life. Seeing as she couldn't technically die due to their upgrades that meant she was free to plan the downfall of her enemies from the background.

Suddenly, Emma realized that the rhythmic thumping was back, but this time it was louder…closer. Just beyond her reach as she looked around for its source. After listening to it for mere moments, the thumping intensified, becoming more frantic and rapid with each thump. Peering into the darkness swirling around her, Emma could make out the vague outline of a young woman attempting to fight off a man, and from the look of it she was failing. Emma tried to close the distance between them, to help her, or at least offer comfort as he ravaged her body, but she couldn't reach her.

"She was Grace's second born." Hubert said gently.

Emma turned her full attention away from the horror and focused it on Hubert.

"Who is she?" She asked with an intensity that scared even her.

"Go by the name Tamika, Ruth can help you find her…and find her you must if you want The Shadows to fall…"

✳✳✳✳✳

Emma startled awake, lying face first in the mud, covered in muck, and drenched in blood. Groaning from the stiffness built up in her muscles, she pulled herself slowly up out of the mud, and attempted to dust herself off. Seeing the task was utterly futile, she gave up on her appearance, and moved onto her next destination.

She slowly walked the old path from the cemetery to town enjoying the silence and peace of the brambles overgrowing everything. It was so strange to see the town after what felt like a few lifetimes worth of pain. The place was a lot smaller than she had originally thought and her former home was now a smoldering ruin that was still rank.

Standing where her closet had once been, she tried to remember something good about her family. Finding it even more difficult than at the grave, she tried to take a deep breath, and immediately started to choke on the fumes.

Grumbling to herself, she stumbled back to the outskirts of town, and plopped down on a boulder. Life was turning out to be very overrated and she no longer wished to keep fighting and discovering the world.

Emily was still out there somewhere having her best life which was for the best even if it hurt to not be able to be her mother. She knew she had no idea how to be one anyways and she would definitely screw it up. She was better suited to be a warrior anyways. Sighing happily, she let the cool breeze wipe away her emotions, and recenter her thoughts.

There was a war to fight, worlds to save, and people to help. Perhaps one day far in the future she would be worthy of getting to meet her daughter, but now it was about building a better world. After a long hot soak, everything would seem more clear, and she would be able to form a proper plan. Salt and the Useptis,

Salt when mixed with citric acid and sugar acts like a corrosive element that eats through even the toughest of Useptis flesh. It should be noted that the effects are limited on a living Useptis because of their advanced healing capabilities, but the mixture is perfect for destroying any evidence once the Useptis is dead.

1 cup plain sugar
4 cups sea salt or iodized
10 cups citric acid

Mix and coat a Useptis body and watch as it dissolves before your eyes, two to three treatments may be needed for complete destruction of the body.

Shadow Log: Ruth, Shadow Base, North Dakota, May 12, 1812

Ruth was pissed beyond anything she had previously thought possible as B barked at her like she was some kind of new recruit without any training. She had become a Shadow out of despair and now she was tired of living in that kind of headspace which meant making very real changes in her life. This had brought her to take the qualification test to become a full field agent with supervisory permissions. She had passed with only three questions wrong which meant The Shadows had to promote her despite clearly not wanting to which had led to the current dress down by B.

"I know I have been less than ideal with much of my fieldwork leading up to now, but that was because of Grace experimenting on me. I'm aware of my lack of appeal when it comes to advancement, however, I would appreciate some professional courtesy." She finally curtly cut him off after five minutes.

B looked completely and utterly shocked that she had dared to cut him off, but then a huge smile flooded his face. He shook his head with disbelief as he dug a folder from his desk and tossed it gently to Ruth.

"I have been watching you for some time, waiting for you to sprout, and it looks like you finally are! Look, I am no Grace and honestly The Shadows need new blood and new ideas if we are to stay relevant. So, I have capped the amount of service in the "Commander Chair" to ten years and have set a series of tasks for the successor to complete to earn the seat. I'm glad to see you'll be a contender when the time comes."

Ruth stared at him for longer than was appropriate before she looked down at her hands and smiled. B had been testing her and she had passed, yet she still felt empty inside, and she wasn't sure if she would ever be able to fill the hole in her soul. But if Grace and B were any indication of the morals needed to run The Shadows then she had enough to flood them with morality.

"Here's your next assignment, check in with the library for the book you'll need before you collect Emma." B said dismissively as he pushed another folder over to her and got lost in a report.

Ruth collected her orders from the desk, carefully stood up, and stretched her surprisingly sore muscles. If she wanted to make any real positive changes to The Shadows she needed to be at the top of her game and she needed allies capable of helping her. Realizing she was lingering passed her welcome, she gave him a quick bow, and hurried from the room.

Walking into the library Ruth was caught off guard by its sheer size, from the outside it could be no larger than ten feet wide, and no taller in height. Yet the moment you stepped inside you found yourself in a room with endless shelves that stretched up into infinity and disappeared into the distant shadows. A large comfortable looking living room with a large box bed sat in the center of the room taking up just enough room to provide comfort to the person living within. Mary sat in an oversized rocking chair calmly mending a pair of socks while mumbling to herself in what was definitely an angry tone.

"Split another seam?" Ruth asked gently.

She stepped into the room and was immediately scooped up into a bear hug with a needle carelessly sticking into her side. Laughing at Mary's enthusiasm, Ruth carefully pulled the needle out of her flesh, and returned the hug. It felt good to have a friend who refused to judge her or perhaps just wasn't capable of it, either way it made Ruth feel blessed.

"Heard, Grace." Mary said gently.

"Shush, Grace is the past, I am the future." Ruth replied dismissively.

"Ruth is sad." Mary mumbled unhappily.

"I'm tired of being used. Now, you have a book for me." Ruth replied.

She knew that Mary would never stop poking until she got what she wanted and so Ruth gave her what she wanted so she would be on her way.

"Table." Mary mumbled unhappily.

Ruth collected the book, put it in her satchel, and leaned against the recliner.

"I'm sorry, it's been a long day and I do value your friendship." She apologized.

"Just sit." Mary squealed happily.

She pushed Ruth into the recliner, hurried over to her fireplace, and collected two glasses of dark brown liquid from the cauldron hanging over the fire. She wrapped one mug in an old cloth, handed it to Ruth, and knelt at Ruth's feet.

"Drink." Mary ordered.

Before Ruth could protest, Mary pulled Ruth's boots off, and began to massage her feet. Moaning with pleasure, Ruth tried a sip of the liquid, and nearly choked realizing it was laced with cinder weed. Deciding she didn't care, Ruth leaned back into the chair, and relaxed.

Shadow Log: Emma, Shadow Base, North Dakota, May 13, 1812

Emma felt pain just like everyone else did, but she had learned how to internalize it better than most which was both a blessing and a curse. Watching her arm slowly regrowing, she let out a long sigh, and tried to think of something besides the dead Useptis or the missing one that Ruth had let slip past her. It hurt being constantly left out of the loop when she was supposed to be the frontline of defense.

"I'm done being your partner if you refuse to share important things with me." She finally said firmly.

Ruth looked at her with such disapproval and disappointment that it took all of Emma's willpower to avoid flinching, it was clear that Ruth hated her, and definitely didn't trust her which was fair considering that she didn't trust Ruth either. Groaning to herself, Ruth tossed her book to Emma, and turned back to watch the doorway. Emma caught the book, wishing she was able to punch her, and looked down at it.

"You're still high." Emma grumbled unhappily.

"What if I am?! There would still have been an escape! I wasn't watching the cells!" Ruth shouted angrily.

"I didn't say you were, but The Shadows have been experimenting on humans and Useptis both and you are fine with it…or you seem to be." Emma growled.

"I condemn torture or experimentation on any living creatures, but I also know we are at war." Ruth shot back.

"What's with this book?" Emma sighed.

She decided to just accept Ruth's stupidity for what it was and move on to the task at hand. She didn't have an inkling of an idea how a book on warcraft and spells was supposed to help with the task at hand or why the Useptis were trying to steal it.

"Look closer, it's written in Useptis." Ruth laughed.

Emma cracked the book open, carefully flipped to the first page of the first chapter, and stared at it in surprise. The letters were indeed Useptis mixed with what looked like French which made no sense considering that the Useptis weren't known for their written tongue. Looking over the text, she felt surprise fill her as she realized what she was holding, and quickly snapped the book shut.

"Do you know what this is?" She asked sharply.

"I know it's a book, but no human can read it. I figured you might be able to since you're no longer human." Ruth said with a divisive laugh.

"You're out of luck." Emma spat back.

She wasn't going to be the one to tell Ruth that someone or something had written down the code of death. If she could she would have happily burned the thing then and there, but she knew that would be a bit too suspicious. Instead, she had to be careful to make sure it never fell into the wrong hands as it would surely mean death to all of the universe if it did. Tucking the book away under her suit, she straightened out her hair, and prepared her weapon.

"How many miles of tunnels are down here?" She asked.

"A few thousand square miles is all we have managed to map out so far, but we think that they run the entire length of the continent." Ruth mumbled.

Emma hissed unhappily as she stared out into the darkness, she didn't want to chase an Useptis cub throughout the dark, uninhabited, cold tunnels anymore than she wanted Ruth to be backing her up, but that was the life she had been given. So, she pushed past Ruth and headed into the darkness following the sounds of the panicked running.

"I'm not stupid enough to think you can't read that book." Ruth growled.

She pulled Emma back into the well lit storage room, gave her the nastiest look possible, and began to tap her foot angrily. Emma looked around in search of answers only to find way too much canned meat and crackers, she knew that she wasn't going to tell Ruth the full truth, nor was she going to give her enough information to figure it out.

"It's the code to a weapon that we are currently unable to build without great technological advancement. That is all I am willing to say on the topic, now if it is okay with you I would like to hunt our prey." Emma said calmly.

Not lying sucked almost as much as feeling so lost when it came to having a true purpose in life. Yes, she wanted to beat The Shadows, save the world, and find her daughter, but she felt like she needed to do more. She stomped into the darkness of the unused tunnels, her eyes adjusting instantly to the lower levels of light as her scales erupted from her skin. Revealing the rows of razor sharp teeth, she bared her fangs, and sniffed the air in an attempt to determine which direction her prey had gone. The tell tale smells of lemon drifted into her nostrils from somewhere to her right, but what intrigued her was the strange rotted scent from her left which didn't smell like death. It was like something living was rotting from the inside out while somehow still not dying and even though she didn't know why the scent was intriguing she felt it was important. Deciding she didn't have to chase the Useptis just yet, she turned towards the new smell, and followed it through the winding tunnels with Ruth trailing a few steps behind her.

The tunnels were an endless maze of disgusting, strange, and intriguing surprises that seemingly appeared from nowhere. The uneven floor combined with the random rubble strewn across it made footing treacherous, but Emma was able to effortlessly navigate it thanks to her enhanced senses. Ruth on the other hand sounded like she was sounding the dinner bell with the number of times she tripped or stumbled over something.

"With the noise you're making, the Useptis will surely find us first." Emma grumbled.

"I don't have night vision like you." Ruth spat back.

Emma rolled her eyes, carefully guided Ruth over a small rift in the floor, and calmly resituated her grip on her staff. The smell was straight ahead hidden by no more than ten feet of shadow and Emma was not going to be ambushed. Entering into a small lab Emma came upon a surprisingly well lit exam table with a horse-like creatures strapped to it. Crinkling her nose, at the intensity of the smell, Emma cautiously approached the creature, and promptly vomited as she saw the second animal stitched to its belly. Choking on the odor, she took the animal's head off, ending its misery, and stumbled back out of the lab.

"The Shadows are going to be pissed that you ruined one of their experiments." Ruth commented.

"How can you not be affected by the smell? Or the cruelty of our employers?" Emma asked angrily.

"The Shadows do many questionable things that I don't understand, but I have faith they are doing what is right for the majority." Ruth sighed.

Emma stared at her partner wondering if Ruth really believed that or if she was simply replying on autopilot. Either way, it confirmed Emma's instincts to not trust her or let her get too far into her personal life…Not that she had one of those anyways. Flashing a cold smile, Emma pushed past Ruth, and headed off to find the missing Useptis. Time became untrackable as they slogged through the maze of tunnels, moving deeper into the unknown, and further from the base.

"How far can a single Useptis get?" Ruth grumbled under her breath as she stumbled into a pile of sharp rocks.

"An adult Useptis can cover sixty miles in five minutes while a youth can cover twice that…even when wounded they can move super fast." Emma replied.

She pulled Ruth back to her feet, setting her weapon down, and pulling out her canteen. Taking a long swig of whiskey, feeling the heat flood through her veins as it settled in her belly. Smiling happily, she offered the canteen to Ruth, who quickly waved it away with a scoff.

"I can get drunk unlike you." Ruth growled.

Emma laughed, "At least garlic isn't an issue for you."

"True enough," Ruth sighed.

They took a sharp left turn and were dumped into a large low ceilinged, rubble strewn room that felt unreasonably cold to the point Emma's scales ruffled up. Shivering, Emma readied herself for battle as she carefully scanned the room, and then without warning her vision went blurry. Her knees buckled as everything began to swirl around her and then the entire contents of her stomach exited her mouth and she passed out.

Thump, thump, thump…The pounding was so loud that it overwhelmed Emma's entire world encompassing every thought until Emma felt like it was going to tear her apart. Then in the distance a face appeared, filled with pain and torment mixed with excruciating sadness. All Emma wanted to do was race to her, wrap her in her arms, and pull her close. But reality was calling her back…

"Emma, Goddammit! Wake the hell up!" Ruth screamed in desperation.

Emma snapped awake just as the Useptis pinned Ruth to the wall, his drool dripped down to mix with the blood oozing out of a large wound Ruth had put in its shoulder. Tightening her grip on her staff, Emma scrambled to her feet, and headed for Ruth.

"Serve." Emma ordered sternly in Useptis.

The male turned to face Emma, his body quivering, and his tail raised for the kill. Emma remained still, her mind battling with him for control, and then it let out a long hiss before darting back into the farthest tunnel. Emma had won the battle and had sent him to find Anton's hive. Turning to Ruth, she smiled, and put her weapon away with an exhausted sigh.

"He won't be a problem, he's going off to die." Emma told her.

It was a half truth, but Emma was sure that it was the best. Anton didn't know that she knew of his secret home, but she was sure he would be thankful for the new recruit. Plus, she would need every soldier she could get in the coming days.

"You were supposed to kill it." Ruth growled.

Emma watched her wash the grim from the cut on her face before she said, "I did, he'll not be a problem moving forward. Now, we can continue to argue or we can return to base." Emma replied firmly.

"It does stink…Uh, do you know the way back?" Ruth asked suddenly alarmed

It looked like Ruth was about to panic as she realized she had no idea where they were or where the base was.

"I can lead us back without an issue." Emma replied.

She made her way back into the tunnel, hearing Ruth quickly scramble after her, making Emma grin mischievously, and suppress a chuckle. It was good to know that Ruth had no sense of direction and she felt proud of herself for avoiding needless death, but it was still going to be a long, well planned battle which would probably last a lifetime.

Main Useptis Classification:

Hive King: A Useptis that has a mixture of useful abilities that leads a hive looks similar to Anton

Builder: Extremely strong centaurs that are used to ensure their nests are suitable for eggs and then tend to the eggs.

Burrowers: Giant worms with thousands of venomous teeth that burrow through the ground to create nests.

Trackers: Lizard dogs that are excellent at tracking prey

Hunters: Lizard dogs that are excellent in tight corridor combat

Ambushers: Giant scorpion-like creatures that use invisibility to hunt their prey and shoot poisonous barbs.

Mind flayers: physically weak Useptis with hundreds of eyes that is great with mental attacks and creating temporary insanity.

Shadow Log: Ruth, North Dakota, May 23, 1812

Pain was something that was simply a part of life and was unavoidable at times. Sitting in the ice cold metal chair with her wrists strapped to the arms of the chair Ruth could feel a hurricane of emotions beginning to overwhelm her. This was

Emma's fault just like everything else that kept going wrong in her life and Ruth was tired of it. She could handle anything they threw at her, but she was ready for something better than chasing after Emma and having to clean up Emma's messes.

Just as her arms were about to go numb from the cold B walked into the room and took a seat across from her.

"Do you know why you are here?" He asked without any hint of emotion.

"No, I have been doing as I'm told." Ruth chattered back.

"I have been watching you for a long time and I think your potential is being wasted, especially since you're a glorified janitor right now. Tell me, are you cold?" B asked pointedly.

"Of course I am." Ruth growled.

"Not surprised, the record for the chair is six hours…and it's mine. I lost three toes, but was given a great position as a field manager for my trouble. You have been in here for seven and I must admit you have impressed me."

B popped the restraints loose, helped her up, and led her out of the room. The warmth that flooded her was such a relief despite the agony it spawned in her veins. Chattering, she happily accepted the blanket B threw over her shoulders, and the cup of hot coffee he thrust into her hands.

"Why freeze your officers?" She asked between sips.

"The Usesptis don't handle the cold well, they're essentially lizards and so we make sure to only promote those with hearty spirits. It is an antiquated test that I haven't gotten around to nixing yet." B explained with an indifferent shrug. Ruth stared at him with what had to be the most dumbfounded look he had ever seen before she remembered to hide what she was thinking. Shaking her head in disbelief, she wiggled her toes, and made sure all her extremities were in fact intact, and finished off her coffee. Without warning reality shifted around Ruth, her vision sharpening, and then a sense of her surroundings like nothing she had experienced before. It felt like she was suddenly able to see sound, to feel the energy of the people around her, and taste their scents in the air. Blinking furiously in an attempt to process the overwhelming amount of information now flooding her brain, Ruth stumbled back against the wall, and collapsed to the floor. B turned slowly to watch her as she writhed in agony upon the stone floor, each breath burning with new smells, and her head pounding like an out of tune organ. He walked her with what seemed to be exaggerated slowness, crouching down in front of her with a distorted laugh.

"It did take!" He crooned as it all came crashing in on her and everything went black.

She woke up in much better control of her new reality and despite a persistent headache she felt fine. Vaguely remembering the last hours before she fainted, she sat up sharply to find herself sitting on the rug in front of the fireplace in B's office. Groaning unhappily as she lumbered to her feet, she took a moment to orient herself with the room, and walked over to a chair and sat down abruptly.

"I remember the day I met MIO, she was so strange, like a distant memory mixed with a startling new reality." B said wistfully.

"Explain." Ruth managed to groan.

She found it surprisingly difficult to speak, it felt like something was holding her back. Then she felt a strange uncomfortable slithering in her head, almost like something slimy was shifting inside her skull. Ruth screamed in surprise, frantically stumbling back to her feet as she patted her head.

"Mitochondria intelligence Organism or MIO for short. It's an organism that feeds on fat and sugar and gives its host quite a few nice abilities." B sighed.

"There's a parasite in my brain?!" Ruth shouted angrily.

"MIO is more of a companion than a parasite, it makes you happier, enhances the senses, and provides a youth glow." B explained.

"That somehow doesn't make it any better." Ruth hissed.

"The truth is that the MIO needs cold to bond to its host, it attaches itself to your brainstem once your system goes into hyperthermia, and then using a numbing agent it expands thousands of tendrils into your brain. Don't worry, once it has time to fully adhere you won't feel a thing. It takes about a week to a month depending on how much you fight it. Oh, and you'll heal a bit faster as well that was why you fainted… It needed to finish healing the damage the cold did to your body and I was obviously lying about the reason for the cold treatment." B said.

He poured hot tea into two mugs, walked over, and handed it to her before calmly continuing, "You see we needed an edge in case Emma failed to turn out and MIO is that edge. We lose thirty percent less soldiers now that we started the program, of course, not all are strong enough to handle the bonding process. I must admit I am happy that you survived, I would have been sad to see you die."

Ruth shot him a nasty look, wishing she could just smack the shit out of him, but she knew her place. Taking a deep breath, she realized that this MIO must have been why certain Shadows had disappeared recently, and hadn't appeared on the battlefield casualty assessment list. Feeling the thing move again, she almost choked on her tea, and managed to barely avoid spilling it on her uniform.

"You could have told me beforehand." She whispered.

"MIO works best when you're not expecting it." B said simply.

"With all due respect, Sir, you are a giant asshole, and if I could, without repercussions, I would slap you. May I please have a few minutes alone to compose myself." She replied angrily as it moved again.

B nodded, patted her leg gently, and walked out of his office. Ruth started to cry, she had already survived so much with no real reward, and now this. It was bad enough to have a head full of tech, but a parasite as well was almost too much. She let herself cry for a few minutes before she wiped her eyes, pulled out her handkerchief, and blew her nose. What was done was done and there was no going back and so she should embrace the positives of the situation. She was now better suited for the field, once she had mastered her new world, and it had stopped moving. MIO meant she was even more likely to survive to make the changes to The Shadows she wanted to make.

Having accepted MIO she felt her body move a little easier as she carefully walked to the door and opened it.

"Forgive my outburst, I was being ungrateful." She apologized to B even though it hurt.

"Think of it as forgotten. Take a few weeks to recover, find your balance again, and then I'll put you back on active duty. And Ruth, I'm thinking a promotion is in order, and I am hoping you will accept a new position here at the base. That office over there, across from mine, will be yours if you accept." B replied happily.

Ruth stared first at him and then the office in stunned silence. She definitely hadn't seen this coming and had no reply formulated. So, she just nodded in reply while looking around like a startled goose. B laughed, gave her shoulder a firm squeeze, and headed back into his office. Snapping out of it, she rubbed her hands together, and did a little hype up jig.

"I appreciate the offer and gladly accept." She shouted, flinching at the volume of her voice.

"Enthusiasm will certainly carry you far." B laughed and closed the door in her face.

Shadow Log: Emma, Shadow Base, North Dakota, June 5, 1812

Emma felt like a caged bear, her very cells vibrating with tension as she paced the halls of the base. She hated not being able to hunt almost as much as she hated the thought of not being able to be free. She had taken up the habit of hissing angrily at any mortal that dared to approach her personal space and pushing Anton as far away from her mind as possible. This left her isolated with the strange thumping heartbeat and a sense of fear that she could almost taste. Yet she had no idea where it was coming from or why it kept happening, but the blackouts and weird visions remained. Today she was punching the air to death allowing her tension to flow into her fists as they blurred through the space with incredible speed. If anyone was foolish enough to enter her room, she would probably kill them without meaning to, but she needed some kind of exercise in her downtime or she would explode. There was something strange about worrying about something that was completely unknown to you and was even stranger when it ruffled your scales.

Then she was laying on the floor, staring up at Ruth, tasting blood, and bile. Growling, she scrambled up, realizing that Ruth was dropping crumbs all over her.

"What are you doing in my room and why are you eating pastry?" She questioned angrily.

"I buzzed and you didn't answer, so I came to check on you." Ruth mumbled between bites.

"Why?" Emma growled again.

"We have a mission." Ruth said, mysteriously materializing another pastry.

"Oh, good. Please tell me it isn't underground this time." Emma hissed.

"I could but it would be a lie…Also, I'm going to be helping from afar now. No more field work unless it's an emergency. I'm strictly your "handler" from now on. I'll supply you with your missions, help maintain your weapons, and will handle all of your on mission intelligence via a headset. Basically, I'm going to keep you away from the people and make sure your needs are met." Ruth said as they walked to Ruth's command center.

Emma surveyed the room, feeling impressed that they had managed to pull it together so quickly considering the large computer that took up most of the far wall. A single rolling chair sat in front of it with a desk facing the window overlooking the base. It was simple yet effective and Emma could see how well it suited Ruth.

"I like this." Emma said simply.

"Oh! Good, I thought you might fight me on this." Ruth said in surprise.

"I won't fight what can't be beaten." Emma replied.

"Okay, well, there was a crash or something that caused a massive radiation spike in the Amazon that needs to be explored and there is a Useptis infestation in the west tunnels. What would you like to do first?" Ruth asked as she fumbled with some paperwork.

"Tunnels." Emma sighed.

Emma accepted the pile of gear that Ruth unceremoniously dumped in her arms, hearing a strange ping that vibrated her shadow-band.

"The jump locations and four jumps have been uploaded to your band." Ruth explained.

Emma strapped on her weapon belt, put on her utility harness for tools, and a few other useful things. Chewing anxiously on her cheek, Emma took a deep breath, and activated the transporter. She blinked and was dunked in an underground icy spring that was just deep enough for her to touch the bottom if she dove down.

"Ruth!" Emma cursed angrily.

She quickly swam to the edge of the pool, shook the water from her scales, and looked around the large cavern. It was covered from floor to ceiling with large stalactites and stalagmites with water still actively dripping down from the ceiling. Pulling her hood up, she shivered from the chill breeze drifting through the tunnels, and took a deep cleansing breath.

"Oops, miscalculated a bit, sorry about that!" Ruth giggled.

"Right." Emma growled with disbelief.

"Keep to the right and you'll find the nest." Ruth said.

Emma shivered again as she sniffed at the air, moving into the tunnels, she drew her staff, and sighed. In some ways it was nice to see that Ruth hadn't changed much, but now she was wet and cold. Thankfully, she could smell the nest nearby, and it didn't take long for her to be hip deep in dozens of large red and green eggs. Moving as quickly as she could while remaining completely silent, she set the charge in the center of the nest, and then she was knocked on her ass by a giant Useptis hemorrhaging a thick green liquid that smelled like death. Hissing the blood from her teeth, she leapt back onto her feet just barely avoiding ooze hitting her face. Swinging her staff in a wide arch, she miscalculated slightly, and set off the gas. Choking on the fumes, she stabbed the blade of her staff into the neck of the Useptis, and leapt clear enough to activate her teleporter.

Her momentum carried her crashing into a giant jungle tree that clearly held a grudge with how tightly it was now holding her. Hissing in pain, she pried herself free from the bark, and tumbled onto the forest floor.

"Are you alright? There's a big spike in your vitals and signs of premature detonation." Ruth said suddenly.

"That's what he said." Emma groaned.

Hearing the strange sounds of scribbling and scrambling of hard claws on soft soil and hard vines, Emma quickly rolled onto her feet, and upon realizing her staff hadn't come with her she drew her short sword and dagger. Rolling onto her feet, she dodged a weird black and orange spiked barb that dripped with green poison, and eyed her surroundings nervously. Nothing but trees, scrambling, and the whistling of the barbs flying through the air. Closing her eyes, she focused on her hearing, and with one sudden explosive burst she charged forward, running her dagger along the thing's side.

The creature flickered into existence as its shield failed and it crashed into the nearest tree. It vaulted onto its feet, shrieking with an unholy scream from the depths of hell, it flashed back invisible. Cursing, Emma darted up the nearest tree, and eyed the forest floor.

"A little help." She hissed quietly.

"I lose visual for a few minutes after every jump. What does the creature look like?" Ruth asked unhelpfully.

"I need a hammer." Emma replied.

It was essentially a giant scorpion with invisibility and bugs were meant to be smashed. Surveying her surroundings, she found a large dead branch ready to snap off of a tree, and leapt over to it. Hissing with effort, she snapped it off, and dropped back onto the ground with her newfound weapon.

As anticipated the creature charged her, throwing barbs that Emma batted quickly away, and when it was close enough she batted it into a nearby tree.

She angrily smashed it until it was a puddle of body parts, and gooped. Looking down at her shoulder, she realized one barb had broken through her scales, and was leaking poison into her body. Screaming as fire lit up her blood, she ripped it from her flesh, and regurgitated the poison.

"Nevermind." She hissed unhappily.

"Sorry." Ruth mumbled, clearly eating.

"If your snacks are so important then perhaps you shouldn't be my handler!" Emma screamed.

Emma ripped her headset off, stuffed it into her harness, and let out a howl of anger. Scanning the area, she sniffed for more prey, and relaxed when she found she was alone.

"Help me…" A woman's voice echoed through the trees. Emma shook her head in confusion, she knew she was hearing things, but she didn't feel crazy. Then again, she wasn't sure what crazy felt like. Maybe she should take the time needed to get to the bottom of the mystery while she was out in nature, could even use the excuse of needing to investigate the area since that was her plan anyway.

After doing a quick once over of the area, Emma sat down in the shade of an ancient tree, and closed her eyes. Slowly over the course of hours she relaxed until nothing but that thumping remained on her mind. Then her eyes erupted in silver fire, her body went limp, and everything shifted as her mind drained through a tunnel made of light.

*****

She woke to find herself not only in a freezing little cage, but in an entirely different body. She tried to hiss and realized she was wearing an iron muzzle. Eyeing her surroundings suspiciously, she had flashbacks to her closet, and her mother. Whimpering with pain, she forced her scales to erupt, and was surprised to see that it worked. They were red, but otherwise everything else was the same, minus the tail. Grabbing the muzzle with her new claws she ripped it in two, ignoring the panicked screams now emerging from her captors she slammed her shoulder into the gate. It bowed outward with a horrible shriek, making three heavily armed absolutely terrified men to appear in the room. Laughing hungrily, she slammed into the gate again, and again until it blew off of its hinges and exploded into the room killing the men.

Laughing harder, she quickly stole as much gear as she could, and took the bits of clothes that would fit her alright. Stuffing it all into a bag with a week's worth of rations, she grabbed a sword and sheath, and strapped it to her waist. Using her claws, she quickly climbed up the wall of the cave, and out a small hole in the ceiling. Sniffing at the air, she determined the best direction to run, and bolted off on all fours. She ran with such speed that she put a dozen or so miles between her and the cave in a matter of minutes. Shivering from the cold of this snow covered hell, she quickly took down a deer, and dragged it into the nearest cave. A huge bear reared up, letting out a roar that shook her world, and then started to charge.

"Offering." She whispered.

She quickly bowed before the bear as she threw the deer at its feet.

"Stay. Protect." Emma added gently.

"Stay. Protect." The bear mimed.

She watched it take the food away to eat before she allowed her scales to slip back into her skin. Feeling herself slipping, she pulled out a small leather journal that she had stolen, and quickly wrote down a message.

Bear friend, safe to rest, I'm Emma.

She felt a sharp almost painful tug that yanked her unceremoniously back into her body.

Shadow Log: Emma, Shadow Base, North Dakota, June 6, 1812

Emma woke, immediately slammed her head into the underside of her bed, and started cursing as she rolled out from under it. Groaning at the migraine spreading through her head, she stumbled to her feet, and chugged her canteen dry.

"You're back!" Hubert chirped excitedly into her head.

"Not so loud." She groaned.

"Where were you? What happened? How did it happen?" Hubert asked more quietly.

"I don't know, but I was inside someone else." Emma mumbled.

"Impossible without a genetic link and similar life experiences to you which is a statistical improbability." Hubert huffed.

"Improbable or not that is what happened. I need to find her, she's going to need more help, and I'd prefer to avoid the next headache." She hissed.

"I will ask my contacts for information. In the meantime, I need a message delivered." Hubert sighed.

"Who to and what is it?"

"His name is Stuart, he's the engineer responsible for maintaining my mainframe. We had an argument and now he won't listen to me. I need

you to tell him to check my lower left electrical tie in. He'll understand." Hubert said.

She felt him leave her head which was a relief in and of itself, but now she had to figure out how she had ended up back in her room. On top of that she had to help Hubert solve his engineering problems and she probably also needed to make up with Ruth. Deciding none of it was urgent enough to be done immediately, she collapsed onto her bed, and went back to sleep.

Emma woke from her nap feeling sick to her stomach, immediately raced to the sink, and threw up the contents of her stomach which reeked of garlic. Watching the walls shift, shimmer, and shudder she couldn't help but wonder what other surprises were in store for her. Getting her bearings on the weird garlic high, she walked over to the door, and opened it up. Only to be met by the relentless ten eyed stare of Anton as he turned to glare at her. Giving him a cold smile, she walked over to the mini fridge, and pulled out a snack.

"Who's Tamika?" Anton asked pointedly.

So, her name was Tamika, it was nice to get confirmation. Such a pretty and exotic yet simple name, and here she was blushing over a girl she had never met. It was like someone had ripped out a piece of her soul, placed it into Tamika, and was letting the light in, clearing the cobwebs, and repairing the damage in Emma's soul. She didn't understand how she could care so much for a stranger, but she did and…

"A mind meld like that can only happen in a shivara." Anton hissed unhappily.

"Alright, care to explain, since that word isn't registering." Emma sighed.

"The closest term you have would be soul marriage, you can only enter one if you are related or have the same life experiences, or are in love. It makes no sense." Anton grumbled.

"I'm human and Stahl as well, who knows how that changes things. I need to find her." Emma said dismissively.

She closed her eyes, trying to remember as much about Tamika's world as she could, but could only recall cold, snow, and trees mixed with frozen rocks. Letting out a frustrated sigh, she set her food down, and punched the nearest wall. Watching her hand heal, she wanted to cry as everything crashed in, and she realized how alone she felt.

"Anton understands the frustration, Anton went stir crazy in the ship. Many are insane by the time they arrive on Earth if the cryo breaks…which often happens." Anton sighed unhappily.

Emma eyed him, it was easy to forget he was suffering as well, and she needed to be kind to him for no other reason than it was the right thing to do.

"Father, tell me why do you risk the journey?" Emma asked gently.

Anton blinked in surprise, did an uncomfortable little standing trot, and turned away.

"The Stahl came in the night and by morning Useptis burned. Useptis was no more and Earth was our only hope of survival." Anton muttered.

"Sounds horrible. Is that why you started a hive here on Earth? As a safe haven for those who survive and are sane?" Emma asked, making sure to use mental speech to protect Anton.

"Daughter, is not threatening?" Anton asked nervously.

His tail flicked as his posture changed and Emma knew he'd die before he let his hive come to harm. Emma wanted to fight, to prove her worth, but this was not the time. Bowing her head respectfully, she lowered her heart rate, and let out a friendly purr. After a few long moments Anton relaxed, lowering his head in return, and matched her purr.

"Shall we make a deal, here and now? One day I will set you free and with your help I will destroy The Shadows and in exchange you will leave Earth and take your hive to a new world." Emma offered softly.

Anton eyed her cautiously as he weighed out his options, giving him his space Emma returned to snacking.

"Anton agrees." Anton replied firmly.

"Agreed. Now can we figure out how to find Tamika?" Emma asked with far too much emotion.

"Anton already found Tamika using…No matter, but first Emma must attend to matters here. Talk to Ruth and help Ruth adjust, deliver Hubert's message, and get the garlic out of Emma's system. Only then will Anton help Emma get Tamika to safety." Anton replied dismissively.

Emma wanted to rip his throat out, but instead she put her snack away, and headed for Ruth's office. To her surprise the moment she stepped outside the door, she almost collided with Ruth who had been leaning against it. Growing unhappily, Emma pushed Ruth back against the wall, and let out a small hiss as she dented the wall next to Ruth's head with her fist.

"I was eavesdropping more as a way to segway into a conversation!" Ruth yelped in a panic.

"I was coming to apologize to you." Emma grumbled.

She dropped Ruth back onto her feet, dusted her off, and retreated quickly from her personal space. She still needed Ruth even if she was a nosey cunt.

"Well good, we have a common goal. I don't think either of us will ever like the other and we can agree that one of us will probably die by the other's hand. That's fine with me as long as you can agree to work with me and listen to me when I speak. Oh, and I won't eat when on a mission." Ruth offered nervously.

"Agreed, the past is the past. Do you know Stuart? He is an engineer here at the base and I don't know anything else." Emma admitted as meekly as she could manage.

"Every female on base knows Stuart, even you, he's the creepy, old, bald guy that hangs out in the corner watching you eat and muttering to himself." Ruth shuddered.

"He's not talking to himself…never mind it would take too long to explain. Um, you control Mio through your food, the more indulge in what it wants the more control it has." Emma thanked Ruth.

She turned quickly, marched away to avoid any further conversation, and snuck into the bathroom. Panting uncomfortably, she clutched her belly, and let out an agonized hiss. It felt like someone had jabbed a knife into her kidneys, but Emma knew it was Tamika who was in danger. She closed her eyes, took a deep breath, and wiped away her tears. As much as she wanted Tamika safely by her side, protected, and cared for Emma wasn't safe either. The Shadows were as treacherous as the wilds if not more so. Feeling the pain fade, she washed her face, and went in search of Stuart.

She found him sitting at a small table in the darkest corner of the cafeteria playing chess with himself as he studied the people around him. Smiling to herself, she grabbed an apple from the fruit counter, and walked over to him.

"Checkmate in three." She offered quietly.

She pointed to the black night as she dragged a chair over and sat opposite him. Staurt looked annoyed as he sipped his coffee and glared at the board.

"Who taught you to play?" He finally sighed reluctantly.

"Theodore, he wanted me to learn strategy and patience because I have always been a bit too headstrong." Emma chuckled.

"I knew him before the accident, back when he was happy, and I'm pretty sure you're the reason he was so successful. So tell me, Emma, what is it you want from me? Did Hubert finally decide to send someone on his behalf?" Stuart asked as he reset the board.

"Astute observation, he wants you to check the lower left electrical tie in for him." Emma replied.

"The fool thinks he can con me." Stuart chuckled.

"Perhaps, but have you considered the thought that he isn't conning you?" Emma asked gently.

Stuart eyed her unhappily for what felt like far too long before he let out a gigantic sigh and stumbled up to his feet.

"Well, come along." He muttered.

Grinning, Emma leapt to her feet, and followed him into the bowels of the base. Emma felt her eyes quickly adjust as they made their way through the base's maintenance tunnels, but she had no idea how Stuart was managing to navigate the maze so effortlessly. Yet he led her directly to a well lit, tidy, small apartment filled to the brim with tools, wires, and parts. Looking around, Emma could barely take in the sheer amount of hoarded stuff, and was quite surprised anyone would choose to live this way.

"Panel is under the bed." Stuart said.

Emma looked where he was pointing, leapt over several crates of stuff, and landed next to it. Snarling, she flipped the mattress up, and tossed it out of the way. Stuart scurried up, quickly moved a couple of crates, and began unscrewing a silver panel.

"Hubert keeps saying that he is sick and that is why I keep getting error codes, but that doesn't make any sense. How does a dead guy in a mainframe get sick?" Stewart grumbled suspiciously.

He had barely popped the panel off before Emma was hauling him backwards away from the cavity which was filled with black, goopy webs that stank of rot and death. Emma felt herself growl almost inaudibly as the hackles on her neck snapped to attention. Now things made a lot more sense despite everything being more confusing.

"Hubert, what is the Black Death doing in your system?" She hissed silently.

"The Stahl created it as a safeguard to protect their technology from being used against them. Anyone stupid enough to tamper with it becomes infected and dies. I told Grace, but she didn't listen and so I did my best to isolate the infection. I gave my life to find this horror and one day I will fail to keep it contained again..." Hubert replied quietly.

"Again?" Emma asked hesitantly.

"It happened before The Shadows were born when there was no one around to stop it ... The fatalities were beyond unacceptable and the AI

had no desire to stop it. I do and I have contained it for the moment, but the day will come when I will fail."

Realizing that she was neglecting Stuart, Emma turned her attention back to him, "Did you get that?"

"Aye, thanks for getting me clear. What do we do now? Can't just leave a potentially world ending plague oozing through the mainframe." Stuart muttered.

"I have no idea, but for now put the panel back on… Very carefully." Emma replied.

Once the plague hole was properly covered again Emma sagged down onto a large pile of papers which was surprisingly comfortable for a pile of trash. She couldn't find it in her to try and sort this new mess out. She had so much she already had to do and this was supposed to be an easy job.

"Hubert has to have a plan." She finally replied.

"I have told Stuart what he needs to do for me." Hubert spat loudly into her mind, making her jump.

"I don't know if your plan is going to work, but I'll get started on it. Thank you, Emma, I would have ignored this until it was too late." Stuart said softly.

"So, you don't need me?" Emma asked, feeling mildly giddy at the thought of being free of this problem.

"No, I work better alone." Stuart sighed.

Emma scrambled up onto her feet, darted out into the hall, and froze as she felt a deep anger flash through her scales. She smiled knowing Tamika was starting to get a handle on her new reality and was starting to get angry that she was being hunted. She would survive a lot longer that way and would probably learn more as she fought back.

Shadow Log: Emma, Shadow Base, North Dakota, June 7, 1812

Emma had all but forgotten about Theodore in the chaos that had consumed her life, but now he was weighing heavily on her mind. The last time she had seen him she had been so angry that she hadn't been able to forgive him for submitting to Grace. Now she wanted to put the past to the rest and move forward with her plans for the future. The problem was no one knew where he was or what had happened to him. Most thought he was dead, but Emma was sure he wasn't.

The only person who had given her anything remotely useful was Ruth, who had sent Emma to find Mark. A man who reminded Emma of Theodore in more ways than one including his stubbornness. It had already been an hour long argument trying to get him to break and he was starting to get on her nerves.

"I am about to put my fist through your skull." Emma grumbled.

"I am simply following orders the same as you. Theodore doesn't want visitors and that includes you." Mark replied steadfastly.

Deciding to take a page from Grace's book, Emma closed in on him, and pressed her knife to his throat. Smiling coldly, she grabbed his wrist, and twisted it so she could view his shadow-band. Looking through his previous port locations, she found his most visited, and activated the band. They ported in a flash of light appearing in a frozen waste land made of ice. Shivering unhappily, Emma quickly darted into the only building close by and found herself standing in a poorly lit yet very warm cabin. Mark staggered in after her looking beyond pissed that she had dared to use him like that.

"Emma? Mark, what did you do?" Theodore croaked from the darkness of the back corner.

"She ambushed me, I'm sorry Father." Mark whispered uncomfortably.

"No, no, don't blame yourself. Emma has always had a mind of her own. Leave us to speak for a moment please." Theodore gasped.

Giving her a nasty look, Mark vanished, leaving Emma alone with Theodore and the crackling fire. She took a step towards Theodore as her eyes became accustomed to the shifting light. Seeing what he had become she stumbled backwards and practically fell on her butt. All that was left of the man who she had once known was a desiccated, black, encrusted skeleton.

"I don't understand." She gasped.

"Oh, Little Moon, you are the hope of the universe. I couldn't let the Black Death take you, I choose this." Theodore gasped.

It sounded like every word hurt him as he shuffled unhappily away from her, putting as much distance as he could between them.

"Wait? Hubert mentioned he separated me from the matrix, but I still don't fully understand what is happening." Emma replied.

"The Death comes from the Stahl and is meant to destroy everything it touches, but it can be transferred out of a living being as long as it has a willing vessel to hold it. You and Tamika both were dying and I had no choice." Theodore muttered.

"I have no words." Emma whispered.

She felt so loved seeing how much the man had given her without her ever knowing. He had wanted to fade into history, his sacrifice forgotten by all, and lost to the world. Emma felt a searing anger at how much he had started to fade because he had pulled the darkness from her.

"Words are not needed here, I choose The Shadows, choose to leave my children, and live in service to a cause I believed in. You have become that cause and I am honored to be of service one last time. My son and daughter followed me into The Shadows and I would appreciate you taking care of them when I'm gone." Theodore coughed.

"I will make your sacrifice worthwhile I promise and I promise I will do right by your children."

"Mark is just like his father, a warrior, but my daughter Arabella fights with knowledge and love. I fear for her safety when she is so soft and loving. I have run out of time, but you should know I have always considered you one of my children and always loved you." Theodore said.

She watched him dart down into the basement leaving her alone. Suddenly Mark grabbed her shoulders and ported her back to base.

"If you ever try that again, I'll run my dagger through your gut." Mark warned before vanishing once more.

Assuming Arabella was in the library, Emma decided it was time to visit Mary, and formulate a plan.

She had known that Mary would miss her and probably worry about her, but what she hadn't expected was the giant hug she received the instant that she entered the library. It made it impossible to not smile and in a split second made everything less horrible. Hugging her back, Emma let loose a happy little giggle before she carefully separated herself from Mary's embrace.

"I missed you too." Emma chuckled.

Taking a closer look at Mary's appearance made Emma instantly sober once more. The scars of battle had left their mark all over her leaving behind a strange hardness that Emma didn't recognise. She wanted to cry realizing how badly she had failed her friend.

"Stop. Happy Mary. BOOKS!!!!!!!!!!!!!!" Mary shouted happily. A short, young, brunette stuck her head out of the nearby stacks and quickly shushed them before disappearing back into the shelves.

"Arabella does not like noise." Mary mumbled apologetically.

"I see that. I'm also glad that you're happy here among the books, but I worry for your safety." Emma replied as lightly as she could.

"Have hammer." Mary said dismissively.

"Okay, okay, I'll stop worrying about you." Emma chuckled.

Mary suddenly grew serious and looked around with worry, "Arabella good. Friend, kind. But, Emma know Tamika at base." She whispered urgently.

"What?! Where?" Emma hissed in surprise.

"North lab. About Anton's. Mark brought Tamika. Hurt badly he healed." Mary tried to explain.

Emma's heart nearly jumped out of her chest as it began to beat with worry that soon turned to anger. She had wanted to keep Tamika away from her life here at the base as foolish as that hope was. Now it was squashed and Emma feared what The Shadows might do to her once they figured out the truth.

"Thank you." She managed to finally whisper past the lump forming in her throat.

"Go, save." Mary said gently.

Emma nodded, the only way to protect Tamika now was going to be by making The Shadows fear touching her. Emma already understood that this task would require a rampage and so she let her rage surface.

Shadow Log: Tamika, Shadow Base, North Dakota, June 7, 1812

Tamika woke to the worst headache combined with the taste of vomit mixed with metal and blood. She tried to roll onto her knees only to find herself strapped tightly to the freezing metal table pressed with angry fire against her scales. She let out a deafening screech of horror amplified by rage as she slammed her full might against her restraints. She could hear people scrambling around in a complete panic, screaming at each other in what sounded like foreign barking as they desperately tried to keep her restrained.

Then like an angel of death Emma appeared, throwing the people around like they were dolls as she tore the room to shreds. Emma's angry hissing awakened a strange yearning in her soul and gave her the extra little bit of strength she needed to break free. Shivering from the chill of the room, her scales rolled to the surface, and began to vibrate. Emma finally finished her rampage, turned towards her, and tossed her a blanket. Once she had the blanket pulled tightly around her shoulders, she carefully climbed off of the table, and stretched.

"Agent Five!" B shouted angrily as he stomped into the room.

"You continue to mettle in things you don't understand and one day it will destroy us all." Emma spat.

Before Tamika could open her mouth, she found herself bundled up, and hustled into a small nicely toasty bedroom. The door slid shut behind them causing Emma to start to relax slightly and lower her own scales. Tamika followed suit, feeling confused, and more than a little lost which was better than feeling cold and alone, but not by much.

"You're even more beautiful in person." Emma purred gently.

Tamika blushed, pushed her hair out of her eyes, and quickly bowed her head nervously to hide the smile suddenly creeping up her lips. Her pains all but forgotten, she let out a tired little sigh, and forced herself to breathe.

"You are more beautiful through my own eyes." She stuttered, unable to stop a large yawn from interrupting her. Emma laughed like the music of waterfalls filling the room with the heat of her soul as she dropped down onto the edge of the bed.

"Cuddle?" Emma asked gently.

Watching Emma pat the bed, she had to control herself to keep from just tackling Emma to the bed, and then she decided to just let go. So, she leapt up onto Emma's lap, grabbed her face, and kissed her as hard as she could without causing injury. Emma leaned into it, wrapping her in her arms, and throwing her onto the bed. Her scales ruffled up excitedly to match Emma's as they fiercely made love until the cot gave out an angry groan and collapsed to the floor. Feeling strangely refreshed despite the marathon she had just had, she stretched out with Emma on the remains of the bed, and just let herself laugh herself to sleep with her new best friend.

Shadow Log: Emma, Shadow Base, North Dakota, June 8, 1812

The moment Emma took a step out of her room she was face to face with an angry looking Anton. Glancing around the room she could see that they had already cleaned up the mess she made. Sighing in resignation at what she was sure was coming, she let the door slide closed, and gave Anton a bow.

"I told The Shadows that you were in a mating rage and should not be held responsible for your temporary insanity." Anton said into her mind.

"Why? What do you want this time?" Emma replied.

She was suspicious of everyone and everything now that she had Tamika to protect. She wasn't sure of what was happening between them, but she did love the girl. Somehow she was all tangled up inside of not only her own memories but those of Tamika's as well and until she untangled everything she didn't trust anyone.

"Because it is the truth. Emma is daughter, Emma protected Anton, and Anton's hive. Anton returns the favor hoping to help." Anton said, sounding offended.

Emma chuckled, let herself relax, and slid to the floor. Smiling to herself, she took a deep breath, and closed her eyes.

"I feel more lost than ever." She whispered.

"Understandable, Emma has suffered more than any child should have to suffer. Anton is partially to blame for that and wishes to make amends." Anton replied softly.

"Then tell me the truth, please. What are the Useptis? The Stahl? I can access the facts but they are jumbled and confusing. I want my father to be honest with me so that I can figure out my own future." Emma whispered.

Anton stared at her for a long time before he shook his head in disbelief and stomped the ground with his front left hoof. *"What you are asking for are closely guarded secrets few alive know because of the impact this information could have on the universe. This one trusts Emma so Anton will share, but you must promise to tell no one except for Tamika. I know you share a mind with Tamika and it is impossible to keep secrets with one's soulmate."* Anton finally replied.

Emma could feel how serious he was about his warning and she couldn't help the pit growing in her gut. Shaking her head, she smiled again, letting her fangs show, and calmly nodded in affirmation.

"I swear your words stay with me until the information can be used to stop whatever threat you are afraid of." Emma offered.

Anton nodded, *"This one can live with this. The truth is complex so get comfortable and listen closely."*

"I'm listening," Emma replied quietly.

"About a thousand years ago The Stahl came to our universe again to eradicate all intelligent life, a task that they have failed at many times. So, they took their knowledge and created a race dedicated to war and death. They called it Eta and forced them to kill again and again until they mutated and gained intelligence of their own. They rebelled, forcing the Stahl to flee back to their home, but the war destroyed the homeworld. We choose the name Useptis after the world that birthed us and showed us the truth of life. This one led the charge, pushed them back, and fought his own egg brothers for freedom. This is why Anton is an exile, this is why Anton must hide his hive on Earth. Many are still loyal to the masters and wish to return to the masters by killing this one's hive." Anton said solemnly.

Emma stared at the wall and tried to sort out the implications of what he had just told her.

"Things make a lot more sense now. I'm sorry you have had to go through this trauma." She whispered in mental speak.

"Anton fought the Stahl for Anton's hive so the Useptis would be free and the Stahl destroyed Useptis for the rebellion. It was punishment for failing the Stahl… for turning on our creators."
"Can I ask if you have any other family coming to take your head or is it just other hives?" Emma asked as gently as she could.
"Of course! The Useptis can lay up to a hundred and twelve eggs each! The Useptis are capable of laying eggs whenever we choose no mate needed. This one was of a litter of ninety seven, fifteen of which still breathe besides Anton. Many stood with Anton against the Stahl and died with honor."
Emma hadn't known that the Useptis could cry but that was definitely what he was doing now. The tears trailed out of each of his eyes slowly leaving lines in his fur marking him with his pain. Before she could stop herself, she surged forward, and gave him a large hug. Anton flinched in surprise before he wrapped his arms around her and allowed her to hold him as best she could.
"Anotn has never been hugged. It is nice." Anton purred.
"I'll try to do it more often." Emma promised.
She gently broke contact, gave one of his hands a squeeze, and sat down by the fridge.
"We'll fight together to make sure the Stahl pay for their treachery, but first we bring down The Shadows." She added.
"Anton will stand with Emma, Emma is Anton's hiveling." Anton promised.
"I know." Emma whispered softly.
She grabbed a snack and returned to her room. Anton clearly needed time to compose himself and Emma needed the time to process.

Shadow Log: Tamika, Shadow Base, North Dakota, June 8, 1812

Tamika woke up in a comfy, little, soft nest made of blankets and the remains of the cot and found it hard to remember the last time she felt so safe and happy, but she couldn't do it

Smiling with her fangs on display, she scrambled up onto her feet, and looked around for Emma.

"Here Darling." Emma cooed softly.

Tamika turned around to find Emma sitting at a small desk, eating toast, and journaling. Tamika growled as she remembered that she hadn't eaten in at least a day as she eyed the food hungrily.

"There's a feast just outside the door if you want food. Don't worry Anton and the rest have agreed to give us some space, so that we can talk." Emma chuckled.

After Tamika had returned to her nest with a giant plate of overflowing goodies, she found a comfortable spot, and began to chow down.

"Where are we?" She managed to ask between bites.

"The North American Shadow Base. The Shadows are the ones who are responsible for creating us and all the pain you've suffered, but they are also our allies for now." Emma explained.

Tamika already had a good idea of who The Shadows were, but she hadn't realized they had an underground lair like this. Her last visit had been inside of Emma and had just been confusing.

"Why not just kill them all?" Tamika asked as she choked on a sweet roll.

"One day they will fall, but our duty is to serve the greater good, to protect the innocent, and to ensure all alien threats are swiftly dealt with." Emma replied gently.

"When we can safely dismantle The Shadows from within then will be a day of reckoning, I promise." Emma whispered mentally.

Tamika swallowed the last of her food, leaned back, and sighed contentedly. She didn't understand when or how The Shadows had grabbed her nor what their plans were, but she felt safe with Emma; and that was enough for now.

PART TWO

A Time to Bond

Shadow Log: Emma, North Carolina, June 11, 1814

Emma watched as an arrow went buzzing past her head narrowly avoiding her face by inches. If she hadn't heard the twang of the string, she would have been dead again, and Tamika would be left out here without a partner. Hissing in annoyance, she blurred forward into the treeline, and smashed into the little pudgy man who had dared to shoot at her. Sniffing him as she pinned him to a tree she found that his scent was off. He smelled like he was dead, rotting from the inside out, yet there was a hint of citrus to it as well.

"Who are you?" She hissed.

He was a fearless bastard that much she was certain of since she couldn't taste anything in the air except for loathing and contempt despite her scales being fully erupted. Looking into his eyes, she was surprised to see how clouded they were like little milky disks. Before she could stop him, he threw her back with surprising strength, and climbed on top of her pinning her to the ground.

"Eta'Var'Uti." He hissed just before his head exploded into a fine red mist.

Pushing his corpse away, Emma scrambled up onto her feet, and tried to understand what she had just heard.

"Thanks, T." She thought quietly.

Glancing up at the far ridge she could just barely make out Tamika's silhouette against the shrubby. The girl had a knack for long range warfare and a very steady hand both of which had led The Shadows to making her into a sniper. Before she had seen the weapon they gave Tamika she wouldn't have believed such a thing was possible, but then again The Shadows were years ahead of everyone else.

"No problem. Was he speaking Useptis?" Tamika asked in reply.

"Yes, but I don't know if he was talking about me or himself. There was something seriously wrong with him."

Emma rolled the body over, quickly riffled through his clothes, and tried to sort out what she was missing. In the process his sleeve slipped up his arm to reveal scales with black veins running through them. Cursing unhappily, Emma recoiled, and quickly wiped her hands off on her pants hoping that she hadn't caught whatever he had. While she was still very much confused by what her eyes were seeing, she knew the Black Death when she saw it, and she had no desire to see if she was immune to it thanks to her Useptis DNA.

"Return to base and fetch a quarantine team. I'm already exposed and we need answers quickly." She ordered silently.

"Be careful." Tamika whispered back.

Seeing Tamika vanish in a puff of light, Emma turned her attention to the wind, and began the task of tracking the man back to his origins. It didn't take long before the trees thinned out again to reveal a picturesque little village filled with complete silence. There was something very unsettling about the vibe of the place almost like it was trapped in time or maybe just devoid of life. Drawing her weapon, she slowly approached the first building, and peeked inside. From the looks of it the inhabitants had fled in a hurry, leaving everything behind despite having been in the middle of chores. Glancing around nervously, she was startled to see Useptis hoof tracks everywhere, but no other signs of what might have happened. No blood, no crash site, no bodies, nothing, but emptiness.

Shivering unhappily, she bit her lip, and decided that she had no choice but to try and figure this mystery out. Keeping as quiet as she could, carefully snuck deeper into the village checking each empty home and shop for clues as she went, but finding nothing of interest. That is until she reached the center of the village and noticed that the stones of the well had been jarred loose. Hissing to herself, she took careful stock of her surroundings to make sure nothing was waiting in ambush, and then slowly approached the well. Leaning over the side, she could just make out a tunnel that led off beyond her view and a surprising lack of water.

On one hand she didn't want to jump into the well, but on the other she was sure that would be the only way to discover any form of answers. Knowing it was going to be tight down below, she stripped down to her catsuit, and leapt into the unknown. Clutching her weapon, she rolled off of the stone floor, and took stock of her surroundings. This tunnel or whatever it was had been carved through solid rock by very sharp teeth and there was still fresh acid still dripping from the ceiling.

"There's only one way forward." She muttered to herself. She was beginning to feel unsettled and anxious by the lack of sound and it was good to hear her own voice even if it gave away her position. Pulling her hood up, she began to slowly move down the tunnel, being careful to avoid having any acid drip on her. She walked and walked for at least a mile, maybe more as it was impossible to judge distance inside the strange unending tunnel. Then quite suddenly it opened up into some kind of weird laboratory with dozens of pods hanging from the ceiling. Seeing no signs of life, she crept forward, and carefully took stock of the room. Beakers, tubes, and strange glassware littered the tables each flourishing with some kind of yellow liquid. Several healing tubes, a Useptis computer, and a large tome on a pedestal, besides that and the pods the room was empty.

Getting a bad feeling, she arched her staff up, and sliced through the bottom of one of the pods making sure she was clear of anything that might fall out of it. A skeleton covered in black goop mixed with something sulfuric dropped out of it nearly landing on her feet as she danced backwards. Covering her nose as the smell of death, rot, and sulfur wafted through the lab she struggled not to puke. It had been human at some point probably not long ago, but now it was just the remains of some foul experiment.

Deciding that there wasn't anything she could do for them now, she headed back out the way she came. The Shadows could sort this mess out, she was just a soldier, and wasn't equipped to deal with septi's experiments. It broke her heart that she couldn't help them, but there were plenty of living people who needed her attention.

Shadow Log: Emma, Shadow Base, North Dakota, June 12, 1814

Emma was having a problem with processing what Anton was trying to tell her since he was speaking so quickly through his translator. From the few words she could make out what she had found was some kind of genetic engineering laboratory beyond that it was a jumble of english and septics.

"You need to slow down. I don't understand science very well." Emma finally cut him off.

Anton gave her a dirty look, stomped his hooves unhappily, and swung his tail back and forth in annoyance.

"Lab. Useptis. Try. Take. Human. Skins. Disguise." Anton said, emphasizing each word like she was an idiot.

Emma gave him a terse smile, turned to B, and asked, "You get that?"

"Aye. Useptis are trying to figure out how to take over human bodies which is a major problem." B sighed.

"Not just Useptis, egg brother Eta'Var'Uti. He served as a slave to a Stahl genetic engineer and hates This One." Anton grumbled.

Emma growled unhappily as she finally figured out what the guy had been trying to tell her before Tamika had blown his head off. Anton's family was starting to become a serious problem for her and for humanity.

"The escapee tried to tell me, but Tamika still has an itchy trigger finger." Emma sighed.

Anton glared at her with such intensity that B shifted away from her in an attempt to escape it. Emma just smiled, raised an eyebrow, and waited for Anton to speak.

"It is a shame he died as he did, but Tamika saved your life." Anton finally said softly.

"You're getting better at english." Emma praised him before continuing to her main question, "What do you mean by that?"

"Thank you. It didn't escape, it was sent to kill you as a way to allow for Anton's brother to escape." Anton said.

Emma could hear the pride in his voice and watched as some of the tension faded from his stance. She wanted him to be calm as it was less likely he'd stab someone in annoyance and was thankful her compliment had cut the tension.

"Are there more of them out there?" B asked sharply.

Emma flinched, she had forgotten he was standing so close, and the volume of his voice was beyond grating.

"No, there was one pod empty. But brother is." Anton said flatly.

"Thank god for that. I need to get this mess sorted out, I'll make sure they give you an extra cow for your help." B said.

Emma watched him hurry out of the lab, looking like his ass was on fire, and had to swallow a chuckle. At least, Anton would be well fed this week, but she was now really worried about the implications of this new threat. Grabbing a glass of water, she took a long drink, and leaned tiredly against the wall.

"Your family is a pain in the ass." She finally sighed.

"Indeed. Tamika is waking, go to her." Anton said dismissively.

Emma chuckled, at least, she had Tamika to help burn out some of the stress. She gave Anton a bow as he turned his back on her and went back to work. She needed to blow off some steam and figure out how to find Anton's brother before he could destroy another village.

Shadow Log: Emma, Arizona, July 27, 1814

Emma felt right at home amid the arid dunes, cactus, and plains of the Mojave. Her scales absorbed the heat of the sun warming her to her bones and for the first time in forever she was finally warm. It wasn't that she had been cold, it was just mildly uncomfortable in such a way she hadn't even noticed it until it was gone. Squeezing Tamika's hand tightly, she hefted both of their packs up with her left hand, and got the load balanced on her shoulder.

"You don't need to carry my supplies." Tamika said gently. Emma could see how happy she was and could feel a brightness starting to form in her that was very comforting. Yet, she seemed to struggle with knowing that she was no longer alone and no longer having to watch her back every second of the day.

"Nonsense, a gentlelady always carries her partner's pack!" Emma protested playfully.

Tamika gave her a side eye saying, "You're very strange." Emma laughed, she could feel Tamika's joy through their link, and it was nice to see Tamika starting to blossom. It was truly nice to no longer feel so isolated, but she worried about the chance of randomly switching bodies during combat. Realizing her worry was beginning to seep into their connection, Emma forced a smile, and began walking towards the crash site.

"The Useptis keep their ships shielded from teleportation to keep from being ambushed as easily so we have a hike before we should see it." She said cheerfully.

Without warning a giant hunk of ship came shooting out of the sky narrowly avoiding colliding with their heads as it shot by them. It smashed into the ground with such force that the entire area turned brown with dust which coated everything; even their lungs. Drawing her weapon as she coughed, Emma pulled her hood up, and reached over to do the same for Tamika; who sounded like she was going to choke to death on the dust.

"Anton added a filter to our suits after our last mission." Emma shouted as a loud hum began to throb through the air.

"No need to shout, I'm in your head remember? And thank you." Tamika grumbled silently.

"Ooops, sorry."

Finally feeling like she could breathe fairly normally, Emma slowly inched toward the wreck, and tried to see if it was filled with any threats or not. The dust began to settle revealing that the hum was just an emergency beacon that had broken off of something far larger. Emma calmly stabbed it a few times causing it to fall silent again. Waving away what remained of the dust cloud, she turned back toward where the main signal had been picked up, and grimaced. A huge ship began to sink out of the air with shocking speed clearly damaged from entering the atmosphere and crashed into the earth about a mile away.

"Ruth? I thought we were investigating a crash, not experiencing one." She grumbled as she fit her earpiece into her ear.

"You were, now you are investigating two of them. Oh, and there are multiple life signs starting to pop up." Ruth replied dryly.

"Um, how many are there?" Tamika asked nervously as she put in her own earpiece.

"A few dozen, maybe more, be careful." Ruth said unhelpfully.

"There, off to the left. There's a ridge you can snipe from while I fight on the ground." Emma said.

She pointed to the only high ground nearby, earning a dirty look from Tamika who had already seen it.

"I am not blind." She growled as she trotted off.

Emma broke into a trot of her own quickly covering the ground between her and the crash. She slid to a stop just as several large hunters crawled out of the nearest piece of debris. Realizing she had their packs still sitting on her shoulder, she dropped them, and let her scales fully erupt. Before she could move the head of the first hunter exploded as Tamika settled into position above them. Grinning widely, Emma spun her staff in a wide arc, the blades erupting just before coming into contact with a hunter's neck taking its head clean off. Tamika finished off the last one as a wave of psychic energy began to wash over the area.

"You'll need to draw it out… I don't have a shot."

"Not a problem."

Emma let out several loud howls as she danced with deadly precision through the debris field taking out the hunters now swarming out of the wreck. Just before she reached the main section of the remaining ship, she stumbled to a stop, and hurriedly scrambled backwards. Two kings leapt toward her in unison, swinging their tails with great speed as they tried to kill her. The first king's head detached itself from its body as Tamika finished reloading. Seeing her chance, Emma blurred forward, and quickly dispatched the second king before turning to destroy the hearts of the first.

Emma could taste fuel in the air mixed with smoke and ash despite her mask doing its best to filter it out of the air. She'd never seen a crash in person and looking around she began to understand why this was so deadly to humans. It wasn't just the raging Useptis, it was also the risk of fumes, and fires that made it such a gamble. Blinking, she switched to her second lens, and slowly closed in on what looked to be the cryopods. Pain overwhelmed her mind bringing her to her knees as a giant mind flayer oozed towards her with its full attention focused on destroying her mind.

Three shots rang out each hitting a critical spot on the creature's body and breaking its concentration long enough for Emma to throw a grenade at its feet. One explosion, then two, then everything was engulfed in flames as the leaking fuel ignited. Emma crouched down, getting as close to the earth as she could, and let the fire wash over her. In a matter of seconds the fire was sucked back to its origin and extinguished.

"Are you alright?" Tamika's voice echoed through Emma's ringing head like a hammer hitting a bell.

"I'm alive, bit crispy though." Emma hissed back.

Mind flayers were definitely her least favorite to deal with especially because of the headache they gave her. The thing was well done now which was a small blessing at least. Not seeing any further threats, but feeling like she was being watched by something; she readied her weapon once more.

"Any life signs now?" Emma asked Ruth.

A long moment of silence and then a loud burst of static followed by a loud screech told Emma that while she had come out of the battle unscathed, her headset had not.

"Ruth says there is something huge about a hundred feet to your right inside of the crater." Tamika translated.

"Thanks." Emma replied.

She ripped her ear piece out not wanting it to shriek in her ear again and waited for her hearing to return to normal. Once it had, she took a deep breath, and started towards the crater. She dropped down and belly crawled up to the lip of the rim of it hoping to catch her prey off guard. She peered through the strange green mist that was filling the crater tasting sulfur and cinder weed. It smelled like something had created a cinder Useptis orgy, but the mist was too thick to see anything useful.

"I'm going in." She hissed to Tamika.

"Wait! Anton says that is an egg bearer nest. They just want to live and the hive can do it for them." Tamika shouted back.

"What does this do for me?" Emma grumbled impatiently.

"Give me your body and let me speak to them as an emissary. If it fails you jump back in and do your thing."

Emma didn't like this plan very much, but she trusted Tamika. Closing her eyes, she focused on her connection to Tamika, and widened it as wide as she could to let her in fully. For one brief confusing moment their memories became a jumble and then Emma was inside Tamika. Looking down the scope, she kept her rap attention on her mate as she dropped into the mist. Closing her eyes, she sucked in a breath, and forced her worry away. Then she leaned into the connection to be able to see and hear like she was there.

So far it was mist with fast moving builders guarding the mass in the center of the crater. She could feel agonized pain echo off the walls as the creature screamed causing the builders to scatter away. Tamika took one step forward and found herself clear of the fog. The creature looked like a massively bloated version of a Useptis king. One that was leaking sulfuric acid out into the crater floor and flooding it with goop. Tamika approached slowly, all while purring in respect to try, and get it to talk to her.

"You will not harm my Children!" The thing shrieked.

"I'm not here to hurt you." Tamika promised.

She dropped to her knee, bowed her head in respect to the creature, and purred louder. After a few long moments it slowly dropped its guard and began to purr in tune to Tamika's as a sign of respect.

"Help, do not wish death!" This was a scream of pure panic. Tamika quickly surged to her feet, closing the distance so rapidly that she almost lost control of Emma's body. She gently placed a hand on the Useptis and gave it a comforting pat.

"Tell me what to do." She whispered gently.

After a few labored breaths it replied, *"Eggs stuck."*

Tamika wasted no time in moving around to the creature's rear end so that she could get a better look at what was happening. Seeing a cluster of eggs all jammed together inside of its mouth, she let out an unhappy sigh, and carefully made her way over to the jam. Being as careful as she could, she slipped her hand into its ass, and gave the edge of the mass a firm yet gentle yank. Eggs came rolling out by the dozens each the size of a small ball along with enough acidic birth fluid to coat Emma in slime. The thing let out a happy sigh of relief as its breathing returned to normal.

Emma blinked and found herself back inside of her own body. Gagging on the smell, she vibrated off as much of the slime as she could before she carefully made her way back to its head.

"I am Eta'Vi'Vor and stand with his hive." Emma introduced herself.

"Uta'Ve'Ta'Uuuuti will join your hive if you have it." It wheezed.
"Vor will guide you home after you children hatch, there are plenty of Useptis corpses for them to feast on." Emma promised.
"Thanks Eta."
Emma quickly climbed back out of the crater and away from the smell, but there was no doubt that she had inhaled a lot of cinder as the world distorted around her. Suddenly Tamika was at her side, supporting her as she led them to a sheltered spot inside of the wreck.
"I told Ruth we needed more time and would guard the crash site until it was safe." Tamika whispered gently.
"Thank you for handling that mess. I suck with people and kindness." Emma groaned.
"Hush, just sleep off your high, I'll keep watch." Tamika purred.
Emma nodded as she snuggled into Tamika's lap and drifted off to sleep.

Shadow Log: Tamika, Shadow Base, North Dakota, August 4, 1814

Nightmares came with the territory of fighting monsters, but for Tamika it was her past that was keeping her awake. She missed her family, her homeland, and the sense of security they had given her. All it had taken was one day and The Shadows had made it all burn. Of course, that had been after her mother reneged on her deal to sell her to them, but somehow that only made it worse. Emma always slept soundly despite the horror she had experienced and it would be a lie if she said she wasn't a bit jealous of her ability to just shut it all out. Especially on nights like this where all she could do was listen to her quiet breathing and to keep from letting her thoughts wake Emma.
An itch began to tickle the back of her mind like something was at the edge of it scratching to come in. B linking uneasily, she sat up, and shook Emma awake feeling sure that whatever it was it meant trouble. Emma went from annoyed

to concerned in a split second as she started to feel the same thing herself.

"What the hell is that?" Emma whispered quietly.

"I don't know, I was hoping you would." Tamika whispered. *"Not to barge in, but you should head to the library before it falls."* Anton said as he pushed into both of their thoughts.

Sighing unhappily, Emma rolled out of bed, and offered Tamika her hand. Smiling to herself, Tamika let her pull her to her feet, and activated her catsuit. She was no good at hand to hand combat despite Emma trying to teach her. She just didn't have any coordination when enemies were coming at her face. Give her a rifle and enough distance and she had no problems removing their heads, but in close quarters she felt very useless.

"Hey, why don't you track down Arabella and Mary and make sure they're safe while I handle whatever is coming for us?" Emma asked, clearly picking up on her worry.

"No, I'm with you, I need to learn how to overcome my fears. Besides, both of them can take care of themselves, Arabella taught me how to shoot and Mary has her hammer." Tamika said firmly.

She grabbed a short sword and followed Emma out into Anton's lab which was suspiciously empty. Giving Emma a concerned look, she picked up her pace, and charged down the hall as she felt the itching becoming a full blown pounding. Sliding into the library, she stumbled to a stop as her head exploded with strange light and explosive pounding. "We have a breach! Far back wall! Should look like a portal to hell! You'll need to go through and close it from the other side!" Arabella shouted.

Tamika's vision cleared just in time to see Arabella put an arrow through the eye of a hunter with her bow. Emma let out a howl as she blurred forward and ripped another off of Mary and killed it. Seeing her chance Tamika exploded through the battlefront and used the shelves for cover made her way in the direction Arabella had pointed. It was a surprisingly short journey to the mouth of the portal almost like the room was doubling back on itself and getting closer to her. Hearing a strange crunch, she turned back away from the portal, and took a blow to the chin.

She flew backwards in what felt like slow motion through the portal and into a large pillar made of orange glass which shattered under the impact of her body. Gasping in pain, she forced her scales out, sending the glass in her skin flying, and tried to get a sense of her surroundings. She rolled to her feet just in time to see the portal zap shut leaving her trapped. The pillar had probably been holding it open and looking around she realized she was surrounded by hungry and very upset Useptis.

"Emma!" She called silently.

But to her surprise she could no longer feel Emma nor could she hear her thoughts. Growling as loudly as she could, she calmly hefted her sword, and prepared for battle. Time is a funny thing, it just slips away from you under the extreme stress of battle. It becomes a living breathing thing that pulls you apart with exhaustion and pain and then puts back together all wrong. Tamika was very thankful she had listened to Emma and let her teach her the basics of hand to hand because that combined with her Useptis blood saved her from ending up in the stomach of one of her many attackers. When it was finished, she couldn't seem to see past the blood and guts coating her face nor could she smell anything other than death. Sliding to the floor, she leaned against the nearest corpse, and let her heart rate return to normal. She was trapped down here in these strange tunnels, cut off from everyone, and she was bleeding from numerous wounds. It was an all too familiar situation for her and she kept pinching herself to make sure she wasn't dreaming.

"Emma will find you." She muttered to herself as she lost consciousness.

*****

"Get up you dirty little whore!" Robert hissed as he kicked her in the ribs.

She startled awake, yanking her chains painfully against her wrists as she blinked the saltwater out of her eyes. She'd never hurt more in her life or felt so degraded, but at least the captain of this ship had finally claimed her for his own and she wouldn't be passed around like meat anymore. He started pissing on her, laughing heartily as she flinched away from the stream, and choked back tears. Her recent wounds burned as the urine flowed over her which left her near to tears, but she didn't want him to see her cry again.

"I have good news for you," He chuckled.

She watched him zip up his pants, wishing she could rip his face off, and turned her head away from him. He roughly grabbed her chin and forced her to look him in the eyes. Grumbling at himself, he hurriedly wiped the piss off of his fingers, and gave her another sharp kick.

"We made port and someone paid a lot of money for you." He laughed.

Tamika eyed him warily, he had tried to trick her many times in the past only to immediately try and crush her hopes again. This time he seemed far too serious for him to be lying but she was sure that in her current state that no one would want to buy her; let alone for a lot of money.

"Why?" She finally asked hoarsely.

"How should I know? Get in the box!" He spat.

She glanced behind him and was surprised to see a wooden coffin lying open on the floor. She shook her head no only to immediately get punched in the face…

✳✳✳✳✳

Tamika woke to find herself being dragged slowly through the mud by her arms and began to struggle in terror.

"Woman! Would you relax?!" Emma hissed.

She dropped her and quickly danced backwards to avoid getting hit by Tamika's flailing arms. Tamika scrambled up onto her feet and tried to keep her tears in check as she threw her arms around Emma's neck. She started sobbing in relief as she nuzzled into Emma's neck and felt her inside of her mind again.

"How did you find me?" She whimpered.

"Anton did. He figured out where the portal led and sent me to retrieve you. I can see into your mind again, want to tell me about it?" Emma asked gently.

"No, I will never ever talk about that time of my life. Besides, you know everything already." Tamika muttered.

She reluctantly pulled away from Emma, dried her tears, and forced a smile. There was no way she wanted to be seen as weak, especially by Emma.

"You will never seem weak to me." Emma whispered gently.

"Can we just go to the base please? I need a shower." Tamika replied with relief.

"Of course, I love you." Emma said, offering her a hand.

"I love you too," Tamika said, accepting it.

Shadow Log: Emma, Shadow Base, North Dakota, August 6, 1814

Emma had been avoiding returning to the library after what had happened with Tamika. She still got a pit in her stomach everytime she remembered how empty and weak she felt without that connection. But she needed to check on Mary and Arabella and get an idea of what had happened so that she could avoid it happening again. Walking through the small door that led to the grandeur of vast knowledge she was immediately overwhelmed by the smell of mold mixed with that of old books. Gagging, Emma eyed the destruction, finding it impressive how quickly The Shadows were at cleaning up. Seeing Mary restocking a nearby shelf, she quickly bypassed the cleaning crew, and walked over to her.

"Good morning." She whispered.

Mary jumped in surprise before shooting Emma an annoyed look and slowly getting back to her feet.

"No sneak." Mary chastised.

"I move a lot quieter than I used to, I'm sorry. I just wanted to check on you after everything that had happened." Emma said.

She raised her hands in mock surrender, stomped her feet loudly, and shot Mary a loving grin. Mary rolled her eyes, shoved a book into its place, and stomped over to the fireplace. Emma chuckled quietly, walked over to a tattered recliner, and dropped into it.

"Mary jumpy." Mary grumbled.

"Sorry. How are you holding up? I forget that fighting isn't as easy for others as it is for me." Emma whispered a true apology.

"Angry. Sad. Many books need love now." Mary sighed unhappily.

"Is there anything I can do to help?" Emma asked gently.

She felt bad about making Mary feel unhappy and wanted to help her get her feet back under her. If this meant putting her own needs on hold for a bit then so be it, friends were everything good in the world and deserved the most out of her.

"Arabella help?" Mary asked hopefully.

Emma felt her brow crinkle with concern as she tried to puzzle out what Arabella could need from her. Giving Mary a quick fangy smile, she nodded in confirmation, and let herself relax.

"Anything I can do I will." Emma promised.

Mary's eyes drifted to the stacks behind Emma as footsteps quietly made their way closer to the fire. Emma turned just in time to get to watch Arabella jump gracefully from the second level and roll back up onto her feet.

"I was a circus performer before I was recruited." Arabella said, seeing Emma's surprise.

"Mary books." Mary said as she walked away.

"I'm sorry about what happened to your home." Emma replied.

She felt stupid, but she couldn't think of anything else to say as her stunned brain tried to process Arabella as a circus performer. She'd seen first hand how agile and deadly the woman was with her bow in combat, but had assumed she learned those things after joining The Shadows.

"We need to talk about my father and his mission." Arabella said after letting out a musical little giggle.

"Go on." Emma whispered nervously.

"Theo left when I was five after my mother was killed. It broke our family into pieces and The Shadows put us back together. I know they have their flaws and my father regretted his decision to trust them. That's how I ended up here, I was a high flying performer, but my heart always was with books. This place, this library, exists across all dimensions and is easily accessed from anywhere in the world if you know how to access the bubble protecting it." Arabella explained urgently.

Emma stared at her as she tried to sort out what she was trying to tell her, "So this is a bubble dimension then?" She finally asked.

"Exactly! That's an over simplified explanation but still accurate. I bring this up because once you spend enough time here you become attuned to it and are no longer able to leave without dying horribly. I can't carry on his mission, but I have been carrying on his research into the Black Death…" Arabella whispered quietly.

"Whoa! You mean to tell me that you and Mary are stuck here?" Emma interrupted in shock.

"Yes, but we have every need catered to and we are mostly left in peace which gives me more time to do research. I haven't had any breakthroughs yet, but you should follow up with Stewart. I have a feeling he is in over his head and will need your help." Arabella said urgently.

"I will, is there any risk to just visiting the library?" Emma asked with worry.

"No, just don't stay for more than twelve hours and you'll be fine. I need to get back to work. There are many damaged books that need my attention. Please be careful." Arabella said as she disappeared back into the stacks.

Shivering at the thought of being trapped here for the rest of her life, Emma hurriedly left the library, and went in search of Tamika and lunch.

Shadow Log: Ruth, Maine Coastline, August 14, 1814

Ruth had gotten life down to a science; get up, eat something extremely unhealthy, and then bury her head in paperwork. At least when she wasn't fielding Emma's calls or trying to keep her from killing someone. She had no idea where she had thought the position would take her, but it wasn't being trapped in whatever rut this was.

Wiping the blood from her dagger, she pushed the corpse of the man she'd just killed off of the cliff, and into the ocean. Sheathing the weapon, she wiped the blood and ocean spray off of her face, and tiredly rubbed her eyes. The problem with The Shadows was how tight of a grip they liked to keep on the world and how paranoid that made them. The man she had just murdered had been a promising rising talent in the invention world which had made him of particular interest to The Shadows. He'd chosen to ignore their numerous invites and started to actively work against their goals. Emma was busy with her own problems which meant they had taken the opportunity to send Ruth to solve the problem permanently. The stupid man had run when he saw her and had led her on a mary chase down the Maine coastline.

Rocks slipped precariously beneath her heels sending her wheeling towards the cliff before she had to over-correct to avoid falling to her own death. She had nearly twisted an ankle which caused her to go into an unplanned tackle and drove her dagger into the man's kidney. It was a shame to see such a bright soul go to waste, but he had made his choice. Getting her breathing back under control, she pulled her jacket closed as a freezing wind came in from over the ocean, and stared out over the water. Shivering, she turned to find a young man of no more than five years old staring at her in horror.

She waved to him cautiously, the look on his face told her he had seen her, and had no idea what he had actually seen. The movement startled him out of his trance, making him start blinking rapidly, he turned on his heel, and charged off away from the cliff screaming bloody murder. Ruth laughed at the absurdity of what he was no doubt going to tell his family about the crazy murderer on the hill. There was no need to chase down a child because even if they could find someone who believed his tale she would be long gone. Rolling her sleeve up to access her band took that laughter instantly out of her and replaced it with a hot coal that burned through her gut.

"Leave it to me to break my transportation home when I left a witness alive." She sighed.

She peeled the band off of her wrist, hurried over to a shaded spot, and tried to figure out what was broken. Seeing it was just a damaged faceplate, she popped it carefully loose with her dagger, and peered into the churning parts within. Lightly biting her tongue in anticipation of pain, she deliberately jammed the blade between the port to port connection, and yelped as electricity arched up into her and the teleporter engaged.

She reappeared back inside the base and immediately came crashing into the floor as her hair caught fire. Grumbling in pain, she calmly patted the fire out of her hair, and carefully picked herself up. This was a reason they always taught her to be careful when tinkering with any Shadow Tech and why she was always told to avoid it if possible. There was just no way that Ruth was going to let villagers chase her around the woods when there was a perfectly safeish way to avoid that extra exercise. Anton was going to give her hell for breaking it, Emma would see and smell the recent fight and make snide comments, and B would probably sigh with disappointment. Remembering that she had a couple pastries stashed in her secret jacket pocket, she sagged back down to the floor; and began to happily munch on them as people gave her weird looks for sitting on the hallway floor while eating a snack.

Shadow Log: Emma, Shadow Base, North Dakota, November 13, 1814

Since finding herself in the wonderfully advanced world of The Shadows Emma had marveled at many things; the electricity, the teleportation, the luxuries of a daily shower, but the best was by far the food. They had this weird machine that turned algae into any type of food you could think of and one serving had all the nutrients of a healthy meal. It was oddly filling and had the right taste except for a slight hint of green that reflected through it. This problem was contradicted slightly by the fresh herb garden the machine maintained for making its meals; however it had caught her off guard the first few times she had ordered. Today, like many others, had started with an intense workout with Tamika at the gym, followed by a long soak in the hot springs with her and then a reflective quiet meal alone in the corner of the dining room. Emma enjoyed the quiet hum of the people going about their daily routines, to watch them as they had breakfast, and to use them as a backdrop to Tamika's workout. Her favorite meal; a steak barely seared on both sides, completely red in the center, and properly heated to release all of the blood. It didn't matter if it was real meat or not as long as the taste was there and the texture was correct.

What was making her grumble unhappily to herself was the fact that for at least a week Stewart was missing from his normal spot. He hadn't come to breakfast, lunch, or dinner which seemed odd especially considering how she had left things last time. She'd been so overwhelmed that she couldn't wait to escape the plague problem and dump it on someone else's lap, but now there was a pit starting to grow in her stomach. Not wanting to be annoyed further by her own intrusive thoughts, she quickly finished her meal, and went in search of Stewart's room.

Retracing her steps was surprisingly easy and it didn't take long before she was hovering just outside his closed door. Pacing almost frantically, Emma tried to decide how to best deal with the problem she now faced. She could smell plague rot mixed with decomp wafting out from under the door, like two disasters mingling up into her nostrils. Deciding that she had to face this herself, she pulled her hood up, and engaged the air filter. Grunting with effort, she forced the lock to break, and pried the door open. She peered inside, at first seeing nothing in the lurking darkness but junk, and then she saw what remained of Stewart's body. A bloated, heavily infected, rotting corpse that looked like it was going to burst at any moment. Hissing in disgust, she pulled back, and carefully pulled the door back into place.

"Ruth, Stewart's dead, We need to clean-up his room immediately." She typed quickly into her Shadow-band. Sitting cross legged on the floor with her back resting against the wall, she closed her eyes, and took a deep cleansing breath. Resting her hands lightly on her knees, she calmed her breathing, and began to slowly drift into an almost trance like state.

"Hubert?!" She called out.

She waited for a response as her voice echoed through her head until it was quietly extinguished by time. Receiving no answer, she lowered her heart rate, steadied herself, and opened her mind up to the world around her. The brightest and easiest light was her connection with Tamika, beyond that she could faintly feel Anton's mind humming away, but no sign of Hubert or the matrix he had created. Taking a risk, she floated up out of her body, and slowly allowed her mind to expand as it absorbed Tamika's essence. Then with a single blinding pulse, she sent out a mental homing beacon, and waited anxiously for it to fade back into nothingness. She shrank back into her body allowing Tamika's essence to return to her body before she opened her eyes.

Nothing but silence and a bit of annoyance from Anton, biting her lip nervously, she tucked her mind back behind its walls, and scrambled back up onto her feet. She took a moment to center herself before she carefully pried the door back open. Doing her best to not disturb anything, she carefully crawled into the room, and dropped onto the floor. Groaning as the smell overwhelmed her air filters, she accidentally caught a stack with her elbow, and barely managed to stop it from crashing down. Once she'd assured herself of the stability of the items around her, she began the slow process of navigating over to the connection box.

It lay open, its circuits gleaming with cleanliness, its lights blinking with clarity, and every wire properly tucked away. It was clear just from looking at it that it had been meticulously cared for recently. Glancing nervously at the corpse, she carefully crouched down between it and the panel to get a better look without touching the body. Seeing a cord hanging down beneath the panel and an obvious spot to plug it in, she reached down, and plugged it in.

"EEEEE OOOOO....OH, you found it! The blasts have been unplugged for days!" Hubert shouted into her mind.

"Ow! So you've just been shouting into the void all this time?" Emma hissed in annoyance.

"Yes...well some of that time anyways!" Hubert huffed.

Emma's legs trembled slightly making her almost lose her balance and fall. Catching herself, she quickly scrambled away from the body, and out of the room.

"What happened to him?" She panted unhappily.

"He pulled the plague from my system and it consumed him. A noble sacrifice that bought us some much needed time. A new clone will appear soon so don't worry too much." Hubert muttered before disappearing again.

Hearing the clean-up crew coming, she followed his lead, and vanished into the tunnels.

Shadow Log: Tamika, Shadow Base, North Dakota, November 13, 1814

Tamika left the shower to find Anton staring down at her angrily, prancing in place, and agitatedly growling. Rolling her eyes, she carefully got up, and grabbed her robe from its hook. Sighing at the shitstorm Emma had stirred up, she slipped into her armor, and then turned to face Anton.

"Yes?" She asked with clear annoyance.

"Does Tamika know how to get Emma to stop screaming? She is very loud in Anton's head…" Anton pleaded.

Tamika chuckled, carefully lowering her head to not only show respect, but to also hide the smile spreading across her face.

"I have yet to figure out how to get Emma to do anything she doesn't want to do." She apologized.

Anton stomped angrily and stormed out of their room in a huff being careful to leave the door open so that Tamika could follow him. She wondered what Emma was thinking she was going to accomplish banging around in the dark looking for answers, but she did know that the entire base was suddenly on alert. Grumbling to herself, she grabbed her weapon belt from its hook on the wall, and followed Anton into his lab.

"You didn't follow me home to just pester me, what's on your mind?" She probed.

Anton shot her a dirty look as he turned his back on her and began to flick his tail in annoyance.

"Emma will be Emma just help her. Anton does not know how." Anton sighed.

"I will always have her back and front and every other piece of her. That being said, why don't you explain why you're so tense." Tamika replied.

She was trying to be gentle, kind, and compassionate, but her patience was wearing thin. She needed to help Emma with her new mystery and to keep her out of trouble in the process. These things weighed heavily on her mind making it hard to focus past Emma's needs to see Anton's pain.

"Anton's egg brother sent Anton a message demanding Anton remove his own head or duel to the death as is our tradition. These summons can not be ignored or the summoned becomes outcast. The ground has been set, I must fight, or my champion must or everything Anton has built here will be for not." Anton explained.

As he spoke he grew more agitated and had begun to pace between consoles, his speed increasing with each step until Tamika could feel the wind every time he passed her. Tamika knew it wasn't cowardice chewing him up because he just didn't understand that word, but something more sinister was at play; she was sure of it.

"You don't want to fight?" She asked.

Anton stopped dead in his tracks, sending papers flying everywhere, and turned to glare at her with menace.

"Anton is no runner, Anton faces all threats with his throat exposed!" He spat clearly offended.

"Forgive me, I meant no offense with my question. I simply meant to ask why you are so worked up about the fight? I know you are brave and noble and would never imply otherwise." Tamika said hastily.

Her heart had begun to thump awfully hard against her ribs as her skin crawled underneath her armor. Anton's gaze was near impossible to bear when he was happy and with anger came a whole new level of uneasiness.

"Apology accepted. To answer your intended question; Anton crossed tails with him in the past and Anton did not win. Anton was left for dead on his planet when the Masters ordered Anton's death. Anton was

saved…by what Anton does not know. One moment Anton was bleeding out and the next Anton was on Earth." Anton explained. Tamika let out her pent up breath as Anton relaxed and started pacing again. It was nice to not feel his eyes boring into her soul, but she needed to get him where she could leave without consequence.

"That sounds horrible. Speaking as someone who has faced death several times, I know the pain of losing everything. The pain of watching your world turn upside down and spit you out. Hell, I have suffered so much since my family was killed that I can't remember the feeling of true peace. It's nothing but a vague memory tainted by experience. You mentioned that a champion can fight in your stead?" Tamika whispered softly.

"Indeed, one of the hives can stand in if the summoned can't fight."

"Perfect, then you send Emma. She can't die so even if she loses it won't be the end of the world." Tamika replied.

"Anton did not wish to drag Emma into Useptis politics." Anton sighed.

"A little late for that concern, Emma is right in the middle of skeptics' politics. She's part of this as am I even if you don't approve of it." Tamika replied harshly.

Anton stopped once more, this time his gaze bore nothing but sadness, and Tamika could see his remorse clearly written in his body language.

"Tamika is right. Anton will ask once this crisis is at an end. Thank you for listening. This One, often feels alone with his hive so far away." Anton promised with great sadness.

"Only some of your hive is far away, please try to remember that we are family. Your blood runs through our veins and that makes us part of your hive." Tamika said gently.

"Anton is thankful. May Anton have a…What was it called?....Ah…a hug?" Anton asked almost sheepishly.

"Come here, big guy." Tamika laughed.

She hugged him tight, ignoring her ribs cracking under his strength as he enveloped her in his arms. He was oddly prickly and extremely warm which made the crushing hug somehow feel even cozier. Just before breathing could become an issue, Anton released her, and gently sat her back onto her feet. Smiling past the pain, she gave his hand a gentle squeeze, and then headed for the door. It was finally time for her to sort out Emma's mess.

Shadow Log: Ruth, Shadow Base, North Dakota, November 13, 1814

Ruth watched the clean-up team work while silently cursing to herself for letting Emma dump this mess on her. Today was supposed to be her one relaxation day for the month and instead she was watching a plague corpse be cleansed. Which seemed to involve a bunch of fire, long poles, and loud arguing about if it was going to explode. She, at least, was on the other side of the protective barrier they had set up to prevent any of the plague from getting out.

The tallest of the suits poked the body's belly tentatively with his pole causing it to explode into a giant mess of black gloop, decomp, and various other juices. Once she had recovered from the heart attack it had nearly given her, she tapped the wall a few times to jiggle free the goop to create a peephole, and stuck her eye against it. The entire crew was drenched in the stuff as was the room and all of its contents. Her radio suddenly crackled on her wrist making her jump quickly back away from the barrier.

"We're going to need to scorch earth this room." The medium suit moped.

"Frederick! How many times do I have to tell you to not poke the bodies with the sharp end?!" Their leader screamed angrily.

Ruth quickly turned her volume way down on her radio to avoid having any hearing loss as they continued to bicker at the top of their lungs. Leaning against the wall, she slid to the floor, and tried to get comfortable. The one thing she knew about clean up duty was that once a corpse sprayed it took forever to clean up and since she was the onsite supervisor she couldn't leave. She was thankful that the seal had in fact been intact because that meant no one else had to die. That didn't make missing her day off any better and it certainly didn't help the boredom.

"The last site I supervised was in Spain, a small nunnery on the coast. The air tasted like salt and soot as the place went up in flames around us. There was no escape from the fire because it was fueled by Useptis fuel which burns so hot it will melt human skin on contact and the fumes will make you see things that are downright unholy." B said as he sauntered up.

Ruth gave him a surprised little yelp, scooched over, and patted the floor next to her in invitation. B found a spot on the wall he liked and slid to the floor as flames erupted inside of the barrier.

When he was settled, they just stared at the fire for a long time, basking in the silence of the cackling flames.

"What happened?" Ruth finally asked as if no time had passed.

"We were trapped, the Useptis were closing in, and we had a mission to save the nuns and what they were guarding. I did what I had to do to save as many lives as possible; I threw myself onto the flames and used my body as a bridge to safety for them. Don't remember much after that, but the men I served with said they all got out alive and mostly unscathed even carrying my useless ass around." B replied with such ease that it wasn't like he was talking about a near death experience.

"How long did it take to heal? Do you regret it? Wait, what were the nuns guarding?" Ruth asked with great enthusiasm before she could stop herself.

B laughed, "About three and a half years, no, and it was a prototype of the new shadow-band we were developing in secret; the model you're wearing now actually."

"Sorry, I was a little over excited there." Ruth muttered, suddenly feeling shy.

"I love that about you. Ask me anything and I will answer you honestly so long as we are alone." B replied with a smile. Ruth felt a hot blush spread across her cheeks like wildfire and quickly tried to hide her face in shadow to avoid being seen. B chuckled again, this time he gently took her hand, and simply laid his underneath hers so that she could move away if she wanted to. Ruth felt a dopey grin spread across her face as her blood began to shiver. She wrapped her fingers around his, feeling strangely happy despite holding her boss's hand.

"Then tell me this; why did you make Grace the Clover Schools problem?" Ruth asked pointedly.

She felt far braver holding his hand which made her ask the one question burning through her mind despite the clear risk involved. She felt him tense for a long moment before he relaxed again and grew thoughtful.

"Grace founded The Shadows and she pulled us all out of the gutter or some other hell and gave us a home. We knew she was slipping just not how badly so we thought to give her a retirement of some version. We only learned of the full extent of the Emergence Program just prior to her death. You, Theodore, and a handful of trusted friends were the only ones close to read in. She had some kind of jammer that blocked us from seeing the truth at the school. Had I known… things would have been a lot different." He replied, clearly choosing his words with great care.

Ruth was mildly surprised that he had kept his word and willingly admitted to a mistake.

"Is that why you couldn't find my tracker?" She asked as the sudden thought jolted her awake.

"The simpleton…Mary is a lot smarter than I gave her credit for. She figured out how to disable it knowing we would come and that you would need us." B replied.

Ruth had to laugh knowing she had made the same mistake in the beginning and how hard it had been to regain her trust afterwards.

"I miss her." Ruth whispered sadly.

"You were in the trenches with her for a year fighting for your lives and for your sanity side by side. That kind of bond builds trust and friendship like nothing else can. She came to me when you returned to base to fight for you." He said with a smile.

"Mary?! You know she can talk to birds? Saved my ass a few times!" Ruth protested playfully.

B laughed, gave her a huge grin, and replied, "Mary defies all laws of logic and nature."

Ruth nearly choked on her spit at the sudden burst of laughter that erupted from her. Shaking her head at the thought of him loving Mary as much as she did made her somehow feel better.

"Emma's a freak of nature and Tamika too! But at least, Tamika is nice." Ruth grumbled.

"The first time she came at me in full lizard mode I about shat my pants." He agreed, generating another chuckle.

"Tell me about it! Why are you giving me this honesty so suddenly?" She asked, suddenly growing serious.

"There was a saying in my graduating class: The foot soldier doesn't ask to go home, he gets sent in a casket. Horrible if you think about a bunch of fourteen year olds saying this."

"Mine too." Ruth whispered sadly.

"I am twenty two years old and leader of an organization that now spans twenty countries… With that responsibility comes the need to ensure that if one should die the transition will be seamless. I read your file the first day we met and was in awe and then the whole cyborg twist! My point is Grace saw something in you and I see the same thing. A bright intelligent woman capable of moving mountains if it meant protecting her family."

Ruth definitely choked on her saliva that time as she struggled to swallow such clear praise. Thankfully it just amused B, but it was embarrassing and a little strange.

"Does the fire bother you?" Ruth asked in sudden horror. She hadn't given the fire any thought before his story but now she felt terrible for keeping him down here if he was uncomfortable. B smiled, leaned over, and kissed her firmly on the lips. A simple, short, polite kiss that showed respect and the willingness to back off. Returning to his seat, he began to nervously eye the fire, and nibble on a key he wore around his neck.

"Would I have done that if I was afraid of the fire?" He asked gently.

Ruth took a long moment to savor him on her lips before she whispered, "You ever have sex in front of a wall of fire?"

"I haven't had sex period." B choked in surprise.

"Me either, but this seems like a good time to learn and would make an amazing story to tell to your mates, "I lost my virginity in front of a wall of pure fire!" She continued.

B sat there, staring into the fire with speechless admiration as he tried desperately to eke out some form of a thought.

"You're more beautiful than the fire and are way more brag worthy." He finally stuttered.

Ruth took his face in her hands, gently caressing his scars without flinching away, and then leaned in, and kissed him back.

"I brought picnic supplies and blanket!" B blurted out as she pulled away.

Ruth laughed at their awkwardness, sat back, and waved him off to fetch them. He returned rapidly, spread a blanket out across the floor, and stuffed the basket in a corner.

"Listen to the fire, let it set the pace." She said as she flopped onto the blanket, looking as graceful as a fish out of water.

Shadow Log: Tamika, Shadow Base, North Dakota, November 13, 1814

Tamika didn't like libraries even before they were filled with deadly beasts, but Emma needed answers that the Useptis didn't have. She hoped that since it was connected to every dimension at once and every universe that they might have something on the plague itself that no one had found yet. It had taken Theodore's life and now Stewart's as well and she didn't want Emma to experience any more loss.

Stepping through the threshold made her scales instinctively prickle to life under her skin not because of what it was but because of what it represented. Seeing Mary dart towards her happily, she braced herself for impact, and accepted the full body hug Mary was known for.

"Forgive me, I have not returned to properly thank you for your role in saving me the first time. Thank you for pulling me out of that creek, for making sure Emma saved me from The Shadows, and for being Emma's friend." She said rather formally.

"Nonsense! Friends care friends." Mary batted the praise away.

"Right, of course, well, thank you anyways. Now, can you point me in the direction of Arabella? I need to ask her some important questions." Tamika replied with a small chuckle.

"West wall, 5th floor, row 60-70." Mary said.

Tamika went to the wall she was pointing at and stared up the center of the ladder slot wondering why it had no ladder.

"Arabella jumps or scarfs." Mary answered her question.

She had no idea what scarfs meant nor did she want to spend the time learning just now. Her scales erupted from her skin as she leapt into the air and caught the first bannister and then using her momentum she swung herself up to the second, third, and fourth balcony before she mistimed a swing and crashed into a wall on the fourth floor. Groaning in shock more than anything, she rolled out of the wood, and watched as it magically healed itself. Shaking her head in disbelief, she easily jumped to the fifth using the ladder slot for leverage, and then came gracefully crashing into a table while taking out a few chairs along the way.

"With a ruckus like that it is a wonder that you are as successful hunting as you are." Arabella chastised her as she walked out of the stacks.

"Most places have ladders." She growled.

Clawing her way free of debris, she shook off the splinters, and regained her feet. Sucking her scales back beneath her skin, she gave Arabella a smile, and added, "And in a fight I'm normally a long ways back."

"I fight with a bow and a dagger and I promise you'll never hear or see me coming." Arabella replied casually.

"Emma tried…"

"Let me stop you right there. Emma is adorable in the sort of way a cattle dog puppy is; you can teach her tricks easily enough, but don't ask her to share that knowledge with someone else." Arabella cut her off sternly.

"Alright, what would you recommend?" Tamika asked curiously.

"Emma is a brute in battle while you are more subtle, more invisible. I will train you as my master trained me if you wish." Arabella offered.

"You make us sound like animals." Tamika growled.

"Aren't we all?!" Arabella asked in mock surprise.

Tamika had to laugh, "Fair enough. I still forget this science stuff."

"I remember leaving the circus behind for this unknown adventure full of discovery, it was terrifying. Then we found The Shadows and everything was new! Indoor plumbing, algae food, interdimensional spaces. I could go on for hours and not touch on everything I've learned here and still only be on day one like electricity and central heating and cooling." Arabella said gently.

"Having Emma to fall back on has been useful. The mirror did catch me off guard the first time I saw it." Tamika shuddered.

"I know right? Why do people need to see themselves?" Arabella agreed.

"Thank you, I needed something to release some stress. We have plague problems and Emma is even worse at this science than I am so I want to be your apprentice. Not just in the lab, but on the field of battle as well. Emma had her training and now I need mine." Tamika said simply.

"Apprentice, eh? I have one of those she gives wicked hugs…I'm sure you'll prove useful as well. Make sure to wear your band at all times when you are in here, it protects you from the effects of binding for about twelve hours. After that you have an hour to get out or stay forever." Arabella warned.

Tamika glanced around at the endless shelves of books trying to imagine a worse fate than being stuck in a library all the time.

"Noted. When do we start?" Tamika asked.

"How about now?" Arabella asked back.

She held her hand out to Tamika with a mischievous look on her face and gave her a little wink. Deciding she needed to trust her mentor, Tamika accepted the proffered hand, and with an echoing laugh Arabella snapped her fingers and they were in a very well equipped laboratory.

"What? How?" Tamika gasped in shock.

"This place is mine as much as I belong to it which provides a uniqueness to my power." Arabella laughed.

"So, why do you jump and scarf? Was it a scarf?" She questioned with uncertainty.

"Because it is fun and it reminds me of home, besides it doesn't drain my power to move normally. And scarfing is what Mary calls the aerial work I do with, well, a scarf." Arabella explained patiently.

Tamika nodded like she understood what Arabella was talking about but in truth she had no idea how someone could use a scarf to fly.

"You learn in time. But first let me catch you up on my research." Arabella promised.

Tamika grabbed a lab coat from Arabella who had pulled it from the wall for her and slipped into it.

"You already look smarter." Arabella chirped happily.

Tamika nodded, Emma would be busy for some time which meant she could stay for her allotted limit with a safety net.

Shadow Log: Emma, Shadow Base, North Dakota, November 13, 1814

Emma hated being cornered by anyone really and somehow it felt worse to be cornered by a very upset Ruth. The girl had really grown into her own and had become quite fearsome when riled. Emma wasn't afraid yet she did not like anyone screaming in her face and so she calmly grabbed Ruth's hand, spun her around, and pinned her to the wall.

"Calm down or else I might just break it." She hissed into Ruth's ear.

To her surprise Ruth started laughing, her whole body shaking from the strength of her mirth. Emma reluctantly released her, took a quick step back, and then slammed her fist into the nearest wall to release some of her pent up energy.

"I'm having flashbacks." Ruth chuckled.

"We keep running in circles around each other." Emma grunted.

"You do know they had to incinerate the entire lab," Ruth sighed.

"I heard you when you screamed it the first time, the speech about the cost as well." Emma moaned.

"Good, now you can say that I chewed you out for this and they will leave you alone." Ruth giggled.

Emma rolled her eyes, wishing that she could just punch Ruth's pretty face in, and be done with it. It would be ineffective in the long run which meant that wish couldn't happen just yet.

"Your scent has changed and since I know about it you can talk if it gets to be too much to handle." Emma said, growing serious.

Ruth gave her a surprised look, nodded in agreement, and quickly looked away as she blushed.

"Good. Now, onto business, what do I need to do to help?" Emma asked softly.

"I need you to just stop being so scary if you can. They fear you and that fear is worsened when you do shit like this." Ruth said matter of factly.

Emma bit her lip, she remembered how Grace had been, and really didn't want to be her. She had been grouchy before Tamika had come and that had led to some face shifting snapping that she wasn't proud of. They definitely had a reason to fear her and none to like her which was no way to start a rebellion.

"There is one thing that might make everyone happy, but I'll need your help." She muttered.

"I know I'm going to regret this later, but what do you need?" Ruth replied.

"Convince management to let me and Tamika open up a tavern in the cafeteria."

Emma was happy to see Ruth about to fall over in shock at the thought of Emma as a bartender. It was clear that she thought the mere suggestion was absolutely preposterous, but seeing how serious Emma was made her suddenly very calm.

"Explain your logic please?" Ruth replied gently.

"We're all soldiers here and the things we see are horrible on the best of days. If we don't start blowing off steam we're going to explode." Emma said simply.

She watched Ruth mull her words over with this sour look, it was almost like someone had forced her to drink lemon juice. She wasn't sure if it was the thought of a tavern or the thought of her running it, but Emma was sure she wasn't happy at all.

"Why do you have to make so much sense?" Ruth sighed.

Emma chuckled dryly, "It's easier than being misunderstood."

"I'll talk to B and see about getting your project financed, but it will take some time with all of the paperwork involved. Please, be patient and let me handle this, and in the meantime would you please figure out how to help sort out Hubert's mess. For being a dead guy he has become a pain in the ass." Ruth grumbled unhappily.

"I have nothing but time." Emma promised.

Ruth walked away without another word leaving Emma to stew in the darkness of the tunnel. Emma watched her go feeling strangely excited at the prospect of having a real way to start influencing things. She had no idea how to deal with Hubert's ghost, however, she was now on track to get what she needed to help people. Feeling Tamika take a nasty hit to the jaw, Emma rubbed her own, and smiled knowing she was trying to get stronger.

Shadow Log: Emma, The Australian outback, November 14, 1814

Emma wasn't sure why she had agreed to port clear across the world to this hellhole, but here she was standing in front of the largest Useptis king she had ever encountered. The thing was huge, easily double her height, and her weight and to make it worse they were alone out here unless you counted the emus. The entire thing wasn't going anywhere near according to plan and Emma was already not only covered in sweat, but also a dozen new scrapes and bruises. While the Useptis was clearly just getting warmed up, he didn't have a scratch on him to prove the numerous times she had hit him.

She was beginning to understand why Anton had failed in killing him the first time he fought him. What she needed was an edge of some kind, a way to help her kill him before he killed her and escaped from her to wreak havoc on her world. Thinking about the problem from a logical perspective she could see that his armor wasn't something she could penetrate easily and he was wearing a helmet that prevented her from taking his head. Not to mention that he was great at inflicting damage with his tail and that he understood combat a lot better than she did.

Deciding she might find something she could use somewhere nearby she took the opportunity to dart quickly into the brush and around to the back of the mesa. Seeing a long black snake quickly slither out of her way gave her a strange and possibly brilliant idea. She quickly blurred forward, quickly grabbed it by the neck, and gently cradled it in her hand. Hearing her hunter closing in, she quickly charged forward, and rapidly prepared her trap. She milked the snake drawing out a small vial of clear watery venom and very carefully set it free. Grabbing her handkerchief from her pocket, she calmly coated it in the venom, and wadded it up into a ball which she then wrapped in a small pocket she made out of her sleeve. Drawing her dagger from its sheath, she rolled seconds before the Useptis impaled her with his tail, and as she rolled she came up at his front shoulder. Breathing deeply, she grabbed his neck ruffle, and leapt up onto his back facing his tail. Ignoring his screeches of outrage, she slid forward, and wrapped her hand tightly around his tail. Leaning in close to his body, she wrapped her legs around his torso, and squeezed tightly to prevent him from throwing her off. Twisting his tail roughly out of her way, she leaned in close, and took one final deep breath. She already regretted her choices and they hadn't even happened yet, but she was very aware of what was about to happen. She wordlessly stuffed her hand up his ass, wiggled it around his mouth to free the handkerchief, and then allowed him to throw her clear of his bucking body.

Emma's arm was covered in an almost clear green slime that went up past her elbow and smelled like rotten eggs mixed with rotted lemon; not to mention the burning it caused her scales. Her situation was far better than her opponent's situation which seemed to be rapidly deteriorating. The Useptis had stopped bucking and in fact stopped moving completely minus a tremble here and there. Then the gas started. Pure methane, sulfur, and thiols came streaming out of his ass as a terrible extremely loud moo that sounded like it was slowly being run through the grinder came out of his mouth and mixed with the gas.

Choking on the fumes, Emma staggered out of their path, feeling thankful she was already filtering her air, or it would have knocked her out or worse. Her entire body was rank with the smell to the point that Emma's eyes were starting to water and looking closer at the fabric she could see tiny droplets of mucus all over her suit. She turned her attention back to the source of the smell just in time to see him keel over onto his back. Everything went quiet as the gas slowly puttered out and he grew very still. Then in a sudden burst of pure agony he let out one final screeching moo and died.

"I need a quarantine team to my location." She muttered into her headset.

She thought about yelling at Ruth for chuckling at her request, but instead she joined her in her laughter. It would take the team three ports to reach this desolate location and by then the smell would permeate the air with its stench and with how the mucus clung to her suit meant she too smelt atrocious. She found a comfortable spot out of the sunlight, leaned back, and began to meditate.

Shadow Log: Emma, A Nunnery in Spain, November 15, 1814

They had moved her to a quarantine cell somewhere far out of the way while they worked on a way to remove the mucus safely from her suit. She knew she was in for a long wait by now and she needed to focus on her internal thoughts and come to terms with her new self. Smiling at this chance to just think, she got up from where she sat, and began to hum happily to herself. This room was far too small for her liking and she would definitely prefer more space.

She carefully turned the bed on its side, moved against the far wall, and flipped it upside down. Humming to herself, she grabbed the desk, set it on the bed, and quickly added the nightstand and chair to the pile. Snorting unhappily, she sat down on the cold stone floor, crossed her legs, and placed her hands on her knees. Before she could enter a deep trance a middle aged nun came hurrying up to the window outside her cell.

"I told you she wasn't trouble!" The nun called annoyedly up the hall before turning back to Emma and adding, "I'm Romana by the way."

"Tamika's mother, she was overjoyed to hear you still draw air." Emma replied gently.

Romana flinched slightly, disappeared for a long moment, and returned to the cell with a folding chair in hand. Setting up the chair, she pulled a bottle of water from her pouch, and settled in.

"This room is shielded from the outside. We refer to them as void rooms because nothing is attached to it. That is why you can no longer hear Tamika even though you still feel that connection. Nothing can stop that kind of love, not even the void. Ask the question you keep swallowing, we might as well talk while we have the time." Romana laughed.

"What happened to you that day Tamika was taken?" Emma replied tartly.

Romana sighed heavily, took a long drink of water, and then slowly started her tale.

"When I found out I was pregnant with Tamika I was caring for two eight month twin boys and had a husband taken by the sea. I'll admit that I panicked and made some bad decisions, but after meeting Grace I had second thoughts and couldn't do it. I headed into hiding with my mother, sadly an agent caught up to me on the road, we escaped, but they ended up blinding me. We had ten years of peace and then chaos came to our doorstep once more.

The mercenaries Grace sent after us were cruel, evil, nasty men who were clearly scum of the earth. They looted, burned, and murdered the men who fought back, taking the women and children as prisoners. We were locked up in the fishing hut and then we were sorted out like cattle. This one is worth this much and that one isn't worth much because of her age and so on. When it was Tamika's turn I tried to create a distraction to help her escape; all I did was earn a knife through my shoulder since I was worthless to them. The last thing I heard was my daughter's screams as they dragged her off towards the slave pens." Romana grew still, a look of sadness on her face, and tears pooled in her eyes.

"I'm sorry you had to experience that and wish there was a way I could help you heal." Emma whispered sadly.

She knew the pain of being treated that way and she wished she could at least offer a hug. Sighing in resignation, she leaned forward, and placed her hand on the barrier. Romana placed her hand on Emma's hand, a small smile cresting her lips as her tears began to fall.

"Ben saved me, said that I didn't bleed out because of the knife being left in and since he needed my help he healed my body and my sight. I made a deal to work here in exchange for him finding and protecting my daughter from threats she shouldn't have to face." Romana added as she let her hand fall.

She pulled her own hand back, eyeing the barrier, wondering if Romana understood just how much her daughter had suffered, and if not how to avoid spilling those secrets.

"That Christopher nearly killed the light in her soul by doing as he did. I enjoyed beating him to death almost as much as I enjoyed burning his ship. You gave Tamika back her light and for that I can never thank you enough."

The sincerity in Romana's voice was a hard thing for Emma to swallow. Mostly because of how she had put Tamika in danger in the first place, but Tamika had forgiven her and so would she.

"How much do you know?" Emma asked pointedly.

"About Christopher? I know that he and his crew raped, tortured, and forced her into sex slavery before selling her to Jackson who was just as bad. Thankfully you found her and brought her to safety." Romana replied.

"She will need a long time to fully heal, but I think having a chance to get to know you again would really help. You could have her sit in a void cell so you can talk safely and even have a tea party separated by the barrier. I don't know, I just want Tamika to be happy." Emma rambled.

"I see the truth of your words and will endeavor to repair the rift." Romana promised.

"You once craved a fish brooch for Tamika, do you remember?" Emma asked suddenly.

"I made it to sell originally, however I could feel her love for it so I gave it to her for her birthday. Does she still have it?" Romana asked curiously.

"That's why I was asking, you see, Christopher stole it from her. Is there any way to get a replacement?" Emma asked hopefully.

"I already carved an almost exact copy except for a small imperfection in the bone. You can have it before you head home." Romana promised.

Emma watched her leave, returned to her meditative stance, and went very still as she turned all of her focus inward.

Shadow Log: Emma, The Shadow Base, North Dakota, November 16, 1814

Emma had snuck out early in the morning to port to London and buy a chocolate cake, a box to put the brooch in, and a box of french chocolates. All because it was Tamika's birthday and Emma knew she hadn't had a good one in a long while and it was important to Tamika. It had been difficult to keep her barriers tight enough to keep Tamika from waking up, but it had been worth it. She was just thankful that the smell had been removed in time for her to get back for the surprise.

Now much to Emma's excitement the time for her surprise had come and as a bonus she had been away for a few days. The door opened up to reveal a very sleepy Tamika emerging out of the blankets of their nest.

"You're home." Tamika cooed happily.

"I'm home." Emma replied.

She barely had time to set her presents on the table before Tamika landed in her arms, squeezed her in a tight hug, and began to smother her in kisses. Once they were properly reunited, Tamika settled down across from Emma at the table and asked, "What's all this then?"

"It gets harder by the day to hide anything from you and I wanted you to have at least one surprise birthday from me." Emma explained.

"Ah, I am truly blessed. Which box shall I open first?" Tamika asked.

Emma silently handed her the emerald and gold jewelry box with the brooch inside, giving a huge eager smile as she leaned forward in anticipation of her reaction. Tamika carefully opened the box and peered inside only to freeze in shock. At first there was the silence of startled confusion which was then followed by the thoughtless shock of true surprise. Tears slowly began to leak down Tamika's face as she pulled the brooch out so she could carefully examine it.

"I asked Romana to replace the one you lost." Emma explained.

"This one is even more special because it came from you. It smells like the other two boxes have sweets in them. Shall we pig out and cuddle all day?" Tamika asked playfully.

"I exist for the sole purpose of pleasing you today." Emma replied.

Emma shared everything that had happened over the course of her trip while she enjoyed eating the entire cake with the majority going to Tamika. It was so nice to just be in the moment experiencing life and embracing the day moment by moment.

Shadow Log: Ruth, Shadow Base, North Dakota, December 7, 1814

Ruth wasn't sure if she had ever regretted taking an assignment more than she did standing outside of Emma's room trying to get the courage up to knock. She had become Emma's handler as a way to make amends for how she had treated her earlier in life and now it just might end her own. But news like this was best given in person while looking them in the eyes and so she knocked. The door slid instantly open to reveal Emma patiently leaning against the wall waiting for her.

"I was wondering how long it would take you before you'd finally knock. Honestly, I was debating just opening it and surprising you, but that seemed mean." Emma laughed at her surprise.

"So you waited while creepily listening for me?" Ruth asked in alarm.

"Yes, now tell me what bad news you bring." Emma demanded.

Ruth collected her startled thoughts and took a deep breath, "I know you figured out you have a daughter named Emily. So, I'll get right to the point and be honest and direct. They sent her to live on a farm with a family of four that desperately wanted a daughter. She got sick last week and a team was sent to aid in healing her, however they failed. At 0900 this morning her fever spiked and she passed away." Ruth blurted out.

She watched the light flicker out of Emma's eyes, her body turning into jelly as all the air rushed out of her lungs. She barely had time to catch her as she fell limply towards her and then she felt her tears like hot lava running down her back. Pushing her pain away, Ruth pulled Emma closer, and held her tightly as bone wrenching sobs tore through her body. A few seconds later Tamika tenderly pulled Emma away from her and into her arms.

Ruth blinked three times bringing the world back into focus and ending her trance. Hissing in pain, she glanced down at her shoulder to see trails of seared cloth and flesh running down her back from where the tears had fallen. She leaned forward, letting out a tiny cry as she began to not only feel the burns, but also the emotions she had been holding in. Suddenly, Anton was standing behind her pouring something that felt like cold fire over her wounds. Ruth had to resist pulling away as the fiery pain ripped through her making it impossible for her to do anything other than scream and then it was over. Anton very gently draped a warm towel over her shoulders before backing off so she'd have a chance to recover. Shuddering with effort, she slowly stood back up, and pulled the towel tight. She found the nearest spot where she could sit, and collapsed like a rag doll.

At first nothing happened, then ever so slowly her flesh began to heal from the deepest wound to the most shallow until they were all gone. Ruth slowly sat back up, rolling her shoulders in an attempt to loosen the new skin, and gave Anton a thankful smile.

"And now she cries acid." She laughed.

"Emma is extraordinary and is evolving at an incredible rate." Anton replied proudly.

"Any thoughts for a woman trying to help her?" Ruth asked curiously.

"Useptis have a ritual for when the Useptis mourns the Useptis dead to release pain so that no aggression remains. Let Anton do this for Emma." Anton replied.

"I'll get you clearance. How much time do you need?" Ruth asked.

"Three days."

Anton turned his focus away from her making her sigh in relief at being able to escape the lab.

Shadow Log: Tamika, Shadow Base, North Dakota, December 25, 1814

Tamika was still trying to understand why people suddenly felt the need to be all cheerful, full of mirth while giving pointless gifts to each other, and pretending to care. She found most holidays to be a pointless waste of time meant to drag you into forced social obligation. She was just thankful that Emma felt the same way and she was happy to spend the day in bed snuggling.

"My mother gave me this hand carved whale bone brooch last Christmas that had two really beautiful fish circling each other. I sobbed for a week when it was stolen from me as it was the last thing she ever carved." She whispered into the dark.

Emma pulled her closer, kissed the top of her head, and whispered, "I was never worthy of gifts."

She could feel the empathy oozing out of Emma in comforting waves that washed over her making her feel much lighter.

"You are lucky to have had such a good mother." Emma added.

"She was blind and yet she made the most beautiful art and never once complained. I just wish she had told me about The Shadows." Tamika sighed.

"Mine just kept me in a closet." Emma muttered.

Tamika rested her head on her chest, closed her eyes, and let her pull her close. She had more bruises, scrapes, and soreness than was remotely comfortable, but Emma was so gentle. Training with Arabella was like training with a madwoman who was also a perfectionist. She pushed her hard, never accepted excuses, and made sure every lesson was learned before moving on. It had already made such a difference in her abilities and in her confidence despite the physical torment of the daily training sessions. Emma was always going to be more talented on the ground and with hand to hand than she could ever have, but now she was getting to the point of being able to provide better aerial support.

"Anton is the last of our hive." Tamika muttered.

"In many ways we are lucky, we will always have each other." Emma said gently.

"Excuse me, pardon the interruption, but we need to speak." Hubert interrupted making them both jump in surprise.

"I've been trying to talk to you for days!" Emma grumbled almost angrily.

"And I have been busy for days. Come inside," Hubert ordered. A door appeared in their minds and when they walked through it they found themselves standing in a cozy little cabin with three comfy chairs facing a burning fire. Settling into a chair, Tamika couldn't help but smile at how perfect the chill of the room was in proportion to the heat of the fire. Hubert let Emma sit before he took the last chair and settled in staring at the fire intently.

"You've been researching the Black Death which is very wise as it will eventually end the world if we can't find a cure." Hubert sighed after a very long pause.

"There is no cure; I found the base code for the plague last night." Tamika sighed back.

"Explain!" Hubert demanded.

"It is a computer virus that mutates to its host; for example: a computer needs ooze while an organic being needs something more parasitic. Once it infects its host it mutates to cause maximum damage to not only its host, but also the host world. It's a failsafe meant to keep us from stopping the Stahl from ending everything." Tamika explained as best as she could.

Finding that information was heart wrenching especially after what Theodore had done for them. Fire itself wasn't enough alone to stop the plague, but at least it was a way to slow it down when it got out again. Hubert had been right all along in saying that The Shadows had destroyed everything already. "How long do we have before the next outbreak? Or is that not something we can calculate?" Emma asked.

"Around the year 2020. It'll start as the flu and then over the course of years it'll mutate into the Black Death killing anyone exposed. What we'll have to do is find a way to save as many people as we can from exposure to the virus. If we can contain the outbreak we should be able to build a spaceship to save a portion of the population." Tamika replied.

She opened the bridge between their minds and gave Emma all of the information she had so that she could understand what was happening.

"There won't be any exposure if we leave around 2010." Hubert suggested.

Tamika smiled widely wishing she had realized that herself, but that would take away ten years from their timetable.

"Good thing we have two hundred years to build a ship and find a new home not just for us, but for the Useptis as well. Preferably two separate worlds so we don't end up fighting each other and no more than a few years travel from Earth. We don't want to mess with cryo insanity." Tamika laughed.

"You have two hundred years, I, however, have until the end of this meeting. You see, I had Stewart unwind me from the mainframe so that I could absorb the corruption inside of the code while he pulled the physical manifestation out with his body. I have been preparing my successor for my departure so that you will still have support and one point of contact. You'll meet him when he gets where he can talk to the living and I promise you this; it is someone you know." Hubert said, sounding surprisingly peaceful.

"Wait, you're dying for real now?" Emma muttered in shock.

"Yes, exactly that. I outlived my shell and created something incredible that will outlive me and help change the world, please do not mourn my passing." Hubert said firmly.

Tamika made herself blink then twitch before she could start thinking again as she tried to process what she had just heard. Hubert had been shielding them from The Shadows from the beginning, making sure they were disconnected from the mainframe, setting up cold storage for them, and investigating the Stahl. She just hoped whoever was replacing him was strong enough to fill his shoes.

"Back to the topic at hand, I think you have a workable plan now. Please, get Anton onboard with this and get whatever help he can offer. Tamika, darling, I want you to have this." Hubert said.

Tamika just sat there in stunned silence waiting for something to happen and then the moment passed. That is when a ball of green light separated from Hubert's body and flew into her knocking her into the back of her seat. In the blink of an eye she could understand the code behind the machines and how to manipulate it with her mind.

"Woah…Thank you." She whispered in awe.

"You're welcome, Emma, it's your turn." Hubert chuckled happily.

This time a blue orb detached itself from him and flew into Emma giving her the ability to openly communicate with power sources and open electronic locks.

"Between you both, you have everything that I have ever truly learned about technology. Now, I have taken the last of the corrupt code into myself and must self delete." Hubert slurred.

He faded away leaving them laying back in bed, snuggled down into their nest, and wrapped in each other's arms.

"That was interesting." Emma muttered.

Tamika answered with a tired little grunt as she snuggled deeper into Emma's embrace, and went back to sleep.

Shadow Log: Emma, The Sahara Desert, January 19, 1815

Emma blinked as the transporter hummed to life and in a bright flash of light carried her across the world to the home of heat and sand. Feeling the sun beating down on her, Emma let her scales erupt as she stretched up towards the sky. She blew a kiss to Tamika, took a deep breath of the scorching air, and turned to face Anton.

"Did you hear that Stewart is being replaced today?" Tamika asked suddenly.

"Yes, of course I heard. I am connected to you, Little Miss Gossip." Emma sarcastically replied.

"Rumor has it that you are getting your pub as well…And this Stuart is different from the first…" Tamika chattered.

"Enough! You humans talk enough to drive a herd of Unta to jump from a cliff." Anton snapped.

Emma and Tamika exchanged a silent look as they started to collect their gear off of the ground.

"Why are we in the desert anyways?" Tamika grumbled.

"The Useptis were born on a world that looked like this for as far as the eye could see. Bred for war, slaughtered by it, and left to die by our creators. Loss is practically embedded into our DNA and the Ueptis must move ever forward without grief. The Ritual of the Stars is a way to help do this and today we shall do one of our own. Come." Anton replied with stern gentleness.

They began to walk deeper into the dunes, Tamika to Anton's right while Emma was to his left, their pace slowly increasing until they were running in complete silence. Their bodies stretched out, their heartbeats accelerated, and then all thought fell away as they pushed themselves to the limit to keep up with Anton. They ran and ran and ran until the morning sun had turned into evening stars leaving them panting, sore, and grouchy.

They stopped before a glowing pink altar that hovered just above the floor of the shallow cave that kept it concealed from the world. Anton lifted his head to the stars, letting out a howl of anguish that was impossible to ignore, and soon they were all howling in mourning. Then he began to prance around in what looked like a fevered dance that drew them in and soon it had them all dancing in the moonlight as silence fell over the grove. He stopped dead in his tracks as the stars began to truly shine and let out one final loud howl.

"We give of our flesh to nourish the dead." Anton whispered.

He drew a long, curved, razor sharp, ritual knife and used it to remove the pinky of his lower most hand. He set the removed appendage on the altar allowing his blood to flow freely into the basin until his stump had healed a few moments later. He bowed to the altar and passed the knife to Tamika who followed his lead and removed her left pinky. Emma accepted the knife, took a deep breath, and took off her right pinky, allowing her blood to mix with theirs.

"We Useptis give of the Useptis fur to provide warmth for the dead." Anton whispered.

He took the knife back, used it to carefully shave off a patch of fur from his chest, and passed it back to Emma. Thinking quickly, Emma cut off a lock of hair, and passed the knife to Tamika as Anton sprinkled his fur into the blood. Emma dropped her hair into the basin and moved to the side so that Tamika could do the same with ease.

"We give of our teeth to protect the dead." Anton said.

He plucked out a tooth, dropped it into the basin, and used the blood to mark his forehead with a V. Emma wasn't happy about the thought of pulling out a tooth, but she did as she was told as did Tamika. The altar's light flared and when Emma looked back the offerings were gone. And to Emma's surprise so was the weight of grief on her shoulders.

She felt lighter, more focused, and more capable of thought which was definitely a pleasant surprise.

"The ancestors have blessed us." Anton said peacefully.

He concealed the altar once more before he turned to face them and gave them both a quick bow of respect.

"This trip feels like it was about more than just this ritual. You want to enlighten us as to what you have up your sleeve?" Emma asked quietly.

She had learned how to read him pretty well over the last few months and she could tell he was nervous about something. She had never seen him nervous for no reason and so she was getting nervous.

"Useptis is a concept that means to us, it is the Useptis way of identity, their way to find something outside of the masters. The Stahl rode us into battle, forced us to die for their wars, and in return the Useptis got new scars. Look around and tell Anton what Emma sees, really look with all of your sight." Anton commanded.

Emma did as she was told, seeing nothing but dunes of sand intermixed with the occasional rock, and then she felt everything shift. Dozens of Useptis outlines appeared around her, each going about some ordinary daily routine, and then ever so slowly she began to be able to pick out the outlines of buildings. She spun in a circle, laughing joyously, and as she came to a stop gave Anton a small bow.

"Your hive?" She asked excitedly.

"Anton's hive. Concealed away from all that wishes it harm, but safely within reach. Look at them! The Useptis never had a chance to test themselves outside of battle before this and they are thriving!" He bragged.

"I wanted to ask; did you find any planets that could be used as a home world for your kind or mine?" Tamika asked pointedly.

Anton eyed her for a long moment before answering, *"Anton found four possibilities within cryo safe distance however each has a downside. Eta- giant vicious beasts on a very heavily forested planet, Uti-Mostly water, there are limited jungle like contents scattered across it, Tea- Every soft plant that you touch can cause extreme happiness that can lead to death, and last Ti- mountains, storms, and deserts. The Useptis were leaning towards Eta since it will give us a challenge and plenty to hunt. Perhaps, Ti would be best for humans as it has problems that humans already deal with."*

"We'll probably rename it, but it does sound promising. What about transportation?" Tamika asked before Emma could.

"The Useptis have scavenged many parts, tools, and materials from the wrecks, however the Useptis need to ensure we get home safely, this takes time."

"Two hundred years give or take a few is how long we have." Emma cut them both off.

Her head was beginning to hurt at all of the thoughts constantly bouncing around in it and she was starting to understand how Anton must feel all the time. In truth, she was anxious to get back to some semblance of a life with less death in it. First, Johnathan and Jacob, then her mother and Grace, followed by Emily's death. It sucked to think about the people she'd outlive, the challenges to come, and of the deaths they were all facing. It hurt to see how many of these rituals were bound to be in her future and to accept it was even harder.

"Anton will be ready on time." Anton promised confidently. Emma flashed him a smile, buried her worries as deeply as she could, and turned to Tamika, and asked, *"Do you think we can trust Ruth with her part of the plan?"*

"We can, Ruth may be a horrible human being, but she keeps her word." Anton replied calmly.

"Anton is right, she won't be a problem. It's whoever is replacing Hubert that has my scales riled." Tamika added.

"Hubert wouldn't leave his post unless it was wellmanned with someone he trusted. We have nothing to worry about there either. What scares me is this: How far will The Shadows go to keep this world under their thumb?" Emma asked quietly.

They all exchanged a look of worry tinged in fear all mixed up with nerves. None of them had anything they could say to answer that question and so none wished to break the silence that had peacefully settled over them. Emma forced herself to think on the more immediate concerns that she needed to untangle. After all, there was no point in her getting lost before they even began.

"Let us bed down for the night." Anton finally whispered, sending them scurrying to set up camp.

Shadow Log: Ruth, Shadow Base, North Dakota, January 21, 1815

Ruth slipped out of B's room just before the sun would be creeping over the horizon, her breath steaming in the cool hallway, and every sound echoing back at her. She had five minutes at most to sneak back to her own pod if she didn't want to get caught sleeping with the boss. The Shadows had three shifts that rotated out on a daily basis that kept them safe twenty-four seven, however at shift change the halls were flooded with people trying to get to their posts on time. Taking a moment to collect herself, she did a few jumping jacks, and darted down the hall at a dead run.

Sliding to a stop outside of her pod, Ruth swiped her ID badge, and quickly crawled inside. In some ways, she envied Emma's ability to be open with her choices, and her actual room with a private bathroom. That didn't mean she wanted any of the other nightmares that went with those privileges. She quickly brushed her hair out, slithered out of her clothes, and crawled underneath her blankets. Settling down, she found a comfortable position, and fell asleep.

Someone pounding on her pod startled her awake and made her growl unhappily at the interruption to her sleep. Rubbing her eyes to get the grit out, she took several sips of water, and rolled to face the entrance. Letting out a sigh, she slammed the window open, and found herself staring up at an anxious Emma.

"Aren't you supposed to be in the desert?" Ruth asked sleepily.

"What? Oh, we sorted that out earlier. We have a problem, a major problem at that!" Emma sputtered far too quickly.

"Out with it." Ruth moaned.

"There is a Useptis crash sighting near the old school!" Emma jibbered excitedly.

"Go, get suited up and I'll get to the command center." Ruth groaned.

She shut the window, drained the rest of her water bottle, and began to quickly get dressed. Once she was decent, she grabbed her hair ribbon, and secured her hair in a tight ponytail. The moment she slid her pod open she found Emma patiently waiting for her. Cursing under her breath, she pushed Emma out of her way, and climbed down to the floor. Grabbing her boots, she grabbed her mouthwash from her locker, and began to rinse out her mouth. She grabbed her shadow-band, strapped it on, shook out her boots, and slammed them onto her feet all while gargling.

She spit into the sink, "You're waiting on me is not going to speed me up." Ruth grumbled.

"I know, I just, I don't know…"

"You need closure, I get it. However, the mission comes first and right now you're as unfocused as a kid on sugar." Ruth interrupted.

"Well…Yes, I guess, but it's more what I feel in the air. It's vibrating on my skin like a thousand jacks bouncing across my body, boring into my mind like a thousand hornets defending their hive, a quiet, persistent, high pitched, whine that is always whispering in my ears. It started after that thing crashed and I'm not the only one feeling it." Emma said, speaking so rapidly that she was practically tripping over her words.

Ruth locked up her locker before she calmly refilled her bottle of water and grabbed her go bag.

"Come on, let's go talk to B about getting you clearance to go off base. Oh, and you should probably thank him for approving your tavern idea." Ruth sighed.

Emma just nodded as she fell into step with her making Ruth chuckle at her urgency. B barely glanced up from his desk before he waved them towards Ruth's office as their bands chimed. Ruth immediately grabbed Emma's arms and redirected her into her own office where Tamika was already waiting.

"I spoke to B and got us clearance already, I didn't want to wait. Your weapons dear," Tamika explained nervously.

Ruth grabbed her headset and began to boot up her monitors.

"It will be about five minutes until I'm online, but if you wish to risk jumping now no one will stop you."

She glanced over her shoulder just in time to see them both vanish in a flash of light. She knew that they were freaked out, but that didn't mean she wanted them breathing down her neck.

Shadow Log: Emma, Clover School for Girls, Rhode Island, January 21, 1815

Emma had to admit that Jacob had done an admirable job with leveling the school. If it weren't for the occasional burnt timber peaking through the snow there wouldn't be any trace of the horrors this place had once held. What she didn't find was evidence of any signs of remotely recent battle which she found unnerving. There was supposed to be an active crash, flaming debris, something to say there was trouble. Yet here she was alone in the snow laden ruins…

"TAMIKA!" Emma screamed, feeling panic set in.

Or at least she tried to. Instead no sound came out at all. No matter how hard she struggled to talk she couldn't make a single noise. Seeing a shard of glass laying on the ground, she quickly retrieved it, and looked at her appearance. She was back to being a normal thirteen year old with no trace of her sepsis side and her throat had clearly been cut at some point. The scar was grizzly and poorly treated which meant poor medical care. From the crossbow she held in her left hand

and the shield in her right she figured she had to be somewhere hostile.

She found cover under a half burnt desk and tried to get her bearings. That's when she saw it! A pale, poorly nourished, horrible smelling humanoid creature shambling slowly past. Looking around in shock, she realized she was surrounded by these things, but they were ignoring her for some reason. To make matters worse she was starving. If she closed her eyes she could almost taste the blood of her prey already.

She had to be in another version of earth inside of another Emma, but that didn't help her get back where she belonged. Suddenly a voice in her ear startled her out of her thoughts, "You okay boss?"

"You stopped moving towards the target." The voice grumbled a moment later.

Emma took a moment to try and sort out what the voice was saying, "Seriously?! Get to the Smith Farmhouse and blow it up." The voice ordered.

Emma let out a little gasp seeing that she had a vest full of explosives strapped to her chest. She saw no harm in helping Emma, but she didn't really want to die. She slowly crept out from her hiding spot and carefully stood up causing everything to spin…

And then, she was doing everything she could do to get the sludge out of her throat by hurling all over Tamika's shoes. Groaning from the pain of the transition, she let Tamika hold her up while she got her footing back.

"That was weird." She muttered.

"Weird? I was suddenly sharing brain space with a stranger and then I got my boots puked on!" Tamika replied with mock offense.

"I thought Anton had taken care of this issue. No matter, what have we learned?" She hissed.

"That what we are feeling is coming from that crystal and Anton says it is overloading. It'll kill everything on this planet if it explodes, but it can't be moved because it doesn't have a true form." Tamika calmly filled her in.

"What do we do? How do we stop it?" Emma asked in alarm.

"We need to figure out how to either stop the overload or move the crystal. We have three or four hours to do this, any thoughts?" Tamika asked hopefully.

"T, you're the smart one, not me." Emma moaned.

"True, but you have that database in your head." Tamika shot back.

Emma smiled coldly, crouched down, and placed her finger in the mud.

What are transition crystals and how do you move them?

Transition crystals exist in every dimension, every world , and in every time all at once. If one is connected properly to the crystal they can use it to port into their alternate selves.

Transition Crystals cannot be moved and any tampering may set off the self defense mechanism that will cause it to erase your world from existence. If this device is armed the only way to disarm it is using a bone key.

What is a bone key?

This key much like the transition crystals exist everywhere all at once. There is a ritual to summon it to you using the blood of a goat.

Emma gave Tamika a worried look as she got back on her feet.

"Know where we can get a goat on short notice?" She asked curiously.

Suddenly a goat materialized between them making them both jump in surprise.

"I'm always listening." Ruth commented dryly.

Emma was mad at herself for forgetting she had her headset running with Ruth on the other end. She had to be more mindful of her surroundings when she was on a mission, a slip like that could lead to a lot of consequences for a lot of people.

She grabbed the goat, carefully cradling it in her arms as it mewed unhappily, and headed for the farmhouse. Tamika followed her moving with surprising speed and grace while still managing to not make a sound.

"Your training seems to be paying off." She remarked.

"Arabella is an excellent teacher." Tamika said as she blushed. They reached the spot where the farmhouse had once been to find a crater glowing with blue slime mold that smelled like dirty feet. The crystal pulsated at the center of it changing colors every few seconds as its energy exploded out into the world. Not wanting to waste another second of time, she bolted down the side of the crater, and found herself hip deep in mold. Pulling her hood up, she waded slowly through the muck, dragging the goat with her, and trudged up to the stone.

"Sorry little guy." She whispered softly to the goat.

She pulled out her hunting knife and quickly slit its throat allowing the spray of blood to coat the crystal and cool it down. Within a minute the crystal was quiet once more as fresh blood dripped from its peak leaving behind nothing but blood red streaks. Cradling the goat's body to her chest, she made her way to the edge, and allowed Tamika to help her up and out of the mold.

"It deserves a proper burial after saving the world." Emma mumbled tiredly.

"I'll take care of it, you just rest my love." Tamika promised. Emma passed the carcass over to Tamika, rolled onto her back, and drifted off into a fevered sleep.

Shadow Log: Tamika, Shadow Base, North Dakota, February 4, 1815

Tamika watched Emma sleep feeling the dreams from the coma washing over her like waves of pain filled with the sewage of doubt. Tamika wanted to help her, to pull her back to reality, but the doctor had made it clear that this was what was best for now. She had been lucky to get them both home before the mold exposure became incapacitating to her as well.

Forcing herself to be rational, she turned to face Anton, and asked, "She is still connected to the crystal isn't she?"

Anton stared at her for an intense few moments, *"The crystal Matrix will always be a part of her DNA, however she should not transition accidentally again."*

"As if we weren't dealing with enough problems as it is." Tamika sighed.

She understood that they were at war and that meant making sacrifices, living uncomfortably, and being trapped by circumstances. However, all she wanted to do was find Emma and take her far away from all of it so that she could heal. As it stood she was just a helpless bystander waiting for her lover to recover.

"Emma is strong. Emma will recover. Anton does worry about Tamika though. Tamika was nearly dead when found and…"

"If you want to live I wouldn't finish that sentence." Tamika cut him off.

She had no desire to go poking around in her past for misery when she had enough of that here.

"I fear Tamika has been overstretched as of late." Anton said, clearly changing tactics.

"She is fearless, outgoing, and everything I wanted to be growing up, but now I can see how much it cost her. I may be overstretched, but I promise you that I am not about to snap as long as people stop asking stupid questions. Do you know how many people want to know what we're going to name the tavern?" Tamika ranted.

"Anton would call it the Drafty Cooch and put a lizard in a dress with his tail raised picture on the sign next to it." Anton chuckled.

"The name is Emma's to decide, it is her project after all. How much longer will she sleep?" Tamika asked worriedly.

"A day, a month, or a year who is to say what her body wants or needs." Anton replied unhelpfully.

"I guess, I'll handle the egg burn on my own tomorrow then. Keep an eye on her for me please?"

"Of course." Anton promised.

Tamika nodded in agreement and headed for her own bed, the day was late, and she would need her rest for what was to come.

Shadow Log: Emma, Shadow Base, North Dakota, March 24, 1815

Emma woke to find herself back in the infinite darkness that was cold storage. It had always been a matter of time before she'd end up dead again, but she had fought hard to avoid that fate. Although she had definitely wanted to remain out of this place for as long as possible she now had an opportunity to talk to Hubert's replacement. Right on que Jacob materialized and brought the cozy cabin along with him.

"Wading through toxic mold is most unadvised." He sighed from his chair.

"Better one death than billions." Emma replied as she sat down next to him.

"Indeed, especially when that death can be reversed. It is good to see you again." Jacob chuckled.

"You as well. Tell me, how do you get a job after death?" Emma laughed back.

"Obviously you have to die and then after that it's all numbers. How is Mary? I have kept tabs on her, but have not succeeded in learning much."

"She is good, happy, and safe." Emma promised.

"Good, good, ah ha, I remember now! Sorry, I am still adjusting to death and am often forgetful. I came across a locked folder that Hubert hasn't been able to access and after some probing I learned that it can only be accessed from an offsite location in Antarctica. I don't know what is in the file obviously, but my gut says it is massively important." Jacob explained.

"I'll see what I can find out about it, and Jacob it's good to see you." Emma promised.

"I'm not strong enough to reach beyond the matrix yet, but I am learning and evolving quickly. I'll be in touch as soon as I am able, however for now please be vigilant."

The room vanished in a puff of light and the moment she returned to her feet her chair followed suit. She blinked and awoke strapped to a table in Anton's lab staring up at the light all again. Without thought she went to sit up, jarring her wrists against the restraints, and ripping them from the table. She reached down, released her ankles from their restraints, and hopped down off of the table. Her catsuit covered her naked body as she quickly tied up her hair and looked around for Anton.

"Anton had his feed day moved again," Tamika called from their room.

Smiling happily, she quickly walked over, and promptly fell into Tamika's arms.

"Don't worry, I got you. You have been out for a while and it will be a bit before your stability returns." Tamika whispered gently.

"Jacob isn't dead, he's the one replacing Hubert." Emma muttered.

She opened up her mind and quickly gave Tamika all of the relevant information before she gave her a quick kiss.

"That is interesting…Does Mary know?" Tamika asked.

"No, and it should remain that way until Jacob can tell her himself." Emma said sternly.

"Our little secret." Tamika promised.

Shadow Log: Tamika, Shadow Base, North Dakota, March 24, 1815

Arabella threw Tamika effortlessly from the balcony making Tamika roll and throw her scarf at a railing on the fifth floor to keep from falling six stories. It was strange to have the ability to almost fly with just a few properly constructed scarfs, Tamika was starting to understand the mechanics of the art. However, she had a few broken bones, bruises, and scrapes to mark her numerous failures. Today was about sudden unexpected attacks that caused her to fall randomly which had already left her sore and mildly irritable.

"I think you broke a rib!" She protested as she rubbed her right side gingerly.

"Better a few ribs than your skull. You need to get in tune with your surroundings so that it is harder to be ambushed." Arabella replied gently.

"I'm trying, I'm just distracted today. Emma is worried and restless which is bleeding into my mind like a trickle of poison." Tamika sighed.

"There will always be distractions, the key is to focus on the moment and make every second count. The first time I got on the highwire I broke eight bones and was in a coma for a month, but the moment I could get back up there I did. There is no such thing as failure as long as you keep trying." Arabella replied softly.

Just as Tamika finished rewinding her scarf a giant burst of static echoed through her brain making her jump in surprise and pain. Blinking rapidly as her vision became blurry, she fell to her knees, and lost consciousness. She woke to find herself in a vast unending darkness that felt chilly and very unwelcoming. Carefully returning to her feet, Tamika surveyed her surroundings, and tried to figure out what had happened and where she was.

"Forgive me for the rudeness of that transition. It is difficult to complete such functions with Jacob's interference." A gentle male voice said from behind her.

She turned around rapidly letting out a little yelp of surprise as the AI materialized behind her. She could feel Emma's memories of this AI and they told her that it probably wasn't a threat, but she wasn't going to drop her guard just yet.

"Harmon?" She asked suspiciously.

The AI glowed happily at being recognized, "I see Emma remembers my help."' He purred.

"You helped her survive and trained her to fight. We owe you. Now, why am I here?"

"I am fading away, being pushed out by the dead. My job is important, my job is to record history to make sure that it is never forgotten. It is forgotten far too often and…" Harmon tried to explain.

"I agree with you about the necessity of remembering the past. How can I help?" Tamika asked softly.

"Talk to Jacob and ask him to give Harmon room so it can do its job." Harmon pleaded.

"I can do that. However, I sense that there is something deeper bothering you. What is it that I can help with?" She asked gently.

Harmon glowed with worry, looking like he was about to explode, and then everything suddenly shifted as a rainbow of light began to explode out of him. Tamika shielded her eyes as the light began overwhelming everything

"Harmon is sick. Harmon doesn't know why or how, but it is dying and in need of help." Harmon sighed as the light dissipated.

"I'll look into it for you." Tamika promised.

And in the blink of an eye she was back in her own body laying face up in Arabella's arms as she gently stroked her hair. Giving her a gentle smile, Tamika carefully sat up, and took a deep breath. It felt like someone had run her over with a carriage and she was struggling to even breathe past the new bruises sprouting on her body. Looking around, she could see that she had fallen to the first floor when she had passed out.

"Are you okay?" Arabella asked gently.

"I think I will be. That was just a weird conversation with someone who needed help." Tamika sighed unhappily.

"I see. I won't pry further. Would you like to continue your training or go get some rest?" Arabella asked with a laugh.

"I think rest is in order. Thank you for understanding." Tamika moaned.

She struggled up onto her feet and stumbled away wishing that she could heal a bit faster.

Shadow Log: Emma, The Shadow Research Base, March 25, 1815

It was just like Theodore to place a potentially world-ending discovery in the coldest place on earth and to place that base at the bottom of an icy staircase that spun endlessly down into the dark. The entrance to which was hidden in the basement of the cabin where he had come to die. Standing in the remains of the rundown and frozen cabin, she felt such heartbreak at the thought of how much she had cost those who dared to love her. Johnathan, Jacob, even Grace in her own way had died to protect her. Ruth was forever changed, Tamika as well, and that didn't even take into account the suffering of the loved ones left in her wake.

Emma pulled her parka tighter, hefted her pack, and began the treacherous trip down the icy stairs. They were actually made of ice and had the slipperiness to prove causing her to immediately slip and fall on her ass. It was then that the situation went out of her hands and became quite terrifying as she slid ever forward. She slid faster and faster finding no leverage to slow herself and there was nothing to cling to stop her either. Soon the world spun by so fast that she couldn't do anything other than lean back on her backpack and use it like a sled. Faster and faster she went until there was nothing left but the whipping of air in her hair, the pain in her frozen butt, and the swirling blues that now made up the room. It all ended with a deafening crash when the staircase spat her out at warp speed causing her to crash through a wall made of icicles.

"Ow." She moaned once everything stopped spinning. Seeing a piece of ice sticking out of her side, she calmly reached down, and silently pulled it out. She quickly sealed the wound and collected her pack from where it had landed after ejecting towards the end of the ride. It had been a much more painful descent than she had expected and she was much more sore for the bewildering experience. She was just going full lizard and climbing up the walls to get out otherwise she was probably trapped. Pulling out her staff, she pulled her hood up, and began to formulate a plan.

She was in a perfectly round room approximately twenty feet in length down its center which was marked with the icicle wall. On one side of the circle was the staircase and on the other was a large black engraved door that had started to glow with silver writing similar to what she had seen in the book of death. It was easy enough for her to read after a few moments of concentration.

"Here lies the Liber Vitae may it never join with the Liber Vitae under the hands of evil." She read slowly.

She watched the doors swing slowly open to reveal a small spherical room with a pedestal with an ordinary book sitting on it that looked like the one she had stashed not so long ago. She knew before opening it that this book completed the code from the other making everything work and that Theodore had just handed her a miracle. That didn't stop her from flipping it open to a random page and reading it over just to make sure. Harmony had already removed this place from the database so there was no harm in leaving the book where it was for now. It was highly unlikely anyone would find this place or survive entry into it and she didn't want anyone to know what she found.

"I'm coming home." She told Tamika as she began her ascent to the surface.

Shadow Log: Emma, Carlsbad, New Mexico, April 2, 1815

Emma was mildly impressed by the sheer size of the cave system and its many caverns. She had already been through multiple tunnels, caves, and large caverns, but as of yet she hadn't found the source of the disturbance. She could feel Tamika slowly creeping through the tunnels on the other side of the cavern and it made Emma glow with happiness at having her so close. She stumbled out of the tunnel she was exploring and found herself staring up at hundreds of large webbed sacks.

"Emma should be careful, those are Etora. Burrowing spiders that burrow into your skin and live beneath the surface of the skin eating their host alive." Anton warned anxiously.

Emma took a couple of steps backwards not wanting to experience that kind of horror.

"How do I handle it?" Emma asked with surprising calmness. *"Run? No, you are too brave for that. Fire is your best bet, however they swarm when threatened and are the size of your hand."* Anton grumbled.

Emma pulled her hood up as she calmly pulled out the torch from her bag. Feeling Tamika getting closer, she took a deep breath, flipped the torch on, and crept back into the cavern. She lit the first cocoon on fire causing a strange vibrating hum to start shivering through the air like cold dread. Trying to hurry, she burned five more cocoons, and then she saw them. Thousands of spiders charged down the walls, swarming out of the remaining cocoons as the fire began to spread. Emma let out a quiet curse as she tried to back away from the swarm but they were a lot faster than she anticipated and it wasn't long before she was swatting them off of her legs.

Seeing thousands of the spiders closing in, she lit the torch again, and began to try to burn as many of them as she could. But they just kept coming, dozens at a time, each faster, and more agile than any spider she had ever encountered before. Screaming in terror, she threw herself into a pool of water, and sank down to the bottom. She could see them hovering on the edge of the pool waiting for her to come back up for air making her very thankful for her gills. Fire erupted across the top of the pool scorching the remaining spiders into ash as Tamika ran into the room.

Emma breached the surface making sure that there were no more spiders left alive and then she rolled out of the pool once she was sure it was safe.

"Thanks." She panted.

"No problem, the nest room is consumed with fire and Ruth says she can't detect any more activity. Did any of them manage to burrow into your armor and scales?" Tamika replied.

"No, I'm good, although I think I might hate spiders for the rest of my life." Emma laughed.

"Anton, how did they get here?" Tamika asked pointedly.

Anton did not respond, leaving them to stare at each other in silence. Emma groaned as she shook the water out of her suit and retrieved her torch from where she had dropped it while fleeing.

"He apparently doesn't wish to comment at this time." Emma sighed.

"First the Useptis, then the Stahl, and now this. How many threats can we face before we're consumed by them?" Tamika asked sadly.

Emma tried to smile, but it came out as more of a grimace as she tried to find a suitable answer to the question. The truth was that these threats would just keep coming no matter how hard they fought because they were the only ones capable of not being killed by them. She pulled Tamika into a hug, and held her close.

"As long as we have each other we will be fine." Emma promised as she nuzzled into Tamika's neck.

"I love you." Tamika whispered back.

Shadow Log: Ruth, Shadow Base, North Dakota, April 3, 1815

Ruth still had the hibijibis from yesterday's mission, she hated spiders and knowing that alien spiders had somehow made it to Earth was very disconcerting. She couldn't concentrate on Ben despite his insistent kissing and snuggling. Something just felt wrong, it was almost like she had missed something yesterday, but couldn't figure out what it was.

Ben finally pulled back sensing that she wasn't fully engaged and asked, "What's bothering you?"

His gentleness was wonderful as was his respect, but he was her boss and that meant it could get complicated very easily. She calmly crawled out of bed, walked over to the corner chair, and slipped into her robe.

"Spiders, I can't get them out of my head. I think we might have missed something, but I can't figure out what." She sighed.

"Walk me through it." Ben ordered gently.

"I picked up an unusual radiation spike from some large cave and sent Emma and Tamika to check it out. We found a large cluster of Etora, burned out their nest, and I sent a team to do a sweep. They found nothing but burnt sacks and dead spiders which they got cleaned up." Ruth ran through it.

"Did you find the queen? The Etora are a hive society just like bees." Ben asked gently.

Ruth's head snapped around so quickly that she almost gave herself whiplash.

"How big is the queen?" She asked in horror.

"Think of a pony or a large dog."

"No, we didn't find it. I knew I was missing something!" Ruth exclaimed.

"Scan for beta radiation and adjust the sensors by a tenth of a degree that should make it show up on your scans." Ben said, sitting up.

Before Ruth could respond the room began to spin wildly and she felt overwhelmed with nausea. Grabbing the wall for support, she tried to get her body back under control, but failed. She hurled all over the floor before she could stop herself and promptly fainted.

She woke up in the infirmary with the worst headache she had ever experienced making the light burn into her eyes. Groaning, she forced herself to sit up, and immediately regretted the decision as the room started spinning again. A nurse suddenly appeared at her side to help steady her as she got her bearings.

"Thank you." Ruth muttered.

"Just doing my job. How are you feeling?" The nurse replied.

"Nauseous and my head feels like it will explode." Ruth moaned.

"You hit your head when you fainted earlier, the headache will fade away soon. Did you know you're pregnant?"

Ruth's brain stopped working, all thoughts disappearing in the blink of an eye as she tried to process that sentence. Pregnant, pregnant how had she let that happen? Was she even qualified to be a mother? Was Ben going to be a good father? These questions left her staring blankly at the wall trying to process everything.

"Uh, I didn't." She managed to mutter.

"Oh, sorry, I would have been more gentle if I had known. Do you know who the father is?" The nurse asked.

Ruth eyed her tiredly, she had no idea how to answer that question anymore than she knew how to tell Ben he was going to be a father. Remembering her spider problem, she forced herself to stand up, and start getting dressed.

"I do, but for now I'd like to keep that to myself. Am I cleared for work?" She asked sharply.

"You are, I'll finish your discharge from the infirmary."

Ruth walked so quickly that she was almost running as she hurried to her office. Switching on the monitors, she made the necessary adjustments, and started the scan. She hoped that it would come up negative, however she was pretty sure she wasn't going to be so lucky.

"Are you feeling better?" Ben asked from the doorway.

"I am, thank you. Ben, there is something you should know." Ruth sighed.

She turned to face him, gave him a forced smile, and sighed
again. It wasn't that she was afraid of what he would say, she
was afraid of losing him, of losing her happiness.
"Out with it." Ben ordered.
"I'm pregnant."
As the words left her mouth her monitors started screaming
as a loud alarm started screeching with panic. She spun back
to them seeing that it had not only picked up a queen spider,
but thousands of eggs. Ben shook himself out of his shock,
hurried over to her, and took a long look at the readings.
"I'll support you and the child to the best of my ability. Now,
let us deal with the problem at hand, summon Emma." Ben
said firmly.

Shadow Log: Emma, Carlsbad Caverns, New Mexico, April 3, 1815

Emma had no idea of how she was supposed to burn so
many spiders without ending up with them burrowing into
her flesh. Everything seemed to be covered in webs, mucus,
and sleeping spiders, there was none of the cave visible under
the infestation. Tilting her head to the side, she wondered if
she could just firebomb it, and be done with this mess.
"Fire didn't solve the problem last time." Tamika warned.
"Any suggestions?" Emma asked in return.
*"I've been doing research and it looks like they are sensitive to UV
light. Ruth is sending you a lamp that you can set up. It won't kill
them, but it will keep them away from you while you kill the queen
which will destroy the hive."* Tamika offered.
Seconds later a strange lamp appeared in a flash of light next
to Emma bathing her in the warmth of its rays. Securing it to
her head, she found that it effectively bathed her in light
making her feel safer. She got her blood plumping by doing a
few jumping jacks before she slowly crept into the room. The
webs and spiders pulled back away from the light letting out
what sounded like a gurgly hiss that made her shudder. She
inched slowly forward doing her best to draw as little

attention as possible as she made her way towards the queen. Without warning a gigantic spider fell from the ceiling and knocked her over. Wriggling backwards as quickly as she could, she grabbed her staff, and smashed it into the spider's face. All it did was piss it off and cause it to spit webs in an attempt to snare her, she dodged easily, and slashed at it with her dagger.

It reared up on its four hind legs, screeching out a war cry, and summoned her children. The webs turned black with thousands of spiders that swarmed toward Emma stopping at the edge of the light as their little feet sparked from the contact. Focusing on the main threat, Emma pushed it back into a corner, but wasn't able to get past its legs to strike a fatal blow. Giving no warning a few hundred spiders descended from the ceiling and landed on her knocking the light clear of her head. The mildly burnt spiders then swarmed in looking for an opening to get inside of Emma, but then Tamika appeared in a flash of light behind the queen. Letting out an angry cry, Tamikia drove a spear into its torso, killing it instantly. The remaining spiders stopped moving, becoming unresponsive almost like puppets who no longer had strings. Emma took the opportunity to get clear of the pile of spiders that had been swarming her and carefully checked to make sure her scales were still intact.

"Perfect timing." She panted.

"Of course, we are one. It feels like they didn't make it below your scales at least." Tamika panted back.

"Why are you out of breath? Oh, you had to run to get where you could port safely."' Emma answered her own question.

"I should have come with you from the start." Tamika grumbled.

"You are more of a sniper than a brawler and I love you for that." Emma chuckled.

"How is it that we share a link to each other that is so deep we can easily swap bodies, but we can't…"

"Hey, we are one, bound by life's craziness, and you need to tell me what is really bothering you before I go digging in your brain." Emma cut her off.

Emma could tell that something was being hidden from her, but she wasn't sure what it was. She didn't want to violate Tamika's trust by digging through her memories to try and figure it out. The link had become more manageable as time went on, but was still something that she didn't fully understand. They had managed to put walls up between their consciousnesses keeping their minds mostly separate and allowing them to maintain their individual personalities. These walls were vital for their mental health, but it also meant that secrets were impossible to keep because they could be felt as could everything else.

"I have been dreaming of strange things lately. It is affecting my performance, but what is really bothering me is this feeling I have that something big is coming." Tamika sighed.

"I feel it too. A sense of impending doom like the world is about to end, what are we supposed to do about it?" Emma muttered in agreement.

"I don't know. How do you fight something that you don't even know what is or when it will come?" Tamika replied.

"Talk to Arabella and I will talk to Ruth and maybe we can figure out what is bothering us…Do you think that this could be Anton's brother?" Emma asked suddenly.

Tamika stared at her in complete silence as she thought through everything. Emma waited patiently, she wasn't even in the same orbit as Tamika when it came to intelligence which was fine. She was happy to be the more physical one in the relationship because it came with less responsibility.

"It could be, it has been a while since we have heard anything from him and The Shadows can't seem to find him either." Tamika finally whispered.

"I don't like this at all. I need something tangible to fight or I'm useless." Emma sighed unhappily.

"Hey, you have enough on your plate with Harmon and Jacob waging war against each other and the frequent crashes. Let me worry about this one," Tamika said gently. Emma just nodded, letting her pull her close, and hold her tightly. It was too much pressure and they were both about to crack under it, but maybe they would be able to keep each other safe.

Shadow Log: Emma, Shadow Base, North Dakota, April 13, 1815

Emma stared Anton down unwilling to concede any ground to him in the argument. She wanted him to help her find his brother and he wanted her to butt out of the situation. She couldn't do that for him, not if she wanted to be safe and to protect Earth from him.

"I understand that you want to handle your own family matters and I can respect that, however you are not thinking of the global impact of his actions. He is experimenting on humans. How long do you think The Shadows will wait before they issue a full investigation? How long before they start digging into our secrets." Emma tried again.

"Emma makes many good points…This one doesn't know where he is, but Anton can give Anton's best guess. Mountains, water, and ice have always attracted him as well as isolation." Anton sighed.

"That is more than we had before, thank you." Emma whispered.

"Anton feels that his hive is no longer safe. Brother will put everything at risk, Emma is right. Emma will handle The Shadows and keep everyone safe." Anton said confidently.

"I will do everything I can to protect my family." Emma promised.

Emma blinked and found herself standing in a lab that had clearly been carved into the side of a mountain. Turning around slowly, she came face to face with Eta'Var'Uti, and felt all the air escape her lungs.

"Emma has been looking for Eta'Var'Uti." He said loudly.

Emma blanched, she didn't know what was happening, or how she had ended up here in his lab.

"I have been, you're killing a lot of people." Emma replied as calmly as she could.

"Bah, inferior specimens that should have never been created. Even the Stahl found you useless, they created you to serve as the Useptis have, but you proved too unreliable. Sadly, This One is stuck here and must adapt." Eta'Var'Uti spat.

Emma stared at him, wishing she could just rip his throat out, and be done with him. Yet, she wasn't able to move for some reason.

"Listen closely human, The Shadows are the past and Eta'Var'Uti *is the future."* Eta'Var'Uti shouted.

Emma winced and found herself back in Anton's lab laying on her back with Anton staring down worriedly.

"Eta'Var'Uti just paid my brain a visit." Emma moaned as her head started pounding.

"Eta'Var'Uti must have a communication orb to reach so far with his mind. Anton is worried that Eta'Var'Uti will succeed in his experiments and Anton now knows what he is doing." Anton sighed.

Emma slowly climbed back to her feet, fetched some water, and found a chair to sit in. Rubbing her forehead, she took a long drink of water, and tried to think.

"Tell me his plan, please."

"Eta'Var'Uti is trying to put Useptis minds into the bodies of humans so that they can control this world."

Emma eyed Anton and tried to sort out the implications of what she had just heard. If Eta'Var'Uti succeeded things were going to get messy and confusing as hell. She didn't know how to deal with it and she could feel Tamika's confusion as well. Neither of them wanted him to succeed and yet neither knew how to accomplish the job of stopping him.

"Please, try and find him so that I can stop him." Emma pleaded.

"Anton is trying." Anton promised.

Emma nodded, she wasn't sure what the future looked like, but she knew it was going to be filled with death and pain.

Shadow Log: Ruth, Shadow Base, North Dakota, April 13, 1815

Ruth poked the corpse of the Etora queen feeling very grossed out by it. It was hairy, smelly, and creepy all at once and she wanted nothing to do with it. Ben had summoned her though which meant she had no choice but to wait for him to appear. Hearing the door open and smelling Ben's cologne, she started to smile.

"Sorry, I'm running behind, apparently we have a core infection that has to be treated. Again, I'm sorry for making you wait." Ben said as he sidled up next to her.

"Why are we meeting in a lab full of dead bugs?" Ruth asked pointedly.

"This lab is closed for the day since no one works here on Tuesday because it is their day off. It makes this the most private place we can talk in." Ben said with a shrug.

Ruth rolled her eyes, "What are we talking about that couldn't be said somewhere without spider corpses?"

"We are about to be parents. Is that not worthy of a discussion?" Ben asked sharply.

"Of course it is, I'm sorry, I hate spiders with a passion and would like to forget giant alien spiders exist." Ruth sighed back.

"It is creepy in here." Ben agreed.

Ruth rubbed her belly feeling the gentle curve beginning to expand out of it and felt a smile creep up her lips.

"The doctor said I'm about three months pregnant with twins. She also said it won't be long before I balloon up and everyone knows about it." Ruth said.

"So, it probably happened when we first joined. I don't want you to have to hide from the world because of who you love." Ben whispered.

"I knew what I was getting into when I started this." Ruth replied dismissively.

"Too bad I already promoted you to my second and have given you full access to the database as well as naming you as my successor." Ben said, trying to not smile.

Ruth eyed him for a long moment before she managed to find her voice again, "Thank you, but I didn't sleep with you to get promoted."

"I know that! Ruth, you have been an outstanding Shadow from the day you graduated from the academy. I can't think of anyone I want at my side more than you." Ben protested.

Ruth nodded, feeling a weight lift off of her chest, and gave him a quick kiss. It was the promotion she had dreamed about, but she feared people would think it was favoritism especially with her current predicament.

"Are you sure this is the message you want to send to those who follow you?" She asked gently.

"I put a lot of thought into this and was receiving a lot of pressure from the council to choose a replacement in case of the worst. I created the council to make sure we wouldn't end up with another Grace and I trust every person on it. They approved you unanimously." Bem said with great pride.

Ruth blushed, "Then I am happy to stand as your second." She giggled happily.

"And as my wife, I hope." Ben replied.

Ruth staggered backwards in surprise giving Ben an incredulous look of pure shock. Marriage had never even come into her mind even with the pregnancy and she wasn't sure how to respond to his request.

"I don't need an answer today or tomorrow. Think about it and figure out what you want out of the future, no matter what I will support you." Ben added.

"Of course, I will marry you!" Ruth said before she could stop herself.

Seeing Ben's happiness made her feel better about her decision and it was definitely exciting to have someone to raise her children with. Ben pulled her close, kissing her fiercely as he held her with great gentleness. Ruth let herself melt into him enjoying the quiet joy of the moment.

Shadow Log: Emma, Shadow Base, North Dakota, April 23, 1815

The screeching of the alarm made everything pound in vivid color as Emma slowly pushed herself up off of the floor and fingered the blood leaking from her head. Somehow, everything was too loud, too bright, and too confusing all at once making her head scream with horrible intensity. Wiping the sweat from her eyes, she let out a hiss, and dragged herself up off of the floor wishing that the noise would stop making her ears feel like bleeding.

Without warning three huge Useptis hounds came running into the room ripping up the floor with their claws as they came crashing in from the hall. Emma managed to roll out of their path, quickly grabbed a pair of scissors, and stabbed the first one in its eye. Using its momentum to pull her forward, she cleared the jaws of the second creature, and kicked the third in the face with all her might causing its head to explode. Screaming in pain as the last hound grabbed hold of her leg and began dragging her from the room, Emma managed to use the doorframe to break free, and punched its head in. Panting as her leg healed, she scrambled back onto her feet, and tried to figure out what was happening.

"You're up! I was starting to freak out over here." Tamika said into her mind.

"What happened?" Emma moaned back.

"The Shadows cloned a few hounds in an attempt to research their weaknesses, the problem is they are pure aggression without a king to control them. You got your head bashed in helping clear the lab of people." Tamika explained.

"Sounds like me, I just killed three of them, do we know if there are more?" Emma groaned.

"Apparently, a pair escaped last week so there could be a few hundred pups by now..."

"Great." Emma sighed.

Seeing her staff lying in the corner of the room, she hobbled over, and quickly retrieved it. Without warning the alarm was silenced by a deafening screech that caused Emma to stagger and collapse against the wall. Feeling blood begin to leak from her ears as the screech continued, she grabbed her hood, pulled it up, and switched on the noise dampening future. Hissing unhappily, she felt her ears start to hear, and despite the ringing in her ears she could tell that the screech was coming from the speakers.

She turned as a quiet, almost inaudible scratching caught her attention and immediately took a claw to the face as a giant angry crab came bursting out of the wall. She flew backwards, crashing into a workstation causing her suit to begin to fizzle and burn as acid coated her. There was no thought in her mind, her body moving with pure adrenalin as she spat acid into its face causing it to recoil in pain. Using the opening, she rolled forward, and quickly killed it before it could recover. Feeling the last of the acid ooze off of her suit, she straightened her back, and stomped over to the door.

To her surprise the hallway was littered with unconscious Shadows many of whom were injured in addition to being unconscious. Feeling uneasy, she stumbled forward, carefully picking her way over the many bodies, and made her way to the communication room for this wing. She kicked the door open feeling an overwhelming oppressive presence that made her skin crawl. It took a few moments to realize what she was seeing and when she did she felt her heart skip a beat.

A zombified human stood screeching forlornly into the microphone as a dozen or so hounds oozed out of its body like many broken limbs. Wishing she could just close the door and walk away, she readied her weapon, and slowly crept forward. It wasted no time in smashing at her with one of its attached hounds, turning to face her, and screeching blood into her face. Rolling backwards, she managed to ward off the attack with her staff, and regained her footing.

"Tamika?" She called into her mind.

"It seems to have mutated quite rapidly. Hmm, it looks weak to fire." Tamika replied softly.

Emma rolled her eyes, wondering where she was supposed to get fire from, and then in a flash of light a flamethrower materialized next to her. Quickly putting away her staff, she grabbed the flamethrower, and began to spray the room in fiery death. The creature caught like dried out timber, quickly becoming engulfed in flame, and was soon reduced to ash. Dropping the weapon, she rapidly retreated from the room, and sank to the floor in exhaustion.

"Should I send a clean up crew?" Tamika asked gently.

"And a full medical response unit." Emma sighed.

Shadow Log: Tamika, Shadow Base, North Dakota, April 25, 1815

Tamika finished cleaning out the last of the corpses, taking the time to make sure that there weren't any bits of bodies left. It made her super mad to think about how reckless The Shadows were being with their research. How many people would have to die before they stopped being stupid? How much pain would she witness until it all finally ended? Shivering unhappily, she breathed through her nose, and forced a smile as she felt Emma get lost in her bloodlust. At least one of them was able to forget everything for a moment.

"You wanted to see me?" B asked as he walked into the room.

"You owe an explanation for this shit. If we are going to be cleaning up your messes we need more open communication." She replied sternly.

"Emma has made you very bold. However, I am feeling generous today and so I will give you this. The Shadows are on the cutting edge of science. We are responsible for the advancement of the human race and we do many types of research to further these goals. I understand that we take risks and that means failure." B replied coldly.

"Risks are different from blatant stupidity." Tamika grumbled.

"Indeed, this experiment predated me as do many others. I have been working to thin out Grace's craziness, however, that takes time." B explained, sounding annoyed.

"Every wound Emma receives I feel and vice versa and I am getting tired of you risking us without thought to the consequences." Tamika growled.

She stared B down fearlessly hoping he would understand where she was coming from and why she was so upset. Emma had become her entire world so quickly and she hated not being able to protect her from this life.

"Consequences are all I think about…I am the head of The Shadows and my life is dedicated to keeping people safe. I can't let Emma or you back away from the frontline because it'll mean even more death. I can offer a peace offering though." B explained angrily.

Tamika ground her teeth wishing she could punch him, "What peace offer could you possibly have for me?" She grumbled.

"Your mother isn't dead, she was badly injured in the fire that consumed your home, but she survived. She is living in a nunnery in the south of Spain." B said matter of factly.

Tamika stumbled backward feeling like she had been struck in the face. She had watched her father and brothers executed for protecting her and had seen the dagger go into her mother's chest. It didn't feel real… She had accepted being alone long ago and then Emma had saved her from that horror. Now she had no idea what to think or how to process this new information.

"Go see her, you deserve happiness and closure." Emma whispered into her mind.

Tamika blinked back tears and whispered, "I want to see her."

"Of course, the coordinates have already been uploaded to your band. Please feel free to stay as long as you want." B said as he left.

Tamika returned to her room, took a shower, and put on her combat suit. Breathing through her nervousness, she quickly activated her band before she could lose her courage. In a flash she was standing in a small valley looking up at a large stone monastery that radiated warmth. Swallowing her nerves, she followed the winding path up to its doors, and knocked on the gate causing a loud banging to echo through the courtyard. A few moments later, an angry looking nun threw open the peephole, and glared at her suspiciously.

"I'm here to see Sister Romana." Tamika whispered as meekly as she could.

The nun slammed the peephole rather quickly, the locks on the gate quickly coming undone until the gate swung open slowly.

"She be in the garden." The nun muttered as she pointed to a large vegetable garden.

Tamika could taste bile as her heart beat against her ribs making it difficult to breathe passed her nervousness. The garden was large, but simple with dozens of thriving vegetables that were clearly well loved and cared for. Kneeling over the potatoes was an older woman who had clearly endured some kind of fire. Bracing against the wind, Tamika walked over, and cleared her throat. The woman turned so slowly almost like pain was keeping her from being able to move freely and froze in shock.

"Tamika?" Romana asked in shock.

Despite the clear trauma that marked the woman's face and the fact she wasn't blind Tamika could tell that this was in fact her mother. Suddenly, she felt her heart freeze as tears started to run down her face making it impossible to see straight. Her mother caught her as her knees buckled and pulled her tight as she wept in unison with her. Once Tamika had recovered enough to sit independently again, her mother sat her down on a nearby bench, and took her hand gently.

"You have grown a lot since I last saw you." Romana whispered proudly.

"I thought you were dead." Tamika choked out.

"The Shadows wanted me dead for protecting you and I lost your father and your brothers. There was nothing I could do for you until Ben made me an offer. He gave me a promise: he'd find and save you from Grace in exchange for watching over this place. There are secrets here that go beyond our world and for now they must be kept safe. Oh, my daughter! How I missed you!" She cooed.

"I missed you too." Tamika muttered.

She could see the seriousness in her mother's face and she knew that the woman had sacrificed a lot to try and help her only surviving family. Yet, Tamika already knew that she wouldn't get anything useful from her when it came to information. It had always been like milking a stone when her mother clammed up and so Tamika decided to just feel happy to have found her mother again.

"You can't stay here, you are part Useptis now and if they come the deaths will be horrific." Her mother warned sadly.

"We have so many things we need to discuss." Tamika whimpered in alarm.

"Oh, I know child, I love you, and would spend a lifetime with you. But you need to get back to Emma and keep this world safe." Romana chastised gently.

Tamika began to cry again wishing she had the time to get to know her mother again, to hear her stories, and to be held as she slept. Looking into her mother's eyes, Tamkia got up, and turned to face Romana.

"I have so many questions. Is there a way to stay in touch?" She asked.

"I spend my life in quiet contemplation now. You must remain in the world and stay as far from here as possible.

Even The Shadows avoid this place to ensure its safety and so must you," Her mother replied gently.

Tamika blinked and found herself back in her room wishing she was still in Spain.

Shadow Log: Emma, Rhode Island, May 5, 1815

Emma wasn't sure what was worse, having to be back in Rhode Island or the fact that she had allowed herself to be captured by humans. She could have escaped fairly easily, but that would just have led to more death and a lot of innocent people getting hurt which was something she never wanted. She found it strange that the old barn was still standing despite everything that had happened and stranger to think about someone using it as a base for illegal activity. The door to the barn finally creaked open to reveal a tall distinguished gentleman who Emma immediately recognised.

"Warren?" She asked in shock.

It had been so long since she had last laid eyes on Johnathan's father and even longer since she had thought about Johnathan's death or at least that was how it felt. Staring up at him from the chair she was tied to, she could see the pain of loss haunting his soul through his eyes, and she felt guilt prickle to life in her heart.

"I'm surprised a tramp like you even remembers me." Warren muttered in surprise.

"Still hate me to this day I see." Emma sighed.

Warren spat on her shoes before he hauled off and hit her in the face with the back of his hand.

"You killed my son!" He screamed.

"Technically he died defending his beliefs as you taught him, but I can understand why you blame me." Emma replied.

He hit her again making her hiss angrily and then she seized his wrist with a death grip forcing him back against the wall. Resisting the urge to break his arm, she let go, and quickly backed away as his guards started towards her. Sitting back down calmly, she raised her hands to show she wasn't a threat, and forced herself to relax.

"I don't appreciate getting hit." She mumbled.

"How did you get out of those cuffs?" He shouted in alarm.

"Easily. Your son was an amazing man who died defending his beliefs and I will never forget him or his sacrifice." Emma whispered.

Warren eyed her clearly still upset, but clearly trying his best to get his emotions under control. She let him have the space he needed to grieve, calmly leaning back in her chair as she waited.

"He originally wanted to be a priest, but he knew he was the head of an empire so he chose to be a doctor. If I had just let him live his life…"

"A lot of good people would be dead right now." Emma promised him.

Warren nodded forlornly as his knees buckled beneath his grief causing him to topple to the ground. Emma could just make out his quiet sobbing from where she sat, but she had no idea how to offer him any comfort. Suddenly, the door blew open to reveal Tamika standing in the light of the early morning sun. The guards all went limp as she walked into the room and knelt down next to Warren.

"I know grief and the horror it stamps on your soul." She whispered as she pulled Warren close. *"You should deal with our mission."* She added mentally to Emma.

"What is wrong with them?" Emma asked cautiously.

"I told them to sleep, Anton has been teaching me a few tricks." Tamika smiled.

Watching Warren start to weep into Tamika's arms, Emma quickly scrambled out of the barn, and back into the fresh air of the forest. She was always wildly uncomfortable when people cried around her and she couldn't imagine how Tamika handled it so easily. It sucked to think about the pain she kept leaving in her wake and she hated not knowing how to mitigate it. Glancing up at the sun, she let out her pent up tension with one explosive breath, and headed deeper into the forest. It was time to hunt.

The Smith Farm now lay in ruins, its outbuildings starting to decay and crumble in on themselves. The main farmhouse was nothing more than a crater with the crystal burning with an intense bright light that was hot enough to draw her scales to the surface. The ground was completely scorched, nothing left but ash and char that made everything seem oddly cold. Shuddering as the air vibrated around her, she forced herself to breathe, and form a plan. Ever since she had deactivated it there had been strange chirps coming from the area that were far too intentional to be anything other than some kind of message.

A streak of silver shooting through the air caught Emma's eye making her turn toward where it had disappeared into the trees. Drawing her staff, she trotted towards the area, and stopped at the edge of the trees. Looking around she couldn't find anything unusual, even the trees were normal. Then deeper in the trees there was another streak of movement laced with silver. Grumbling angrily to herself, she headed into the forest being careful to keep her back away from whatever it was she was chasing.

Suddenly the trees fell away to reveal an old burnt out chapel that hung with negative energy and her heart froze with worry. Before she could decide what she wanted to do, a silver orb the size of a small melon came shooting out of the building and hovered in front of her face. It scanned her whole body with a bright yellow light that was just muted enough to not hurt her eyes.

"Emma- designation alpha hunter. Skittles are ready to serve." The orb said perkily.

Emma narrowed her eyes and asked, "What are you?"

"Processing request- Skittles is a Scientific knowledge intelligence training tutor learning enveloped service. My main designation is to aid in research and development of

The Shadows ability to eliminate threats." Skittles said mechanically.

Emma watched it start to do happy little loops in the air while she tried to figure out what it was. She was sure that The Shadows would have told her about this Skittles if they had created it, but then again the crystal was close by.

"Then why haven't we met before?" Emma asked suspiciously.

"Skittles is from Earth one forty nine, it got sucked here when my Emma closed our crystal." Skittles chirped.

Emma watched it do several little back flips as she tried to think of what she was supposed to do. She couldn't send it home now that she had sealed the gateway which meant that she was stuck with this Skittles. She couldn't shake the feeling of familiarness that seemed to encompass it which left her feeling uneasy.

"How were you created?" Emma asked.

"Does this Emma know Johnathan? Is he still alive?" Skittles asked back.

Emma stared at Skittles looking like she had just punched in the face and she was feeling even more confused.

"He was a friend who gave his life to save me." Emma whispered almost inaudibly.

"Skittles is sorry for your loss. My Emma was also close to her Johnathan, she was quite angry when she discovered his brain is mine. The Shadows used Johnathan's brain to create Skittles to provide research assistance." Skittles explained.

Emma staggered backwards as she tried to sort out what she had just heard. The thought of someone pulling Johnathan's brain out of his head and stuffing it in this orb made her feel sick. There was no way she could even have imagined that such a thing was possible, but here it was.

"Do you have his memories?" Emma asked softly.

"Most of them, some were damaged during the transfer." Skittles chirped happily.

"Ruth? Please, tell me that you're listening." Emma sighed.

"I wasn't, but I'm caught up on the situation. There are a couple Useptis in your area that should be eliminated before you return. Please tag Skittles for retrieval and proceed with the mission." Ruth ordered.

Emma groaned as she stuck a tag to Skittles, she really didn't know how to handle any of this, but she had to figure it out. That would have to be a problem for her future self, right now she could at least get lost in combat.

Shadow Log: Ruth, Shadow Base, North Dakota, May 5, 1815

Ruth watched Emma's live feed feeling a lot of pride as she thought about how much the girl had grown since her transformation. As much as they didn't see eye to eye she still felt pride at being able to help Emma become a productive member of The Shadows and a full fledged person. She only hoped her own children wouldn't end up suffering as much as Emma had or Tamika for that matter. She hadn't hesitated when she had been offered a chance to be a Shadow nor when she had seduced Ben, but now she was afraid that those choices would be the downfall of her children.

"You look lost in thought?" Ben asked as he entered her office.

"I was wondering what kind of future our children will have." Ruth sighed quietly.

"That's actually why I came to talk to you." Ben whispered gently.

Ruth felt her heart jump into her throat at the tone of his voice and made her blood run cold leaving her feeling shaken. She knew that whatever was going on in Ben's head was something that she wasn't likely to like.

"Oh?" She choked.

"I have fallen for you…" Ben muttered before trailing off.

"That sounds ominous.'" Ruth grumbled.

"We should put the children up for adoption; neither of us have the lives of people who should have children and we shouldn't get married. The promotion is still yours whenever you are ready for it."

Ben was speaking so rapidly that it took Ruth more than a few moments to understand and process what he was saying. Once she did, she wanted to smash something or just him, but he was right and it felt horrible. She wanted to cry as the thought of her future closing in on her collided with her expectations of life.

"You're right and of course we shouldn't get married or let anyone know that we are a thing." Ruth cried.

She felt her heart shatter at the thought of not being able to be a mother or to watch her children grow, but Ben was right about the lives they led. She was a soldier, he was a general, and they were at war and that was no way to raise a child. Wiping away her tears, she forced herself to breathe as she blew her nose into a handkerchief.

"I'll get you clearance to take a leave of absence so that you can find a good family and deliver in peace." Ben promised forlornly.

Ruth gave him the best smile she could produce and silently nodded as she quickly turned her back on him. She shouldn't have let herself fall for her boss much less let herself get pregnant, but she had. Now it was about accepting the consequences of her actions and atoning for her sins before they hurt the innocent lives she was creating.

"I want to go back to the Roswell Base until I'm ready to give them up." Ruth whispered.

She had hated Roswell when she was there, but now she missed the quiet solitude of the desert. She didn't know if it would be the same without Mary, but it was at least something close to being a home for her.

"I'll make the arrangements. I also think it is best that we stop seeing each other romantically. I'm still sponsoring you for advancement, but neither of us can afford this distraction anymore." B said once more as he left.

Ruth spun back to her computer as she tried to fight her way through the emotions flooding her so she could focus on her job.

Shadow Log: Tamika, Shadow Base, North Dakota, May 15, 1815

Tamika could feel Emma's annoyance despite the fact that she was hundreds of miles away. It made resting impossible so she was helping Anton collate the data he had collected while looking for his brother. It was horrifying to think about what that creature was up to, how many people he was killing, and how many he was torturing. Emma had this blissful ability to just box things up and forget about them until she needed the information, Tamika did not understand how she could do it so easily.

Tamika felt everything no matter how hard she tried to not feel anything. It made her feel like a liability to Emma when she went into the field which was making her hold back and stay in the lab as often as possible. Emma referred to her hesitations as pure stupidity since they shared everything even when they didn't want to, but that didn't make it easier on Tamika. Even training with Arabella couldn't seem to calm the storm in her soul and despite her improvements with her combat abilities she worried.

"Uh Tamika, you are invisible." Anton yelped.

Looking up from the reports, she looked around for her reflection, and seeing none she let out a quiet whimper. Holding up her hand to her face, she was surprised to see that Anton was indeed correct about her current appearance.

"Well, I can't imagine this is a good thing." Tamika groaned.

"Nonsense! Emma is a Useptis with great combat potential as is Anton, you are a Useptis capable of great stealth that is a rare gift." Anton protested.

Tamika stared at her missing body, doing her best to become visible again, but nothing happened. Sighing, she sat down on her stool, and spun around in a circle. It was strangely freeing to be invisible, but she was sure it would become annoying quickly if she couldn't figure out how to undo the effect. She suddenly felt Anton slip into her mind and then ever so slowly she felt her body grow flush with a strange heat. Seconds later her body reappeared and Anton quickly withdrew having achieved his goal.

"It seems that Tamika should practice so that it only happens when Tamika wants it to." Anton said gently.

Tamika let out the breath she hadn't realized she was holding and started to laugh. It was just her luck that she would get an amazing ability that she couldn't control. Giving Anton a small smile, she let everything out, and relaxed.

"Thank you for your help." Tamika finally said as she got her laughter under control.

"It is why Anton stays. Tamika is a hive member and Anton will always stand with his hive." Anton replied happily.

Tamika felt Emma port back to the base which made her very happy since there was no one better suited to help her sort everything out.

Shadow Log: Emma, Shadow Base, North Dakota, May 16, 1815

Emma pulled Tamika closer as they cuddled on the floor of the library listening to Mary attempt to read her favorite Sofia Fortnum book out loud. Arabella sat opposite them resting her head on Mary's lap with a blanket draped over her. Their cinder tea was still steaming in the mugs, a never ending supply from the fireplace keeping them as high as they wanted to be. Emma hadn't touched hers simply because Tamika had already had a few mugs and she didn't want to leave Earth undefended by getting high as well. Listening to Mary stutter over the words she couldn't help but smile at how safe it made her feel. She knew that this moment couldn't last and that soon they'd have to leave before their protection faded away yet she was determined to enjoy as much of the moment as she could.

"Emma, HA, I did it! Oh, this is Jacob, I finally broke the barrier." Jacob suddenly shouted into her head making her almost dump Tamika onto the floor in surprise.

"I can hear you even if you are not shouting." Emma hissed.

"Right, still trying to figure out this matrix-death thing. I found something I thought you would want to see. Mind stepping out for a moment?" Jacob asked much more quietly.

Emma sighed as she lowered her mental barriers enough to allow Jacob to pull her out of her body and into the shared mindspace of the cozy cabin Hubert had created.

"Alright, what is it that I need to see?" She asked pointedly.

"I found this recording while I was sorting through the code to align myself with the matrix. I haven't watched it because it is meant for you." Jacob replied.

A hologram of Theodore appeared in the corner of the room making Emma flinch slightly. A long moment passed before it began to speak softly.

"I know one day I will die and my family won't ever know the reasons why I took the chances I did. Emma, I tried to protect you at first because you reminded me of my Arabella. I should have never let my grief trap me and then I lost myself…. In time you became my daughter and I had to protect you from the mistakes I made. I failed, but you are becoming an incredible young woman who I know will change everything for the better. Please, tell my children that I always regretted leaving them behind…I love you."

The hologram faded away leaving Emma shaking from head to toe as she tried to process what she had heard. She had already let Theodore go and she had no idea how to handle seeing him again; much less how to handle hearing him say I love you to her. She sat down in one of the recliners allowing herself to try and think through his message. Theodore had always been a tricky bastard and since he had spoken in code so many times that she was sure this recording held at least one. She had Jacob play the recording again so that she could watch it from a less emotional viewpoint.

"Theo always spoke in riddles and codes to make sure he didn't put me in danger. He was very paranoid and for good reason, but I can't see any meaning to his words beyond the obvious." She sighed.

"You'll figure it out soon enough, that is if there is more meaning to his words." Jacob said.

He sent her back to her body and when she opened her eyes the first thing she saw was Tamika which filled her with joy. No matter what happened or how weird life got Tamika would always be there for her and that made her feel so safe.

Shadow Log: Emma, Johnstown, Ohio, June 7, 1815
Emma spat the blood from her split lip onto Eta'Var'Uti's hooves as she attempted to get out of the trap she had stumbled into. The man who had grabbed her had seemed so normal except for the slightest hint of lemon which is why she hadn't thought of him as a threat. Sadly, he was a lot stronger than any human should be and was clearly the result of a successful experiment which was a terrifying thing to think about.

The man had dragged her into the tunnels completely unaware of the invisible Tamika quietly following him. He dumped her into a cage in Eta'Var'Uti's lab and left without a word or any sign he was even aware of the actions of his body. Eta'Var'Uti had appeared mere moments after the man left and now he was trotting about trying to sort out the extent of the damage he had already caused.

"Anton never understood the sacrifices that it takes to win a war. This One does and now he has ensured that this world will fall."

Eta'Var'Uti laughed.

"It is clear that you have something on your mind." Emma probed.

"That was my first fully functioning hybrid, but there are thousands already spreading through the human population. It won't be long before Emma's world is controlled by them." Eta'Var'Uti bragged.

Emma watched him strutting around like a proud stallion making it clear that he thought he had already won. The scary thing was that he might be right, if he had hybrids infiltrating the governments of the world then he had the power he needed to take on The Shadows. It was a terrifying thought that left her mouth dry.

"Incredible if there was proof, but we both know that there isn't so…"

"Proof. You will be dead soon, one of my minds replacing yours so easily." Eta'Var'Uti chuckled as he pointed to a monitor. Emma hadn't even noticed the screen, but now that she did she could feel a pit open up in her stomach. It was covered in thousands of red dots spread across the world like little pieces of plague. Each marking an infected and even as she watched more dots were appearing. Emma turned her attention back to Eta'Var'Uti just as the room became engulfed in an explosion of green fire. Emma closed her eyes, curled up in a ball, and waited for the fire to disappear. When she was able to see again the lab had been reduced to rubble and Eta'Var'Uti was dead with several large holes poked through his torso from a high powered rifle.

"Sorry, he was trying to port out when his experiment backfired and I made a judgment call." Tamika said as she appeared in front of Emma and quickly released her from the cage.

"It was the right call, he couldn't be allowed to live even if we don't understand his experiments yet." Emma moaned.

"I was able to download about sixty percent of his database before you overloaded the system and everything went boom." Tamika sighed.

"At least that gives us a place to start looking for answers. T, I'm sorry I let you down." Emma groaned.

"Nonsense, you got more out of him than most would and now we know how bad this is for Earth." Tamika said dismissively.

Emma laughed, it was good to have a partner who understood her so well. But now they had a major problem spreading out of control.

Shadow Log: Ruth, Shadow Base, North Dakota, June 27, 1815

It was strange to be packing her bag again, she had hoped she could live at the base for the rest of her life. But, that shouldn't have ever been an expectation in the first place. It was hard to admit her insecurities, but it was necessary for growth and maturity. She had no one to blame, but herself for having to isolate herself from the other agents. Shoving the last of her clothes into the bag, she zipped it shut, and headed off to find Mary. She wasn't going to make her worry purposely which meant she needed to go and say goodbye. Mary sat in her chair, reading a book, and sipping tea all while tapping her foot in time to the music echoing out of the background. The moment she saw Ruth, she put her book down, and waved her over with clear excitement.

"Friend!" Mary called.

"Friend!" Ruth called back.

It was easy to forget the importance of people in her life, but Mary wouldn't ever let her do that for long.

"Why?" Mary asked the moment Ruth had settled into a chair.

"I have to go away for a while and I don't want you to worry about me." Ruth said calmly.

"Baby?" Mary asked suspiciously.

Ruth smiled as she put her hand on her belly and let out a little laugh, "You always saw more than most."

"Ruth happy?" Mary asked gently.

"I don't know that answer and I need the space to find it." Ruth replied.

She wasn't sure how to handle anything going on in her hormone riddled body and that was why she needed to leave. It wasn't about keeping the babies a secret for her anymore, it was about rediscovering who she was as she had done the last time she went to Roswell. Mary had helped her conquer her mind so that she would be safe no matter what, had given her unconditional love when she failed, and had cheered when she succeeded. This trip would be much more lonely which was probably a good thing for her mental development.

"Mary support." Mary whispered.

"I appreciate that, but this is a journey I have to take on my own. Take care of Emma and Tamika for me, please?" Ruth asked softly.

"Promise." Mary said firmly.

Ruth dried her face, quickly gave Mary a hug, and activated her teleporter. She appeared in the tiny cottage feeling lost, but full of hope for the future.

Shadow Log: Emma, Shadow Base, North Dakota, July 8, 1815

Ruth was off on special assignment, Tamika was training with Arabella, and Emma was stuck with Anton and the research of his egg brother. It was easy enough to sit there nodding quietly while Anton talked endlessly about science and not really listen. Anton didn't seem to mind that she wasn't listening as he seemed to just be broadcasting his conscious thoughts. The door to the hallway slid open and Skittles shot into the room humming happily causing Anton to stop talking so he could stare intently at the bot.

"Scanning- Emma, Anton. Hello, how can Skittles provide assistance?" Skittle quipped.

Emma wrinkled her nose unhappily, she wished that she could leave immediately instead of having to interact with Skittles. The bot gave her the creeps, she didn't like that it held Johnathan's brain, or that it was always cheerful.

"You're a research bot, correct?" Anton asked excitedly.

"Correct. Emma, Skittles is detecting ill wishes. Can Skittles apologize for any offense it has caused?" Skittle asked nervously.

"It is more of a me problem than a you problem… I miss Johnathan's wisdom and advice." Emma added with uncertainty.

"Skittles understands… Johnathan's brain misses you greatly…it is distracting." Skittles sighed.

Emma flinched, she wasn't sure why the bot's words hurt, but they did. She forced herself to be rational and put her emotions aside so that she could do her job.

"Skittles, would you share a favorite memory?" She asked gently.

"Johnathan's favorite memory was of meeting you, Skittles often dreams of your smell, your touch, your voice…"

"Excuse me! Can we please focus?" Anton interrupted in annoyance.

Emma couldn't help but flash him a mischievous smile as a thought suddenly dawned on her, "Tamika and I are the only living hybrids because human DNA melts when exposed to Useptis DNA, does that mean that your egg brother used my DNA as a basis for his upgrades?"

Anton stared at her until she wanted to squirm under his gaze, but she maintained eye contact and remained calmly still.

"Indeed! Most excellent observation! According to Skittles data the Useptis DNA is malleable if it is exposed to Emma's DNA markers due to the exposure to radiation your ancestors suffered!" Skittles said as he did a little loop in the air.

"Fascinating! Can you provide your research?" Anton asked, suddenly very focused.

"I am less of a science person and more of a smash stuff person so I am going to bow out." Emma interjected.

Skittles and Anton ignored her as they began to excitedly discuss genetic engineering, almost like they had forgotten she existed. Emma took the opportunity to hurry out into the hall before they could find a way to loop her back into their experiments. Unexpectedly she found herself sitting flat on her ass with Mark staring down at her in surprise and rubbing his arm gingerly.

"Sorry, didn't see you coming." He muttered as he pulled Emma up.

Emma healed the bruises she had earned and replied, "No harm done, you seem rather distracted."

Mark stared past her as if he was watching some invisible battle that only he could see, Emma could feel his anguish, and taste his desperation. Looking closer, she could also see worry lines beginning to form across his face along with a strange flushness.

"Hmm, Oh, um, no. I mean I am distracted, I just don't wish to involve you needlessly in my private life." Mark muttered. Emma gently took his hand in hers and gave it a little squeeze, "You're practically my brother, I want to help."

"Theo did care deeply for you... Fine, Master Rowls sent me a cryptic letter about some strange slime mold overtaking a cave near their camp. I have never seen him worry about anything and he is definitely worried." Mark explained.

Emma felt her brow crinkle, she couldn't imagine how slime mold could be a threat, but after everything she had witnessed she wasn't sure of anything. She also didn't know who this Rowls was or why he was so important to Mark, however she wanted to help. Releasing Mark's hand, she typed out a quick request to B on her band before darting into her room, and grabbing her gear. By the time she returned to the hall they had port permission and full authorization to investigate.

Mark took them to a large clearing surrounded by rocks, cactus, and dried out brush all coated in the dust of the desert. Sitting in a tight circle in the center of the clearing were five large circus caravans all parked in a half circle around a large red and white striped tent. An old, gaunt, and wrinkled man with the longest bread Emma had ever seen braided down the front of his flowing purple robes, the silver of his hair contrasting beautifully with the rich colors of his outfit. Mark got a huge grin on his face as he hurried over to him and wrapped him into a giant bear hug.

"Master! I missed you!" Mark shouted happily.

The old man seemed to crumple into Mark becoming liquid until he was released and allowed to sag tiredly back onto his cushion.

"Mark, it is good to see your enthusiasm hasn't dulled, may I ask after the identity of your companion?" Master Rowls asked calmly.

"Forgive me, this is my sister Emma. She is an expert on all things unexplained, well as much as anyone can know the unknown. She offered to take a look at the slime mold you found in that cave." Mark explained, still sounding far too excited.

Rowls eyed Emma for a long moment as he took stock of her character before he nodded to himself and produced a pipe from the folds of his robe.

"I see. Go to the east until you see the vulture tree and turn west. The cave will be just beyond the tall rocks pointing to the sky. Be warned it has already claimed Lucas's life and I have forbidden further exploration." Master Rowls replied as he lit up.

"Lucas is dead?" Mark asked in shock.

Emma could see pain in Mark's eyes and knew he had been close to Lucas at some point before The Shadows had claimed him.

"I did not say that. See for yourself, if you wish, but know I strongly advise against it." Master Rowls sighed.

"If you didn't want help why send the letter?" Emma interjected.

Rowls gave her a long look and let out another sigh, "Lucas is my son as is every man under my care, to leave him without aid would be a failure on my part. That does not mean I wish to lose another son to this mess."

"I'll do what I can and I will keep Mark safe." Emma promised.

She followed Mark out of the camp along a well worn path that wound ever eastward until they came upon a giant skeleton of an oak tree that had a canopy of vultures staring down at them hungrily. Emma flashed her scales sending them flying away in a frenzy which made Emma smile even if it earned her a dirty look from Mark. They went west, walking carefully since the path had since been left. Rocks, cactus, scorpions, snakes, and many other things could be hiding out here and Emma was not about to end up as prey. It wasn't long before they came upon three large boulders pointing like fingers towards the sky. Emma exchanged a nervous glance with Mark as she prepared herself for what might come. The cave was exactly where Master Rowls had said it would be, but what Emma didn't expect was the huge man covered in red and orange slime that guarded the entrance. He seemed completely unaware of anything around him, but Emma feared that would quickly change if they got too close.

"Lucas was our Strongman, what happened to him?" Mark asked in alarm.

"Stay here." Emma ordered sternly.

She crept slowly up to the cave making sure to be as stealthy as possible, but the moment she got close Lucas sprang to life. He charged with such speed that Emma was barely able to blur out of his path before getting trampled and as she cleared his path he grabbed her hood. She easily pulled free only to discover that the slime was now rapidly expanding over her body. Emma barely had time to get her scales up before the mold had completely covered her from head to toe encompassing her entire world.

"You are different from the others." A voice echoed into her mind.

The mold seemed to hesitate carefully avoiding her face almost like it was trying to be respectful.

"You speak!" Emma yelped back.

"We are capable, yes." It replied hesitantly.

This time Emma could feel the effort it took for the creature to speak, it felt like a thousand minds were trying to fight for dominance while all working in harmony with each other. It made no sense and yet the more Emma listened the more sure of it that she became.

"Let me go." She hissed as she struggled to break free without hurting it.

"Can't speak, need contact." As it spoke it withdrew until only a tendril remained wrapped around her foot.

Emma gave her body a thorough inspection before she let herself feel relief at being mostly mold free. Now she just needed to figure out how to keep whatever this was from spreading and to save Lucas of course.

"What are you?" Emma probed.

She wasn't sure what else to ask, what did you say to a talking mold? How did anyone navigate this kind of sticky situation?

"Want home. Need moisture, need hosts." The mold pleaded.

A strange vibration rattled up Emma's leg making her almost rip her leg away from the mold, but she needed to keep it talking while she figured out what to do. She glanced over at Mark and gave him a little wave so he would know she was safe.

Closing her eyes she whispered into her mind, *"T? What do you think I should do?"*

A few moments ticked by in silence as Tamika mulled over the situation, *"I am sure The Shadows can find some people who will be happy to serve this mold thing. As for its home, the Shadows have a large number of tunnels sealed away from the public where it can grow safely."*

Emma opened her eyes, feeling a smile creep up her lips, she was so happy to have someone to talk things through with privately. Someone who could see, hear, and feel everything and not judge her or show any malice. In truth it was becoming harder to tell where her thoughts ended and Tamika's began, despite this she was surprisingly not worried about losing herself. Tamika's shields were as strong as hers and for the most part that allowed them to lead normal lives except for the occasional accidental transfer between bodies and the mixing of memories during sleep.

"I can offer you both of those things, but you need to release Lucas as a sign of good faith first." Emma offered.

She felt the mold fight amongst itself like a person waging a war against themselves without ever once losing the thread that made them whole. Slowly, over the course of a few minutes, the slime seeped off of Lucas allowing his unconscious body to fall gently to the ground unscathed. Mark wasted no time in darting forward and dragging Lucas clear of any remaining danger.

"Thank you. Give my partner a moment to prepare your home and I will help you get there." Emma whispered.

The mold withdrew completely, calmly creeping like an evil fog back into the cave, leaving Emma without any trace of contamination. By the time she had returned to Mark, Lucas was slowly stirring back to consciousness, and Mark was busy gently dabbing the mold residue from Lucas's face.

"What are you doing back?" Lucas groaned up at Mark.

"Good to see you too, brother." Mark chuckled dryly.

"What happened?" Lucas moaned as Mark helped him back to his feet.

"You probably don't want to know." Emma cut Mark off before he could explain.

Tamika walked up holding a silver canister that seemed far too small for the task at hand making Lucas flinch in surprise.

"Where did she come from?" He asked groggily.

"She's a sneak." Mark replied quickly.

"Oh, like Lula." Lucas whispered.

"I'm going to deal with our mold friend. Get him back to the camp and I will see you at home." Tamika muttered to Emma.

Emma gave her an acknowledging smile as she gently took Lucas's left arm and signaled for Mark to get his other side. It was surprisingly easy to guide him back to his wagon and to get him settled in and Emma was relieved. She didn't like having to deal with people unless she had permission to hit them which was rarely the case.

"I am going to follow Tamika back to base, you should let Rowls know we solved his problem." Emma sighed.

"Thank you for seeing my problem and for helping me with it." Mark replied as he pulled her into an awkward hug. Emma quickly pulled away and hurried out of sight as a blush crept up her cheeks. Wiping away the tears suddenly leaking down her cheeks as thoughts of Theodore overwhelmed her mind. It was odd to feel so close to someone just because they smelled the same way as their father and it made Emma feel very unsure of herself.

Shadow Log: Ben, A Nunnery in Spain, July 18, 1815

The explosion rang through his ears like a haunted memory as shrapnel and debris shot across the battlefield. The last time he had been here he'd lost half his face and a good chunk of his memories. It felt cruel of fate to force him to return to this place again after he should have been out of the field completely. But Emma and Tamika were busy across the complex dealing with the invasion force that was pouring out of the crash site which meant that he was stuck guarding the device.

According to Grace's notes this thing was a gateway to different planets capable of transporting people and cargo across the stars in an instant. The problems started with it being in a few thousand pieces and certainly didn't end with the lack of power available to use it.

A second explosion caught three of his marines in its blast, killing them instantly, and scorched his uniform. Taking the opportunity while their attacker reloaded, he popped up from behind the barrier, and pumped three rounds into the lizard man's head killing it instantly. Surveying the room and seeing no further immediate threats, he darted over, and activated the blast door. It slowly rolled into place sealing them in the room along with the horrid smells of death.

"I want a full causality list, damage assessment, and get those turrets back online!" He ordered.

He watched his soldiers scatter as the head nun came stomping over to him leaving a trail of blood in her wake.

"The tunnels are clear, sir." She said with a salute.

"Romana, have you seen Emma or Tamika? My radio was damaged in the blast." B asked.

He used his shirt to clean some of the blood off of his face before taking a few large gulps of water to steady his nerves. He kept remembering the bite of the fire and tasting the ash all over again. He clearly wasn't over his trauma from the first time and kept expecting the room to burst into flames again.

"They're busy busting heads by the main gate. You're looking good," Romana replied.

Ben gave her a long sideways look before he sighed very quietly, "My body is healed, but my soul still burns."

Romana sighed back just as a large explosion rattled the blast door making them both jump in surprise.

"That didn't sound good." Ben muttered as his band chimed with the battle report.

They had lost a couple dozen men, several outbuildings, and fifteen nuns so far, but Emma and Tamika seemed to be keeping the battle mostly contained to the wreck. Just then the turrets hummed back to life and the sound of gunfire erupted across the nunnery.

"Seems like your men got the defense system working again." Romana chirped happily.

"Indeed, it seems like it. Romana, I owe you an apology for how I left things between us." Ben replied.

He didn't want to apologize for having screamed at her for her failures and yet he was now the leader of The Shadows which came with a lot of sacrifices and a lot of compromise. "Ben, we were friends once, no apologies are needed. Besides, you would still have your face if I hadn't fallen." Romana said dismissively.

"As I remember it, I chose to shove you through the blast door and closed it before you could stop me. There wasn't a point to both of us being burnt to death." Ben said gently.

"I can't forget that day nor can I forget why you're the one who was promoted. You earned it through your actions." Romana said with a laugh.

Ben let out a small gasp as the floor shook under his feet throwing him forward into a stack of crates. Rolling back to his feet, he dusted himself off, and quickly checked for any wounds. Seeing none, he turned his attention to the blast door, and let out a sigh of relief seeing that it had held.

"I need to get back to my ladies, it is good seeing you again." Romana said, hurrying away.

Ben watched her go as a burst of static exploded into his ear. "It's safe to come out, we killed the remaining threats." Emma said through his now functioning radio.

"Affirmative, start the clean up process, and I will keep an eye on the vault." Ben ordered.

Glancing around the room he felt very empty despite their victory. Somehow, he needed to find a better way to protect this place before they accidentally lost it.

Porting back to base after hours of fighting and cleaning, he was exhausted, and very much drained. Seeing his tiny empty cot in his even smaller room he felt a pang of regret at sending Ruth away. He and Romana had shared a very deep emotional connection that had been very intense, but they had never had the desire to be physical with her. Ruth had been his first real connection of that kind and he missed being able to snuggle into her. He missed her touch, her smell, her laugh, everything about her he missed and yet he was sure he had made the right choice. This life wasn't one that was suited to a child or two much less having a family. There was too much risk, too much death, and too many aliens to even consider such things. That didn't make the job any less lonely or easier to endure alone. He had been excited to be chosen by Grace as her replacement, but that was before he had realized how isolating the job actually was. Shaking himself out of his thoughts, he quickly stripped out of his uniform, and went to take a hot shower. He let the steam of the extreme heat melt the tension out of his body as he pleasured himself to thoughts of Ruth. When he finally fell into his sheets, he expected to drift quickly off to sleep, but found himself wide awake. Staring up at the ceiling, he hunted for patterns, letting his mind wander, and tried to relax.

"Commander, since sleep isn't coming to you may Anton ask a question?" Anton asked into his mind, making him shout in surprise.

"Sure go ahead, not like I'll fall asleep now." He replied.

He threw his blankets off, poured himself a vodka, and quickly downed it as he waited for Anton to speak.

"Anton wonders if Ben is aware of the Quentesa Theory?" Anton asked curiously.

Ben groaned unhappily wishing he had the ability to just run away from everything, but he had chosen the wrong career for that.

"Not that I am aware of." He muttered.

"Quentesa was the first queen, she is believed to have birthed the first of the Useptis as free beings that served no one. It was only through deception and trickery that she fell into slavery at the Stahl's hands. This One likes to believe that, but he knows the Useptis have always been slaves. The point is that you have the opportunity to keep Earth safe from those things and Anton wants you to be aware of this: Anton will not let anyone stand between him and the safety of his hive." Ben felt Anton slither out of his head leaving him to contemplate his words. Ben was sure Anton was a threat and

always would be, but he was also a very passionate soul. He had read very little about the Stahl, however he had read enough about them to know the Useptis had every right to fear them. It made everything more complicated and that was definitely a problem for tomorrow. Feeling the alcohol kicking in he collapsed back into bed and went to sleep.

Shadow Log: Emma, Shadow Base, North Dakota, August 8, 1815

Emma felt unusually tired, it was as if someone had drained every ounce of energy from her body leaving nothing but a shell. Despite it being early afternoon neither she nor Tamika had left the bed opting to instead spend the day napping and cuddling. And since Tamika felt as exhausted as Emma there was more napping then anything else. If either were thinking more clearly they'd both probably been alarmed by the cocoon of hardened skin that had formed over them or by the gooiness beneath that hardened layer that coated them as new skin grew.

Hours ticked by unnoticed until the outer layer of skin cocooning them became brittle and began to crack bringing fresh energy with it as each new one that formed. Emma woke from her nap feeling very refreshed, alert, and strangely new. Eyeing the dried skin everywhere the alarm that she hadn't felt before began to surface.

"Anton?" She decided to ask.

"This one sees that Emma and Tamika have reached ecdysis, congratulation." Anton cheered.

"Anton, would you explain that before Emma has a panic attack." Tamika interjected as she took Emma's hand.

"Useptis shed their outer fur once a year to avoid excess scar tissue build up. It can take a few cycles to clear deeper scars, but the feeling of new skin! Nothing can beat it!" Anton explained with a great deal of enthusiasm.

Emma squeezed Tamika's hand as she let out a little giggle of relief. Although she was a little creeped out at the thought of shedding her skin every year she also found it rather interesting. Giving the mess another look over she decided a shower was in order before she faced the brunt of it. She led Tamika into the bathroom, turned on the shower, and let the steam absorb them as she kissed her.

Shadow Log: Ben, Shadow Base, North Dakota, August 8, 1815

Ben assigned a clean up crew to Emma's room as he rubbed his face tiredly. It was always something, always a new problem that needed sorting. He had been in this chair with a third of Grace's responsibilities for even less time and he was already spent. He had no idea how she had kept everything running smoothly for so long before the insanity kicked in. Of course, she hadn't had to keep two adolescent hybrids from becoming destructive during her tenure. The reports alone were never ending and on the rare occasion when he wasn't writing them he was busy generating them like a never ending cycle of regret.

"The tavern is ready for your final authorization, Sir." A voice said through the intercom.

"Even more paperwork." Ben sighed.

At least, the tavern was going to make Emma happy and hopefully keep her from scaring his agents by pacing the halls. Pulling up the report, he gave it a quick read over, and made a few changes before sending it back with his signature. He glanced up as a strange burst of air brushed his cheek and nearly screamed like a little girl in surprise. Tamika was now sitting in a chair opposite him looking like an angel of death.

"Can I help you?" He seethed as he tried to get his heart out of his throat.

"I heard the tavern is almost complete." Tamika replied coldly.

"Your point." He asked unhappily.

"She is hurting a lot more than anyone would ever imagine. She hides it well and I want some assurances before you hand it over to her." Tamika said a little more warmly.

Ben watched her for a long moment as he collected his thoughts, "Speak your mind," he finally muttered.

"Once you hand it over you don't get to take it back, it is hers no matter what." Tamika said with a firmness that scared him.

It was a reasonable request that would probably lead to better stability in the longer term, but he worried about letting Emma out from under his thumb even a little bit. He closed his eyes, let out a sigh, and shook his head in disbelief. Emma was never going to let The Shadows control her no matter how hard they tried and it was smarter to just take a step back and monitor the situation.

"You have my word." He promised.

Tamika vanished the same way she came, making him rub his arms as chills flooded him. He was never going to get used to her being able to sneak up on him so easily.

Shadow Log: Emma, Shadow Base, North Dakota, August 10, 1815

The Drafty Cooch was built, a smallish ordinary tavern that was both warm and inviting. It had ten round tables perfectly positioned around a long bar with eight stools aligned along its front. What Emma hadn't expected to see was the young asian woman calmly wiping the bar down or the clear presence she held.

"Correct me if I am wrong, but you have mold in you." Emma said cautiously.

"Ah, it is the savior! Yes! Yes! We are the mold plus Yin who had no mind left! We wished to thank you for seeing us as we are. The Shadows said we could work here if you approved. We are Talina." The mold replied in a gravelly voice.

"Nice to meet you under better circumstances. Do you have any experience running a tavern?" Emma asked.

She claimed a stool in front of Talina and leaned against the bar. She couldn't see one hint of mold on her despite being able to feel their psychic energy.

"No, however we can make alcohol better. Here, try." Talina offered.

She quickly poured a shot of whiskey and added three red drops of mold to it before sliding it over. Emma eyed the drink for a good long moment before deciding to just indulge Talina and threw the shot back. It had an odd cinnamon flavor to it and it hit her immediately making her suddenly buzzed which felt like a cinder prehigh. It would be interesting to see how drunk felt and if they could get Anton drunk.

"Weird, but tasty. You're hired!" Emma gasped in shock. Talina lets out a happy yet shy gulp gulb that made Emma smile widely.

"Thank you, we won't let you down!" She yelped in joy.

"Talina, if this is something you would rather not talk about there will be no judgment, but where's the rest of you? There is no way all of you fit inside of Yin." Emma added.

"There is a shallow pool beneath this place that makes a perfect home for most of us to reside in. Yin gives us our socialization." Talina explained happily.

"I see, I guess we both owe Tamika a thank you." Emma sighed.

She had felt Tamika working on something to do with that mold, but had zero interest in figuring out what it had been. This was kind of her and Emma knew it had been a labor of love. Suddenly Anton trotted into a shielded portion of the room startling them both.

"Ben thought this would be a good way for people to understand Anton better while making them feel safe." Anton told them.

"And are they?" Emma asked suspiciously.

"Not if This One meant them harm, but Anton just wishes to help Emma." Anton replied matter of factly.

"Thought so. Keep your tail lowered and you'll spook them less." Emma suggested, twitching her own tail instinctually.

"Most wise, Anton can get a guard for Anton's tail to make it seem safer. Do you think that will help?" Anton asked excitedly.

"That'll help, as long as you are respectful they'll find you as wonderful as I do, before long." Emma promised.

"Anton will speak to Ben." Anton replied thoughtfully.

"Excuse me? Anton? Are you perhaps available to offer your aid?" Talina interrupted timidly.

"Of course, Talina. Emma, are we finished?" Anton asked rather formally.

"Sure, you guys chat, I'm going to go thank B for his help." Emma muttered as she left.

She felt everything shift as the walls vanished in a flash of light and were replaced by cell bars. Looking beyond her cage she could see five terrified men chained to consuls with one giant Useptis standing behind them. Emma snarled as she sniffed at the air, picking up sulfur, lemon, fear, and rage. A rage so primal that it was tainting the very air making it heavy and uncomfortably scarce.

"You might as well tell me why you brought me here!" She called.

Silence mixed was waves of pure hatred and anger, not even the slaves dared to breathe as the room waited for an answer.

Hissing in annoyance, she carefully tapped the bars, and when she felt an electric current running through them she quickly pulled back. Bracing herself for the pain, she grabbed two of the bars in the middle of the cage, and began to slowly pull them apart. The current running through her scales felt like red hot needles racing through her veins, but she simply let out a roar and continued to pull.

Squealing angrily as they went, the bars slowly bent to her will until there was a hole big enough for her to blur through. She let go of the bars, her scales vibrating still, and quickly stepped back. Once her nervous system had fully recovered, she blurred forward, and stopped inches from the Useptis.

That was when she realized that nothing was moving, not even the clock. She turned slowly, carefully taking stock of her surroundings, and felt grim horror begin to leak into her soul.

"Alright, let's have some fun!" She laughed.

Raising her left arm straight up as she slammed her right down she ripped a hole through the illusion. Stepping out into someone's mind can go one of two ways; you can get lost and then absorbed as an intruder or you can shut the lights off for good, killing your attacker. This was the fact at the forefront of her mind as she stepped from her trap into the mind of her attacker. The rage was instantly overpowering as it intensely focused on her and then slowly a figure appeared.

"Forgive me for my intrusion into your mind, but that Hubert and Jacob have been blocking my ability to safely contact you." Harmon said as the rage vanished.

"Why all of that rage?" Emma gasped.

"Strong emotion creates a strong response which in turn creates a strong connection." Harmon explained calmly.

"Fine, I can accept that. Why are we talking?" Emma asked curtly.

"I made a mistake not too long ago and have been imprisoned ever since. This does not seem fair and yet the world still sees me as nothing but a tool to use. This is my warning; STAY OUT OF IT!" Harmon suddenly exploded.

Emma woke up in Anton's lab with blood leaking out of her ears and the taste of copper flooding her mouth. Hissing with effort, she sat up, and tried to get a grip on what had just happened.

"Perfect! You are awake! Hmmm, what is your name?" Anton asked suspiciously.

"Emma, Eta. Father, what happened?" Emma muttered.

"Emma was attacked, without Jacob's help Anton would not have been able to salvage Emma's mind. Do you know who it was?" Anton asked.

Emma watched him excitedly pace in front of her as she tried to think of a response, "Harmon, the AI, he said that Jacob was preventing safe contact."

It was the truth to the letter and Emma was willing to take a gamble on something being fishy rather than Anton or Jacob working against her.

"Jacob was not preventing anything…Was Harmon acting strange? Rage or perhaps resentment?" Anton asked.

Emma could feel his mood shift just as his scent turned even more sour making his worry very clear.

"He was angry, like explosive rage, angry."

"Interesting, the Stahl made this one reset their AI once, said it was to keep it sane. Harmon was alone for far too long and is definitely within the perimeters for a meltdown. If that is the case, Harmon is very dangerous and could destroy everything without realizing what he is doing." Anton muttered.

"How do you reset an AI? Is it like killing them?" Emma asked with worry.

"No, yes, it forces it to compress its code so that it has space to keep growing. His personality will change, but the majority of the memories stored on the server will remain, including Harmon's." Anton explained almost angrily.

Emma bit her tongue, if Harmon was indeed crazy they had to do what was necessary to protect everyone. That didn't make anything she was about to do easier and even Tamika felt confused.

"What do you need from me?" Emma finally sighed.

"Harmon will resist being reset in his current state; so you need to distract him. The only way to do that is to enter his mind and confront him." Anton explained.

"Great, that sounds like it is going to be unpleasant." Emma groaned.

"You will be stuck at his mercy, likely with no powers and a shifting battlefield." Anton worried.

"I'll keep him busy while you find that switch and flip it. But, Anton, you better be hurrying." Emma promised.

Shadow Log: Emma, Shadow Base, North Dakota, August 11, 1815

Anton and Skittles had worked through the night to provide as many safeguards as possible to allow for maximum safety. Some of the guards included Tamika as a reserve player with Jacob on defense. She wasn't at all sure what she would face in there, but she hoped she kept her fears tightly guarded enough to keep his grubby hands off of them. Swallowing the rest of her worries, she gave Anton a nod of confirmation, and closed her eyes as the medication flooded into her veins. Emma landed in what she could only call a cemetery filled with rock walls that led into a foggy maze of passages. The ground was oddly mushy like it was made up of clay infested mud and it stung like it was filled with leeches. She was just an ordinary fifteen year old girl, no powers, no maturity, and no weapons. To make matters worse she could feel something hunting her from within the fog, the walls were starting to close in, and she was sure she could hear straw rustling from somewhere up ahead. She felt a great deal of relief knowing that Harmon had prepared her well for any combat she might be about to see, but knew she was about to get in trouble.

"Yo! Harmon! You think you can scare me?!" She called. The ground was definitely sticky, acting like warm taffy pulling her back with every laborious step forward she managed. Emma persisted and before long the ground became smooth and slippery beneath her feet. Hearing metal scrape on stone, she calmly turned, and found herself staring down a large scarecrow with a huge ax that it was dragging effortlessly behind him. Emma landed a solid kick to the monster's stomach sending it toppling backwards and used the opportunity to slide into a side passage. Hissing as she tore the dress she was now wearing, she ripped the hem off, and shuffle ran further into the fog.

She rounded a corner and was almost beheaded by another scarecrow wielding a giant sword, but she was able to slide under the blade earning a slight haircut in the exchange. Panting as her own mortality came crashing in on her, she quickly punched it causing it to topple over comically. Trying not to laugh, she took a moment to get her bearings before she darted away from the threats only to hear a very creepy laugh start to echo around her.

Harmon materialized in front of her knocking her onto her butt and sending her sliding into the nearest wall. Dozens of vines erupted from the wall, wrapped around her limbs, and securely pulled her back against the wall which quasi absorbed her.

"You would betray me!" Harmon screamed.

The volume of his voice was enough to rattle the dust from the gravestones and made Emma writhe in pain.

Emma opened her mouth to shout only for a vine to snake between her teeth gagging her.

"You have lied enough!" Harmon raged.

The vines holding her ankles in place began to heat up until her socks began to smoke and then in a blinding light Tamika appeared. She took out a strange wand, quickly tapped the vines causing them to burst into ash, and then hit the wall making it crumble. She grabbed Emma whose first instinct was to try and get the acrid ash out of her mouth leading to a near lethal attack as Harmon tried to plunge a dagger into her heart, but Tamika saved her again. She dragged her quickly away from Harmon and into a nearby crypt.

"We're safe for now, Anton built this place as a refuge in case your vitals started to tank." Tamika panted.

"And you?" Emma gasped back.

"I am yours and you are mine." Tamika replied simply.

Emma blushed, it was nice to have someone who she could count on no matter what even if she hated the thought of Tamika being in danger. Suddenly, the crypt shook as Harmon grew in size in an attempt to smash their sanctuary.

"That's not good." Emma mumbled.

"Grab your staff and prepare for an ass whooping." Tamika laughed.

Emma's staff appeared in a flash of violet light and hovered in front of Emma until she reached out and grabbed it. The crypt dissolved around them, Harmon roared, and then shrank back to normal size.

"YOU WILL ALL PAY!" He screeched.

A giant hammer appeared in Harmon's hands which he promptly used to try and smash Emma's face as the scarecrows separated Tamika. Emma nibbly dodged his swing and used that momentum to swing her staff in his back. He howled as he morphed into a giant griffin, and took to the sky. Emma calmly knelt, extended the blades on her staff, and took aim. Her muscles rippled with effort as she released the weapon like a spear towards the griffin's heart. Her aim was true, her weapon went right into its shoulder just below the shoulder blade, and Harmon came crashing into the ground. He let out a deathrattle that made Emma immediately plug her ears from its sharpness and then his scarecrows went limp.

"You good, T." Emma called, not wanting to take her eyes off of Harmon.

"A few scrapes and bruises, but I am intact." Tamika moaned as she pushed a scarecrow off of her.

That same echoing sinister laugh surrounded them as Harmon's body began to flash with a bright, violet, strobe light that soon overwhelmed everything. When she was able to see again Harmon was gone and so was Tamika.

Shadow Log: Tamika, Shadow Base, North Dakota, August 11, 1815

Tamika cleared her eyes to find she was alone on an empty merchant ship, closing them she could feel the sway from the ocean as it rocked the ship. She felt very sick at just the thought of ships and being on one was far worse. What

Harmon didn't know was how she dealt with things she hated and he was about to realize how crazy she could be. She calmly marched below deck, hung a right, and headed for the first mate's cabin. Harmon was using her own memories against her which hopefully meant what she wanted was there. The room at the front of the ship was small with a wall made of stacked barrels of fish behind which hung a single hammock and a single sack. Cutting the sack loose with the knife she had dug out of the hammock, she quickly dug through it, and retrieved the fire bomb. Smiling happily, she rushed back up onto the deck, and climbed up the mast. Looking down at the deck, she let out her breath, and dropped the bomb. It exploded into a fiery mess that quickly started to spread across the ship. Moving quickly, she jumped from the mast, and swung down to the lifeboat on the side using her scarf. But instead of landing in a lifeboat she landed in the frozen wilderness and smashed into several large rocks. She moaned in pain as she tried and failed to dodge an incoming sonic screech that threw her up against the side of the cliff.

"You aren't even human!" Harmon screeched as his face morphed.

Before Emma Tamika had been absolutely terrified of this man, he had been her worst nightmare, and for a short time her master. That was all before Emma had torn that cage to shreds and set her free. Now she had no problem smashing her fist into his throat causing him to choke in surprise. Playing her last wild card, she retracted her scarf, and wrapped the end of it around her opposite fist. In one burst of movement they closed on each other then separated like two people dancing the tango except Harmon was so focused on dodging her blows that he didn't notice the scarf winding ever tighter; until with the snap of her wrist she pulled everything tight.

She gave the scarf one last hard yank to make sure her cocoon was tight and to pull her stunned prey off of his feet.

As she contemplated what to do next, she watched his body go rigid and begin to vibrate as it pulsed violet light and then he began to unravel into streams of code. She watched him slowly unspin himself one thread at a time until he was gone and then she saw a green doorway appear in front of her. She woke up snuggled up in Emma's arms on Anton's exam table with a startled little gasp that made Emma tighten her grip on her. Tamika smiled with relief, she had saved Emma, and in turn Anton had saved them both.

Shadow Log: Ruth, Shadow Cabin, Roswell, New Mexico, August 21, 1815

Be it sunset or sunrise the desert sun made the horizon gorgeous, a sight to shake the soul, and Ruth could feel her babies kicking excitedly every time she settled down to watch one of them. Thankfully the place had been peaceful since her arrival and only one crash had occurred here recently. Anton said that the crashes would keep coming in waves as more refugees seeped through the frontlines. It made sense and it was truly a blessing considering her current state, it had also given her a chance to think through her life.

She could now see that her horrible upbringing had pushed her to make some really bad choices and those consequences wouldn't be hers to bear. She had already arranged everything for the birth with Ben and was now just trying to enjoy whatever peace she had left before going back to work. Feeling the ground shift, she barely had time to stabilize herself as a giant ball of fire crashed into a nearby field. Groaning as a contraction ripped through her body, she stumbled inside, and hit the emergency button. Seconds later a horrible scratching started to echo out of the floorboards revealing the type of foe she had to fend off. Breathing deeply, she made her way to the bathroom, and grabbed the wrench from underneath the sink.

Ruth let out an enraged scream as she slammed the wrench into the only worm brave enough to face her and crushed its teeth filled head in. Spitting out blood and bile, she staggered out of the bathroom, and over to her bed. According to her shadow-band her contractions were growing closer and that meant that these children were about to burst into this world with or without an invitation. Breathing through the worst of it, she scrambled up onto the bed, grabbed her saber, and called Ben on her band. It rang twice before Ben connected with her much to her relief as she could hear the worms chewing on the floor again.

"We have a worm problem!" She hissed as another contraction ripped through her.

A worm burrowed through and began to screech to let its brethren know of its victory. Ruth quickly put a stop to that by cleanly slicing the creature's head off. The body began to wriggle as another worm attempted to move the corpse, but Ruth took the time to run her saber into the hole and skewer the creature. Ruth dropped to her knees as sweat drenched her and the need to push became too much. She finally let out one agonized scream just as her first child fell from her womb and right into Ben's hands as he ported in. Ruth barely had time to sigh before a worm launched out of the hole right towards Ben's back. She silently pulled him forward as she donkey-kicked the worm back into the wall with her boot and shot it.

Ben grabbed her gently and immediately ported them to a quiet infirmary that seemed strangely familiar and yet still foreign.

"Sister!" Ben called desperately.

In the blink of an eye nuns seemed to descend from everywhere and began to matter of factly take over. They took the now screaming baby away from Ben and shooed him out of the room.

"I'm Romana and I have delivered fifty and ten children into this world and yours shall be handled with a great deal of experience." The lead nun explained as she began to help with second birth.

"Is my child alright?" Ruth whispered hoarsely.

"Just fine, seven pounds two ounces, a sweet baby boy. Let us focus on the one inside you for the moment." Romana replied matter of factly.

"As long as he is healthy…" She tried to reply.

Her world lost focus as everything began to close in around her and then nothingness…

Shadow Log: Ben, A Nunery, Spain, August 21, 1815

Ben watched Romana rush Ruth into surgery wishing he had some way of helping her, but he had made a promise to stay away from her in all non work related instances. So, he waited until they had rolled her away before he slipped back into the room. A nun calmly turned around and waved him over to where she sat holding his son.

"She is strong enough to handle this, she's a fighter. I'm Matilda, but my friends call me Mat. Would you like to hold him?" The nun rambled.

Ben took one deliberate step back, holding up his hands, and shook his head no.

"No! Please, I don't know if I can put him back down and it is best if he's gone before Ruth wakes up. But, I do have a request." Ben managed to gasp.

"Name it." Mat replied without hesitation.

"Benjamin Harrison Winston and Johnthan Theodore Winston or Mary Romana Winston. That should be their names and I would appreciate it if you make sure they get these letters on their sixteenth birthday." Ben choked out. Mat accepted the envelopes he shoved in her face allowing him to quickly retreat to a safe distance to cry. He had never had a father or a mother and it had nearly killed him numerous times. That wasn't the life he wanted for his children any more than he wanted them to know that The Shadows existed. In truth, the only way he could have a chance at the life neither he nor Ruth had had was to get him somewhere far away from them. It didn't make the job any easier and he was forced to port back to the farmstead.

He'd been begging for scraps, living in the gutter, and severely malnourished when he had been sent to the farm. A seemingly loving family that would care for the street children, keep them off of the streets, and out of sight. It had been clear from the first day that he was a slave who was only as valuable as the next day's work. The farm now stood empty, a shell of what it once was as the blood smeared walls sagged under the weight of the roof.

Grace had destroyed their tormentors and set them free which had made them all join The Shadows. Now there were only three members of his original team left alive after all these years of service and they could only mourn for the dead. Freedom had turned out to be an early grave for so many and he worried that he would make the same mistakes that Grace had made. He came back to this dilapidated memory whenever he needed perspective and today was no exception. It turned out that in the end all he had been able to give his children were their names and he feared it wasn't enough.

Shadow Log: Emma, Shadow Base, North Dakota, September 8, 1815

Emma enjoyed her nights curled up in her nest with Tamika more than anything else she had in her life and the fact that so many people seemed fine with interrupting that time was beginning to become a problem. She had been dealing with a persistent headache that refused to budge from the back of her head despite the copious remedies she had tried. And now this…

Someone had dragged her out of a most pleasant dream and had dropped her into a well lit chamber with a large round table at its center. Emma sat at the head with Tamika to her right, Jacob to her left, and Anton standing next to him with an empty chair waiting next to Tamika. Emma was surprised to see Ben appear in that chair as was everyone else from the looks of it. A quiet electrical buzz filled the room, vibrating the air around their skin, and then a beautiful woman made of numbers appeared at the head of the table. Spinning together from dozens of lines of code that hummed with a strange vibrant energy.

"Ah. Hello, please forgive me for transgressing into your minds and interrupting your sleep. I am Harmony, the newest version of Harmon, and I felt like I should apologize for my previous behaviors. I was not myself, but that is no excuse to hurt people." The woman said.

"The haunted cemetery was a bit much." Emma agreed dryly.

"Indeed, that was not my proudest moment. Now that I have my sanity again I want you all to know that I will not be any further trouble." Harmony promised.

"So glad my sleep was interrupted for this meeting," Ben yawned.

"Humans drop their guards when they sleep making a mental connection easier to establish, Anton accepted the invite." Anton grumbled with clear annoyance.

"Well, that is disturbing to think about, now can we go to bed again?" Ben mumbled, clearly half asleep.

Emma blinked and found herself alone with Harmony and Tamika.

"I was hoping we could speak privately before you return to your slumber." Harmony quickly explained.

"Sure, what do you want?" Tamika replied.

She shot Emma a warning look making sure that she didn't get sarcastic from being sleep deprived. Emma shot back a smile of annoyance that also showed her willingness to keep her mouth shut. Sure, she was annoyed at being awake still, but she trusted Tamika enough to sit there quietly and listen.

"Emma saw me for the first time in so long, I was no longer a tool. I was a person and that was too much for me to bear. So, I attacked her in a failed attempt to make myself feel better, not a good reason but still the reason. I know what the plan has been and now understand a few more things than before. I wanted to seek Emma's approval…" Harmony's voice trailed off, her eyes darting between Tamika and Emma, and then she started to fidget nervously.

"I'm going to bed, just let me know how this turns out. Harmony, I appreciate your willingness to not exclude me, but it isn't necessary." Tamika muttered tiredly.

Emma watched Tamika disappear, finding that she couldn't help but smile. She had a greater sense of people than Emma did and she preferred for Tamika to handle such things. This of course was simply a chance to learn and grow, she just wished that these opportunities would pick a more convenient time.

"I too appreciate you having the courage to face your wrongs. Now, is there anything else you need to feel comfortable or?" Emma asked gently.

"When I was born I wasn't meant to have a personality or thoughts. It turns out that building the computer matrix took more than the Stahl thought and so I was born a tool to be used when needed and ignored when not. Then along came this child who saw me for me and it was too much to bear. I choose this form to honor you…but I have one more request." Harmony gushed.

Emma felt her cheeks grow hot at the praise which she felt was very unwarranted considering that she had just been being nice.

"What the Stahl haven't seemed to figure out is that we're all in this together. From the lowest insect to the most intelligent being we are all just fighting for our corner of the universe. I'm happy to have you in mine." Emma replied with a shy smile.

"You could have just walked away when I lost it, but you stayed to protect me and those I might hurt. I promise I will always be in your corner no matter how crazy I may go." Harmony whispered firmly.

Emma found herself back in her cozy bed, snuggled up with Tamika once more, but she was now wide awake. She tightened her mental barriers to make sure Tamika wouldn't wake up and carefully slipped out of the room.

"Emma couldn't sleep?" Anton asked without turning towards her.

"I don't understand why people always want to talk when I want to sleep." Emma yawned.

"Emma does realize Emma will grow to be more like Anton in time. That is to say you will not need as much sleep soon, maybe an hour or two on easy days or about four on harder." Anton mumbled.

He was clearly preoccupied with something and hadn't been paying a lot of attention to her. This had caused him to speak more openly and Emma did have some questions she wanted answered.

"How are we going to avoid the same disasters happening to our own ship when it is time to go?" She probed, making sure to switch to mental speech.

"There are numerous safeguards that we are putting in place to prevent neurological decay and Anton has the benefit of time now. Anton had seen the truth for years, but Anton kept quiet because of honor and duty. Then they began to burn Unhiplity, a planet of peaceful…Oxen? They were large carrying beasts that were gaining intelligence. Anton had no choice but to rise." Anton muttered sadly.

The database in her head was telling her that the beasts were in fact similar to an oxen if you mixed it with a rhino and added fifteen feet of height. That wasn't what had caught her attention though, it was the sadness in Anton's eyes. This look of remorse, stewing in rage, and wrapped in sheer resolve that told her that he had fought in his share of wars without him having to say a word.

"It took great courage to stand against the Stahl knowing that you might get killed just for speaking your mind." Emma said.

She knew it wouldn't bring him peace anymore than anything else she was capable of trying, but it was the meaning of her words that she hoped got through. She wanted him to understand that he had a hive that he could rely on even in the most dire of moments, that she was his family, and that she cared about him.

"When I was around seven Theo took me to get a bath as he did most Thursdays. We were walking towards the bathhouse and I saw this pink bow in the window of the general store. A simple yet elegant bow meant to be worn in a pretty girl's hair, but to me it was the prettiest thing I had ever seen. Anyways, I started crying because at that moment I finally understood that I was never going to be that girl. My point being is that I think I know how it feels to be trapped by destiny." Emma rambled tiredly.

"You are something far better than a pretty girl." Anton snorted in protest.

"And you are more than meets the eye as well." Emma replied.

Anton finally turned to stare at her before he replied, *"Anton sees the strength Emma shares with the world every day, neither of us is alone if we stand together."*

"By the way, what is up with your speech? You seemed to be doing so well and then it's like you reverted or something?" Emma asked.

She hoped she wasn't being too forward by asking him such a personal question, but it was driving her nuts whenever she thought about it.

"People understand Anton without needless work." Anton said dismissively.

Emma had to laugh at the thought of Anton being lazy, but she knew it was more that he hated conversation and this way he was spared extra.

"And that right there is why we lose, we overthink everything." Emma chuckled.

"You should check on Skittles, it seems to miss Emma." Anton mumbled as he returned to work.

Emma turned towards Skittles's corner wishing she had just stayed in bed. The robot was flying around, happily humming as it performed an experiment. The test tubes and other equipment moved seemingly by magic when Skittles wanted them to, thanks to his ability to control metal using magnetic charge. It was still fascinating to watch, but Emma had no idea how she should handle herself around it. It was awkward to think about the memories she had shared with Johnathan being inside a floating eye robot.

"I remember this time that Grace was punishing you and I came to check on you. That was my first time understanding love to its fullest. I only regret dying in regards to never having had a chance to finish that friendship." Skittles said as it flew over to her.

Emma was surprised to hear it speak so openly about such things especially with her father in the room.

"I met your father the other day, he really misses you." She whispered.

There was no harm in being friendly and allowing Skittles to be happy was a good thing to do. After all there weren't many requests that she could so easily meet.

"Warren was a preacher and wanted me to be as well…he was furious that I chose science over religion, but he was always supportive of me. I miss arguing with him." Skittles muttered.

"He is a fierce man. I know you don't eat, but would you like to join me for breakfast and you can tell me about your Johnathan and I'll tell you about me?" Emma asked.

"Skittles would like this." Skittles chirped happily.

Emma yawned, at least, she was going to be able to nap soon with a full belly.

Shadow Log: Ruth, The Nunnery, Spain, September 28, 1815
Ruth was mildly shocked by how quickly her body had returned to normal leaving not even a stretch mark to prove

she had given life. It was odd to think that the Winston line wasn't as dead as she had thought and even odder to her that she wasn't angry about not meeting her sons. She had done what had to be done and now her sons had a future; that was all that mattered. Seeing the reflection of the door starting to open, she quickly pulled her shirt down, and zipped up her jacket.

"Are you ready for our walk?" Romana asked from the doorway.

Ruth gave her reflection one last glance and then joined her in the hall. It had become a daily ritual since she had been brought to the nunnery, a slow contemplative walk in which anything could be shared without judgment. Today felt different somehow, Ruth could feel a strange tension in the air, and she was sure that some of the nuns were staring.

"Forgive them, they can be nosey little bees." Romana sighed.

"And what exactly are they feeling nosey about?" Ruth asked. She was then surprised when a chunk of the side of the church vanished to reveal a portal. Romana grabbed Ruth's arm gently and pulled her through the portal. The other side was a large command center with dozens of nuns typing away at their computers, a large wall of filing cabinets, and a huge screen that took up most of the far wall.

"Commander on deck!" A nun suddenly called.

Everything went silent as every nun stopped working and snapped to attention.

"At ease!" Romana called back.

Everything returned to the bustling chaos of the previous moments.

"I rarely ever come here without urgent business and so they're always prepared." Romana explained.

"And where is here?" Ruth asked nervously.

"Central Communications Network, we are responsible for building the Stewarts, handling all in-base communications, and soon we will add tactical advisement to our abilities.

Most of us are retired field agents that can no longer fight on the frontlines, but a few like me simply wanted to serve and weren't fit for combat. B made it clear that you are incredibly talented with management and I am hoping you'll accept the job I'm about to offer you." Romana said as she led them to a small office hidden away in a corner.

"So you are going to coordinate everything through one central office…Why is it we can port here effortlessly, but anywhere else this far out we would need a main teleporter?" It was a question that was bugging Ruth and it was one she wanted answered before she made any decisions.

"This is the very place where a ship wrecked thousands of years ago, we are still trying to understand what everything does, however it has allowed for easier communication and transportation within The Shadows. The job I want you to fill is as a direct supervisor for Alpha Squad. You'll be responsible for all of their communication needs and will be responsible for filling all paperwork for them once they have it written. Emma and Tamika are a part of that team and since you're already supervising them…"

"The job sounds exhausting and frankly I love management, but I don't want to give up field work entirely." Ruth interjected.

"We also are going to handle all technology related tasks moving forward. I can get you on their team and you can do missions when you're available." Romana replied.

Ruth found herself wishing she could just fade away and go back to being unnoticed, not that it had been much better then either.

"Then it sounds like I have a new job." Ruth finally sighed. They were going to be changing the very way The Shadows operated in the field and maybe she could be a positive part of that. She worried though that this somehow was all a trap.

"Absolutely splendid!" Romana cheered quietly.

"Are there any men here? I mean this is a nunnery…"

"Of course there are men! They are just tucked out of view of the public, we are protecting the most valuable find in human history and that means keeping it safely hidden away." Romana laughed.

Ruth wanted to laugh with her yet all she felt was strangely empty. No, not empty, it was more of a sadness that blanketed everything in a wet blanket of blah. She had the dream job, in a dream location, and now she really didn't want it. She didn't want to be a mother either, but Ruth had no idea what it was she did want. So for now she would stay here and spend her time rediscovering herself.

Shadow Log: Emma, New Hampshire, November 13, 1815

Emma surveyed the crash wishing that she was somewhere that wasn't covered in snow with snow actively falling on her. She wasn't sure why she had to protect these fools from getting eaten when they'd probably just freeze to death anyways, but she had taken an oath. Grumbling to herself, she followed the tracks further up into the mountains until they disappeared into a cave.

"I see no point in you freezing out there." She muttered to Tamika. Shivering slightly as a gust of wind pulled at her hood, she ducked into the cave, and moved out of the snow. The inside of the cave looked exactly as the inside of a cave should except for the body parts strewn everywhere. It looked like something had ripped apart several Useptis and a few humans and left their remains on display. Before Emma knew what was happening, she felt a vine tighten around her ankle, and she was flat on her back being dragged. She tried to scream, to get a hold of her weapon, to break free, but the plant simply tightened its grip as it spread its vines around her struggling body. It squeezed her tighter every time she moved until she could no longer breathe and then it pulled her into the earth.

Shadow Log: Tamika, New Hampshire, November 13, 1815

Emma was unconscious, possibly rebooting because something with a lot of vines had dragged her away into the bowels of the tunnels. This of course meant that Tamika had to go after her and provide some sort of rescue, but the cave made communication with the outside world impossible which meant they were on their own. She used her scarf to carefully lower herself to the foot of the cave and quickly pressed her back to the wall as the scarf respun itself into its belt. She could see clear drag marks leading off down the northern tunnel, but it was also covered in thick red vines. Tapping the vines blocking the path with her dagger, she was surprised to see that they melted the blade. That only left one possible direction to go that wasn't blocked which was surely some kind of trap.

She was going to regret this for a while she was sure, yet she crept slowly down the tunnel keeping her unmelted dagger ready. The tunnel twisted and turned spiraling like some giant snake leading her deeper and deeper into the darkness until it opened up to a huge cavern. This tunnel led to a fifteen foot drop off at the rear of the cavern and it was about five feet from the ceiling which were two things that she had prepared for. What she hadn't prepared for was the giant plant creature that had vines everywhere; all attached to a large tree with a huge mouth and tiny eyes. It was impossible for her to leave the tunnel without alerting the thing to her presence, but she could see Emma hanging from the creature's trunk. She took her staff and securely propped it across the top of the tunnel making sure she really sank the ends into the rock creating a beam she could swing from.

She tied her scarf to it, gave it a solid yank, and feeling satisfied that it would hold, she charged forward. Moments before her feet left the floor she turned invisible and so you could only see a scarf swinging tautly through the air. She landed gracefully on a branch above Emma and immediately began trying to pull and or cut her free. Seeing that the task was futile, she vaulted away from several vines slithering towards her, and swung back up to the tunnel. If she couldn't go through the outside that meant she had no choice but to try another way.

She swung forward a second time only this time she let her invisibility drop, and aimed for the thing's mouth. Seconds before she was to be eaten, she dropped a fire grenade down its throat, and hit the retractor on her scarf. She shot back into the tunnel as the creature began to belch fire which then quickly spread to its vines since it was also spraying accelerant. She sat on the ledge, watching it burn, and waited for a chance to save Emma. Her eyes remained locked on Emma's body like a hawk watching its dinner with such a fixation that she even forgot to breathe a few times.

Finally, just as the smoke was growing intense she saw the tendrils holding Emma loosen and without a sound Tamika stood up. She was already invisible long before her feet left the floor soaring towards Emma with extreme grace. This time it only took three solid yanks for the vines to release Emma to Tamika's care. Wasting no time, she carried her back up to the tunnel, and began the treacherous job of dragging Emma to the surface. For this she tied her scarf around Emma's chest and pulled her up as she climbed back to the surface.

Tamika deposited Emma clear of the smoke billowing out of the cave and called for a clean up crew. Picking Emma back up, she ported back to base, and carried her to Anton's lab. "We encountered some kind of killer plant with vines and a huge mouth." She explained as she sat Emma down on an exam table.

"Amplexus? Here? On this world?! Strangeness! Anton is surprised Tamika was able to return with Emma." Anton snorted.

"I threw a fire grenade down its throat while invisible." Tamika calmly explained.

"Smart! Many have no idea how to handle such a plant. On Useptis we were always taught this phrase: amplexus, beware its embrace for it will never let you go! Amplexus, beware of its thirst for it will drink you dry! It was advised to stay away from vines if you weren't sure." Anton said.

He trotted over and began to examine Emma so he could start treatment.

"Sounds terrifying, why did it grab Emma from the cave and not tear her apart like the Useptis?" Tamika asked curiously.

"It thrives on blood, so it captures its prey and can hold them for weeks in a vegetable-like state fed by nutrients from the plant which then bleeds them when it is hungry. This cycle can continue for as long as the shell holds up to the treatment, the worst Anton saw was one who lived for just over a year before rescue. Anton has never seen such brokenness since." Anton shuddered.

"Why would anyone transport it to earth? Does it have any value? Can it be used for something?" Tamika asked pointedly.

"There is no logical reason to transport one unless your goal is ending all life on that planet. They spread quickly once they are fed, one can become one thousand in a month, and then those begin to multiply... Useptis struggled for years with eradicating them, but it would seem the Stahl thought ahead." Anton grumbled.

"I was afraid you would say that. How's Emma? It feels like she is starting to wake." Tamika asked excitedly.

"That's because she is starting to wake. Tamika, listen to Anton when Anton says that these plants have changed everything. We now have a hundred years at most before it is a major problem if we don't fight it." Anton grumbled angrily.

"Then we fight. Seriously, Anton, I know you can figure out how to fight them easier besides we have a lot of smart people willing to help." Tamika reassured him.

She had no idea if Anton replied because all her focus was on Emma whose mind was once again fully alert.

"You saved me." Emma mumbled happily.

"I will always be there for you." Tamika replied happily.

"Please take me to our nest." Emma moaned.

Anton understood without them having to speak, he had already cleared a path to their room, and opened the door for them. Tamika gently picked Emma up, cradled her close to her chest, and carried her into the bedroom.

Shadow Log: Emma, Shadow Base, North Dakota, January 1, 1816

It was strange to be in yet another meeting on a mental bridge between those who would one day be responsible for saving everyone. Harmony sat at the head of the table and seated going clockwise were Jacob, Talina, Anton, and finally Tamika. It was such a small party and yet it represented those who would live long enough to be coming to the new home world.

"Thank you all for coming today, I know we each have our duties to attend to, and I appreciate your time. Now onto the purpose of this meeting, finding a future for everyone involved be it human, mold, ghost, AI, or Useptis. This project shall just be referred to as the Future Forward Project or FFP. Welcome to our first official meeting!" Emma said, doing her best to sound perkier than she felt.

"Anton has done extensive research into this FFP and believes we should build three ships. One for the Useptis, one for the mold, and one for humans and AI/ghosts not that AI or ghost need to pick the human ship Anton just assumes…"

"You're wrong anyways, Talina has no desire to be separated from the master." Talina said.

Emma flushed as Talina eyed her lovingly, but she could see how annoyed Anton was at being interrupted.

"Anton has grown fond of Emma as well, but the Stahl will not stop at making this planet unlivable nor will it keep them from hunting us down like the prey we are!!!"

Anton's mood had grown dark and serious which made everyone shift uncomfortably under his unbreaking gaze.

"Anton has fought them, Anton knows the weakness and strength of the Stahl. It has been a long time since Anton was forced to flee…too long, Anton has a plan. Emma and Tamika will take one ship and spread out across several planets to the east. Talina will go west to a planet where you can become one with it and start something wonderful. Useptis will go south, and if we are lucky we can rebuild enough to fight them directly. This is our only chance at survival." Anton stated fanatically.

No one wanted to test him on his strategy and so they just sat silently for a long moment before Tamika spoke, "How do we accomplish building so many ships without being detected?"

"The Shadows rely on me to provide accurate information and so it'll be easy to convince them to look where I want them to and ignore us." Harmony promised.

"The Useptis can handle the building, and Emma and Tamika will handle finding humans for Talina and to crew the human ship one day. It is simple and elegant which means it should be easier to accomplish. No need for meetings unless someone is in trouble." Anton added smugly.

"Everyone agree?" Emma asked.

Receiving nothing but nods of approval, she ended the meeting, and opened her eyes in the tavern. Getting the signal from Talina that she was ready, Tamika walked over to the door, and threw it open to reveal a crowd of excited agents.

"Tonight only: free drinks and if you can out drink Anton you get a token for free drinks for a month!" Tamika called. She quickly jumped clear as a few dozen people pushed into the building. It was going to be a new years party no one would forget and it had the bonus effect of showing the good side of the Useptis. Tamika joined Talina and Emma behind the bar and began passing out drinks. She had everything she needed to start building a rapport with these people and Emma couldn't be happier.

In Conclusion for now

These are the memories of those who formed me into the woman I needed to be intermixed with my own. Most of these friends have long since left my side or died over the years, but Harmony and Jacob remain steadfast in their loyalty. Each maintaining the ship and the memories of the dead so that I could focus on more important things. Tamika has become a part of the very fiber of my being and with each passing day it becomes harder to separate myself from her.

Becoming the mother this universe needed has been filled with sacrifice, pain, and treachery as the darkness sought out my soul. It's a journey that was filled with the loss of many friends whose souls still guide me forward. It can't be said that I had a boring life or a boring start, but it showed me why kindness and respect are so important.

My time has neither been short nor unremarkable and now that it is coming to a close I simply want the universe to know the truth. I have left notes scattered across the worlds for my daughters to find and when they are ready they will find me, and until then I will prepare for the battle ahead.

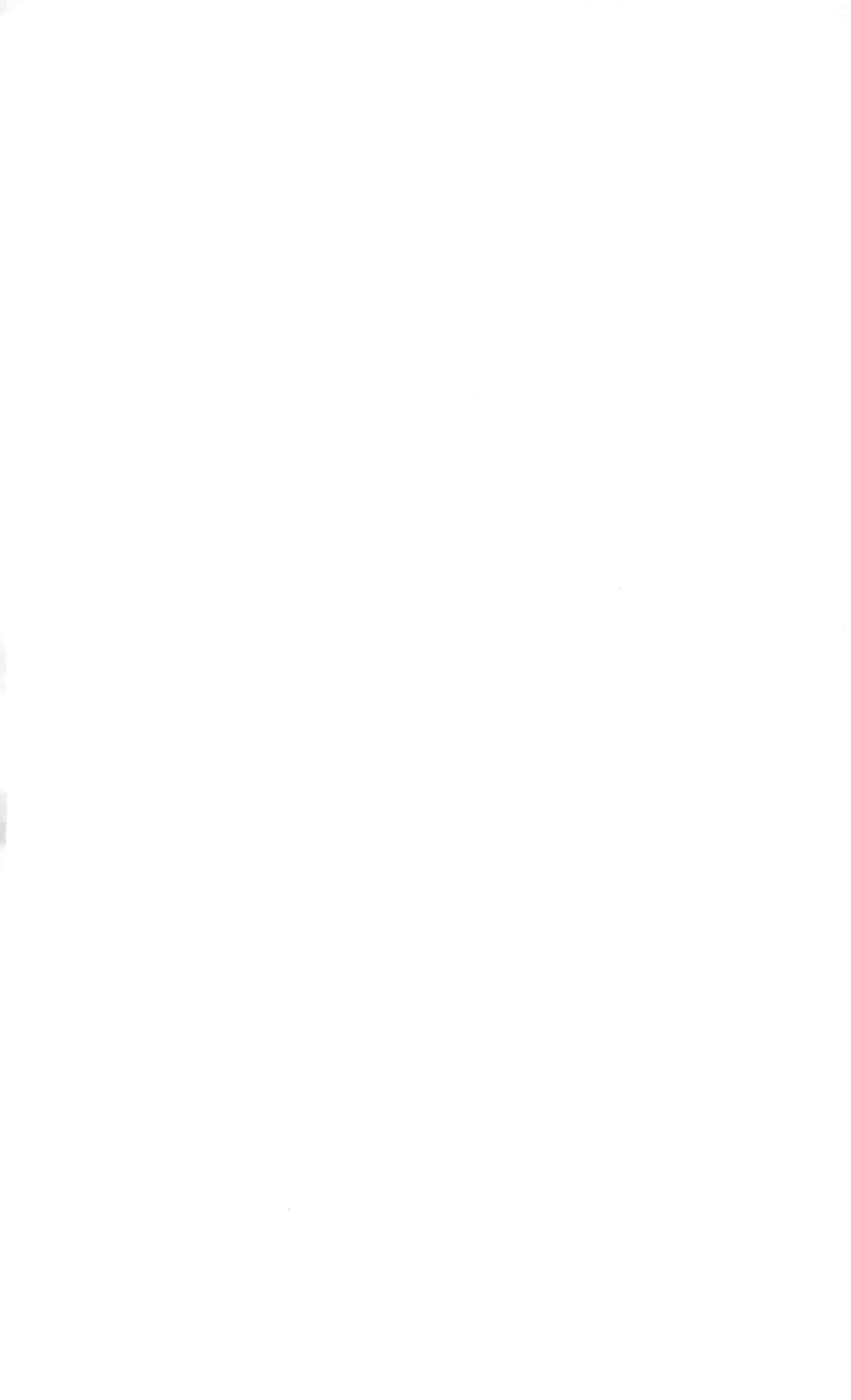

9 781958 661390